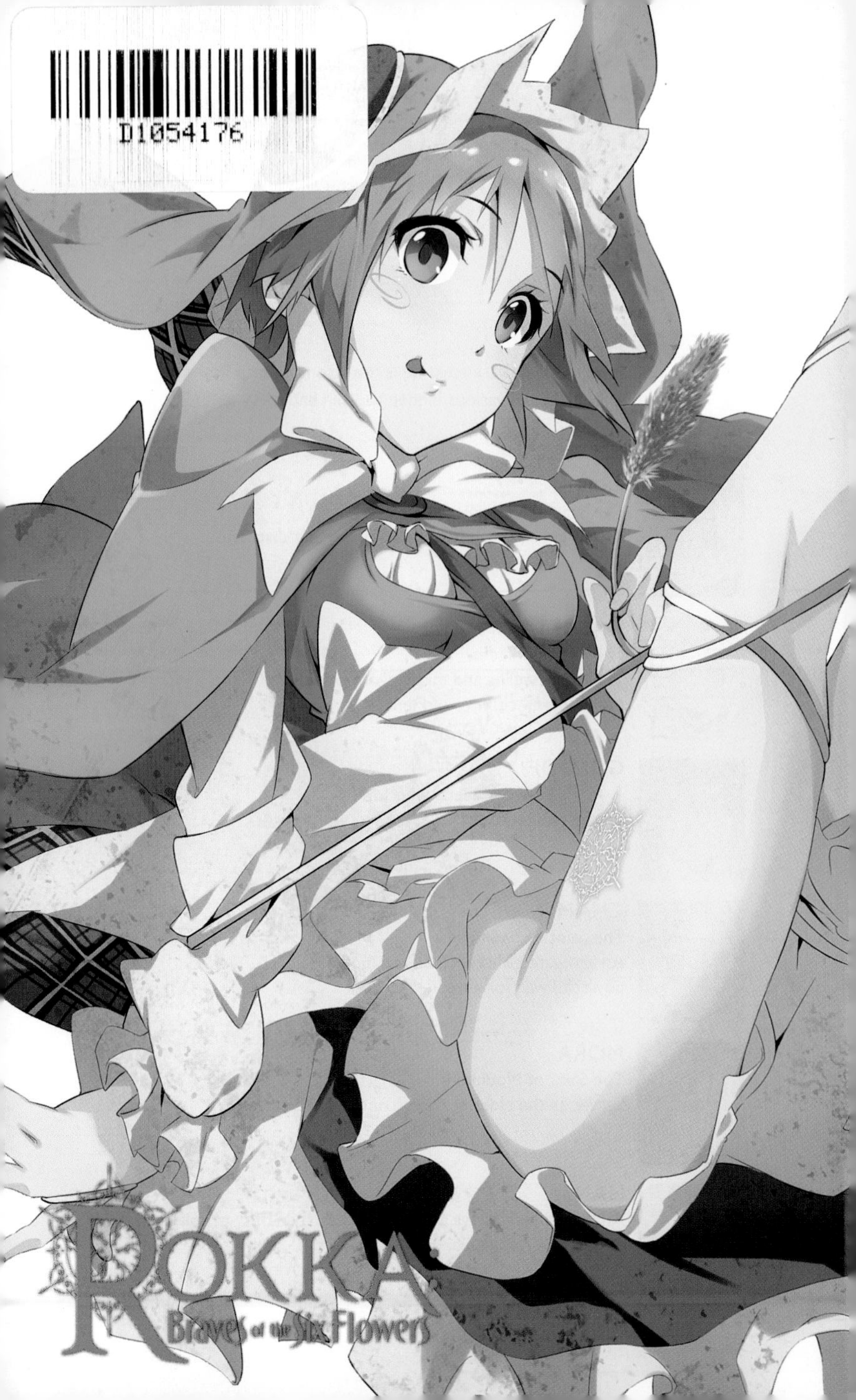
ROKKA
Braves of the Six Flowers

CHARACTER INTRODUCTION

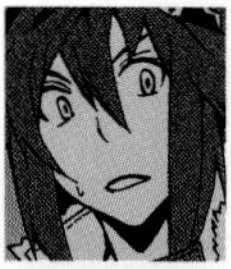

ADLET
A boy who declares that he is the strongest man in the world. Utilizes various hidden tools in battle.

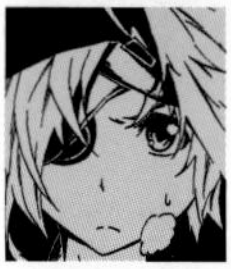

FREMY
The Saint of Gunpowder.
A cold girl who tends to keep others at a distance.

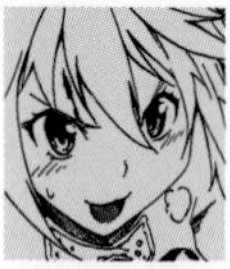

NASHETANIA
The Saint of Blades.
The freewheeling and mischievous princess of the powerful country of Piena.

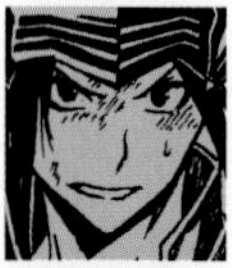

GOLDOF
A young knight of Piena who loyally serves Nashetania.

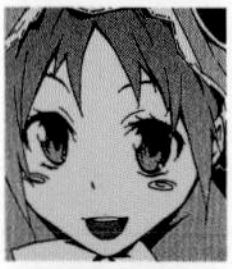

CHAMO
The Saint of Swamps.
An arrogant girl said to be the most powerful warrior alive.

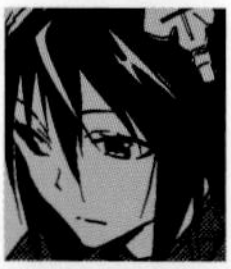

MORA
The Saint of Mountains.
Serves as the elder in charge of the saints.

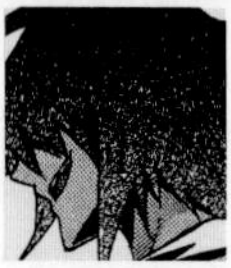

HANS
An assassin who uses an otherworldly style of swordplay.
Speaks in a catlike manner.

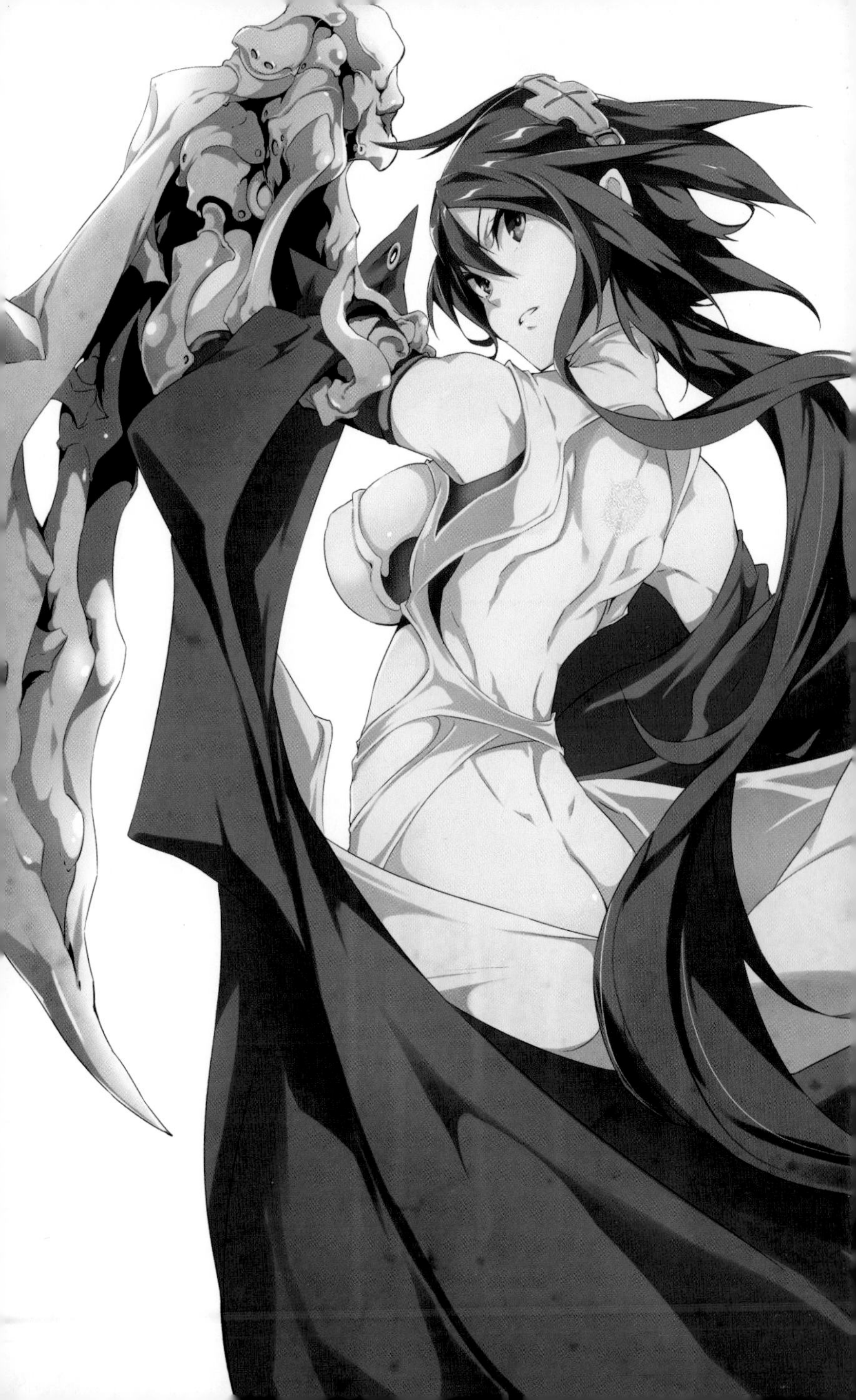

Contents

Episode.09 005

Episode.10 047

Episode.11 089

Episode.12 127

Episode.09

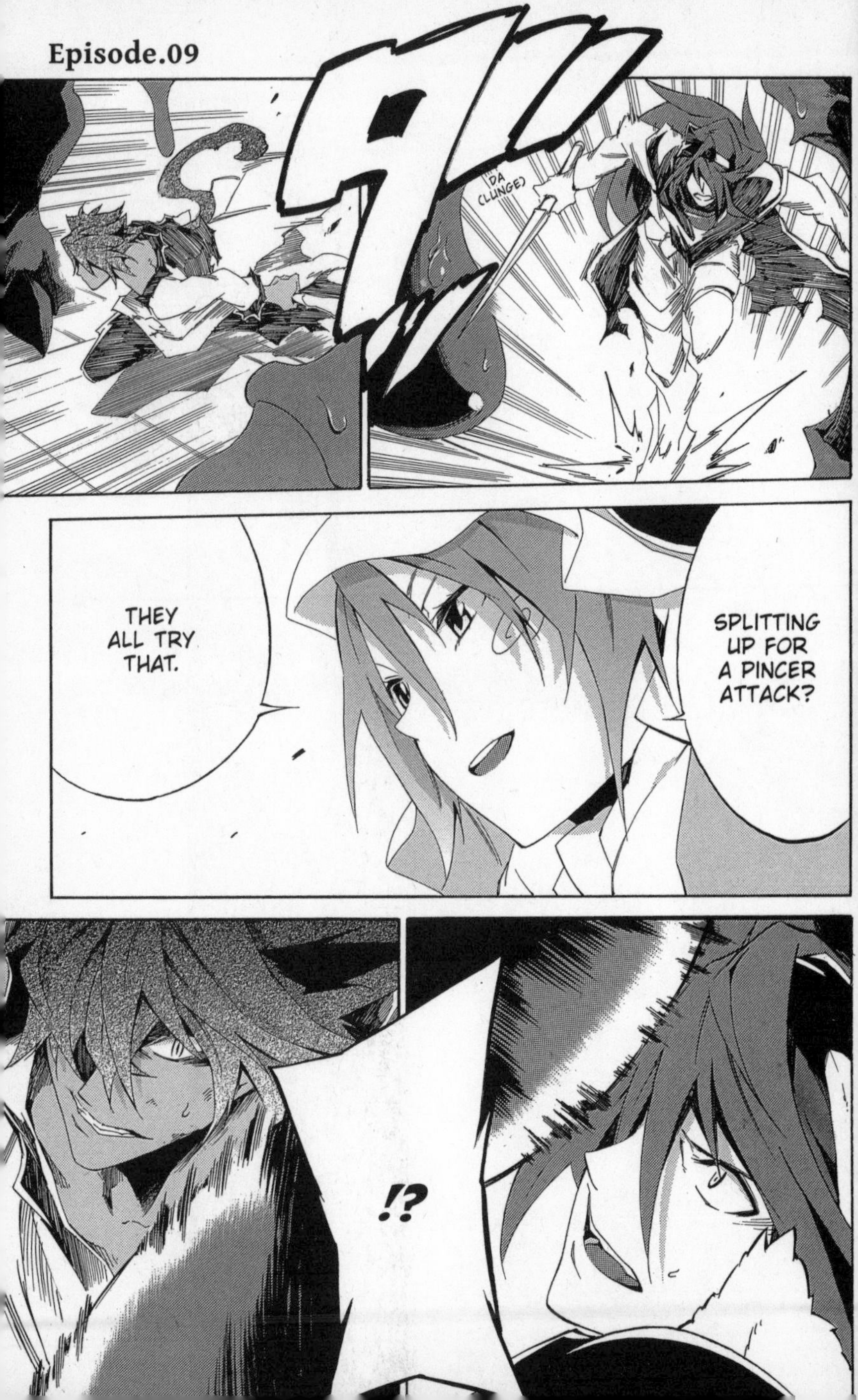
DA (LUNGE)
SPLITTING UP FOR A PINCER ATTACK?
THEY ALL TRY THAT.
!?

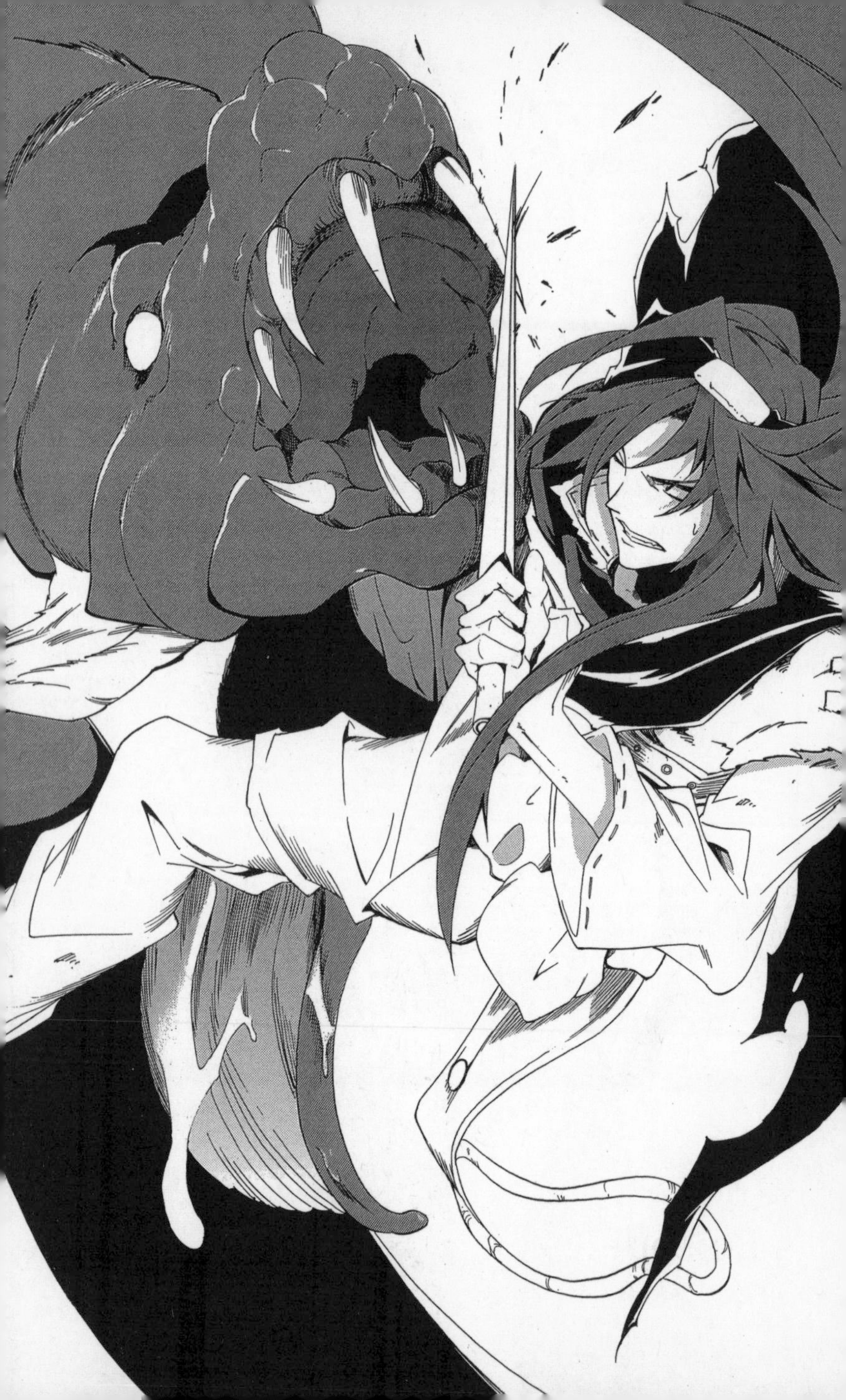

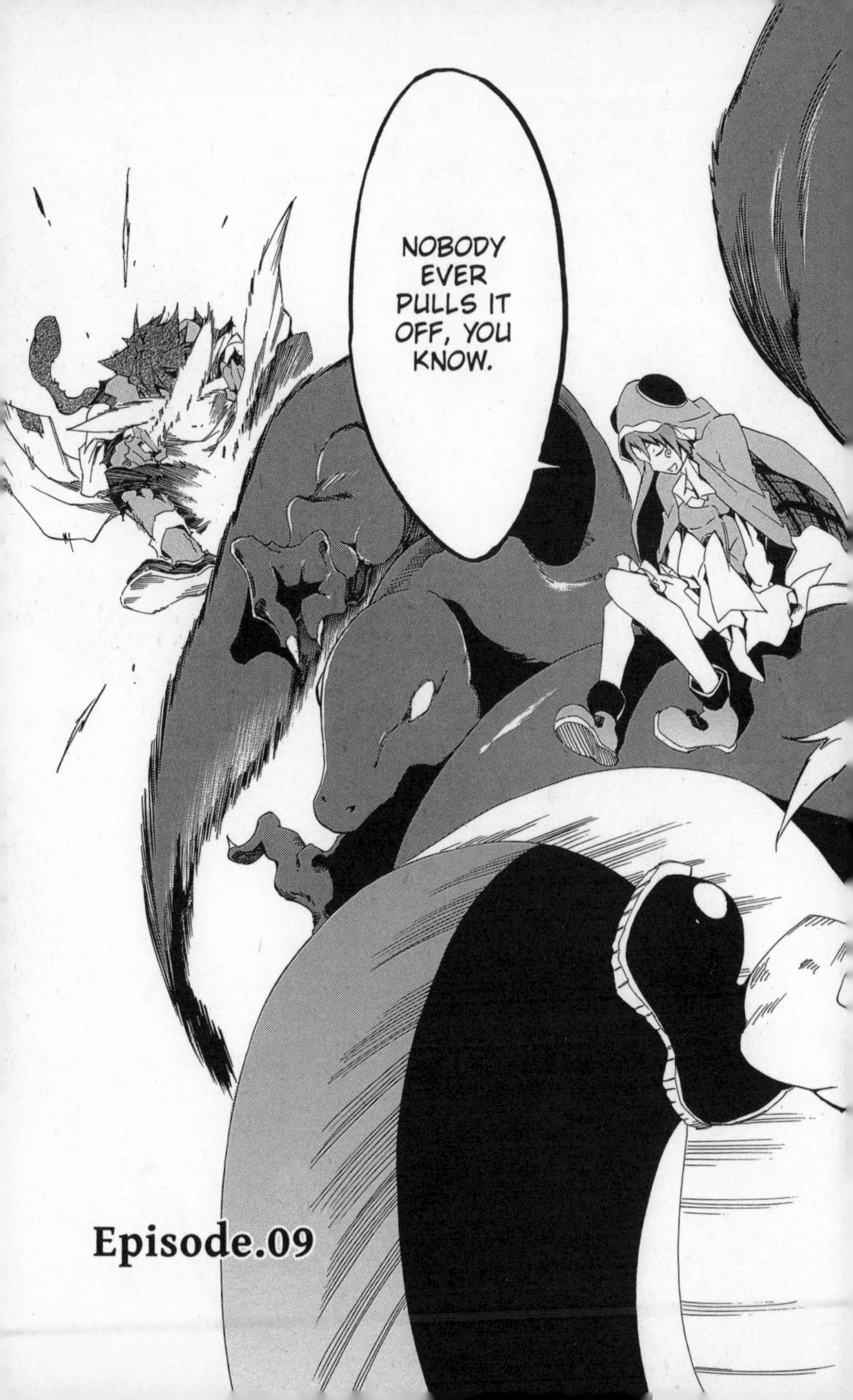
NOBODY EVER PULLS IT OFF, YOU KNOW.
Episode.09

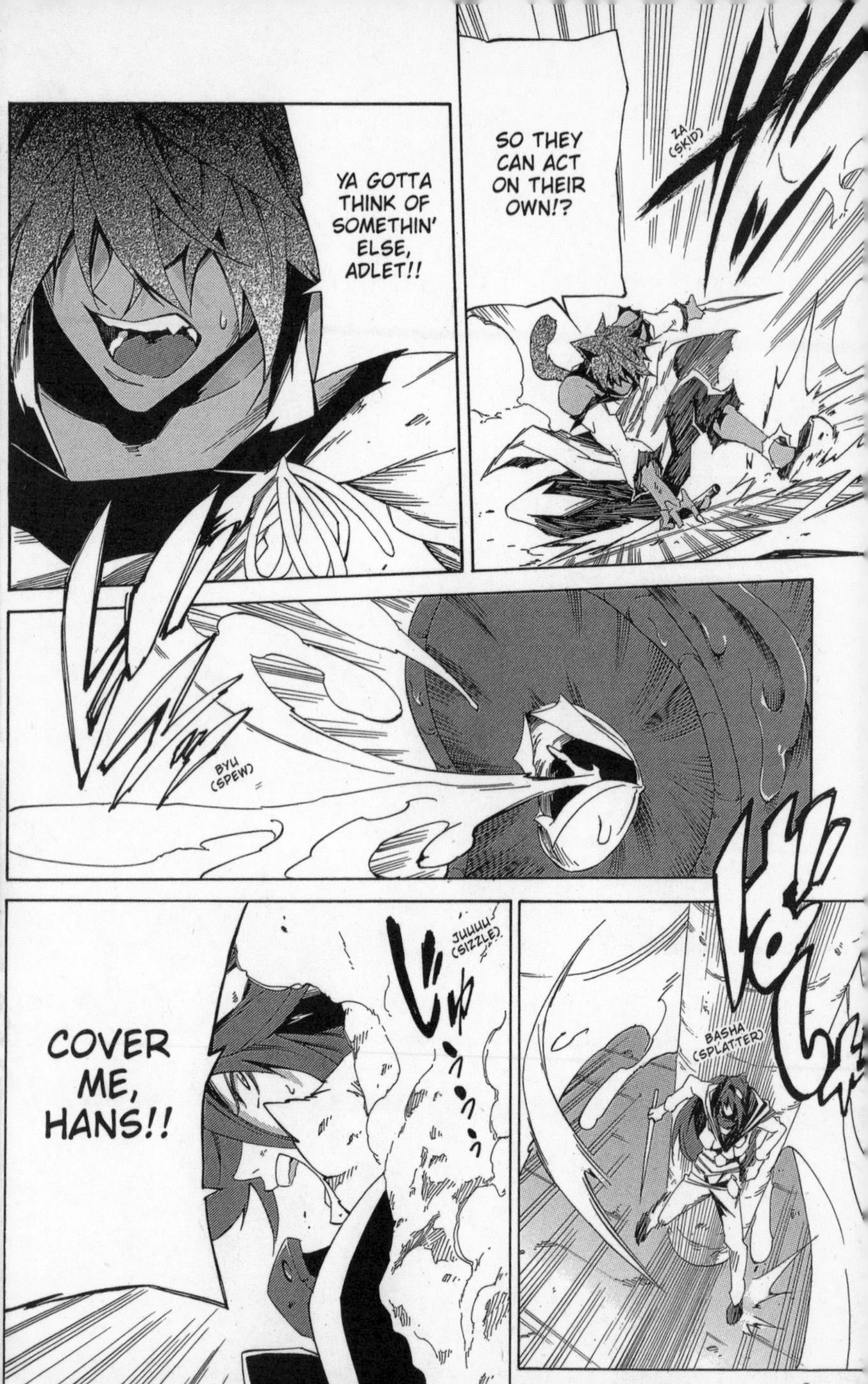

SO THEY CAN ACT ON THEIR OWN!?
ZA (SKID)
YA GOTTA THINK OF SOMETHIN' ELSE, ADLET!!
BYU (SPEW)
BASHA (SPLATTER)
JUUUU (SIZZLE)
COVER ME, HANS!!

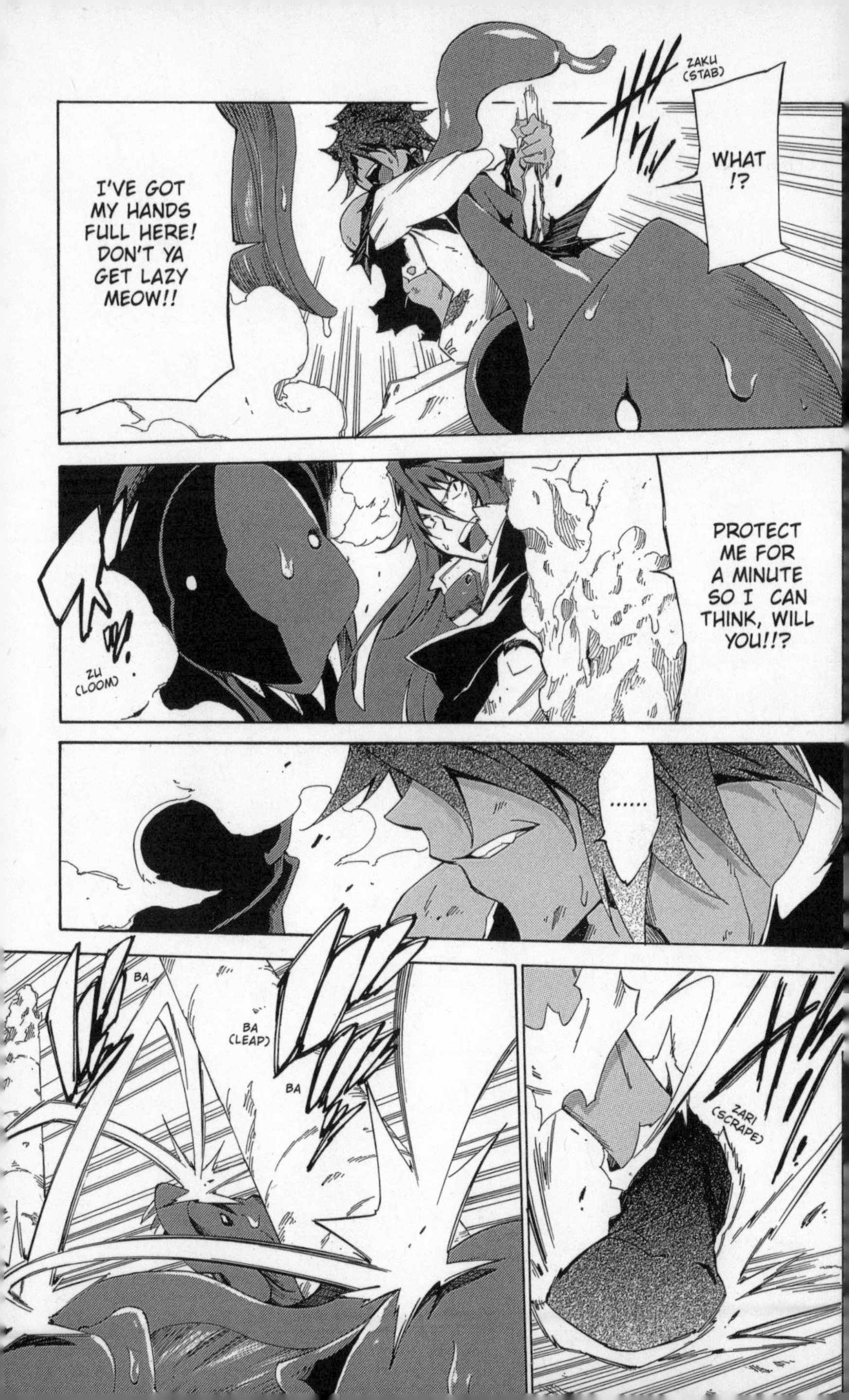
ZAKU (STAB)
WHAT!?
I'VE GOT MY HANDS FULL HERE! DON'T YA GET LAZY MEOW!!
PROTECT ME FOR A MINUTE SO I CAN THINK, WILL YOU!!?
ZU (LOOM)
......
ZARI (SCRAPE)
BA
BA (LEAP)
BA

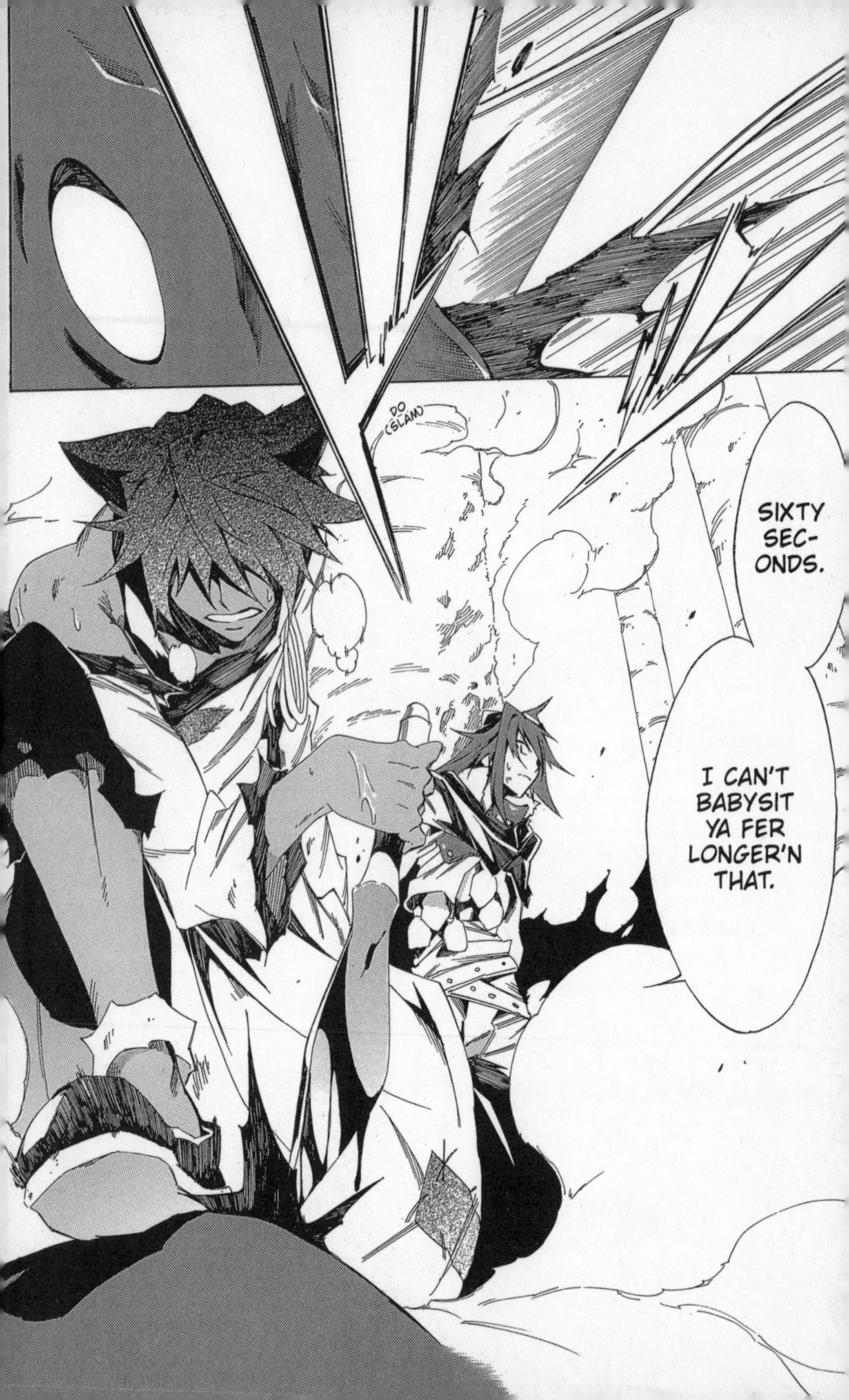
SIXTY SEC-ONDS.
I CAN'T BABYSIT YA FER LONGER'N THAT.
DO (SLAM)

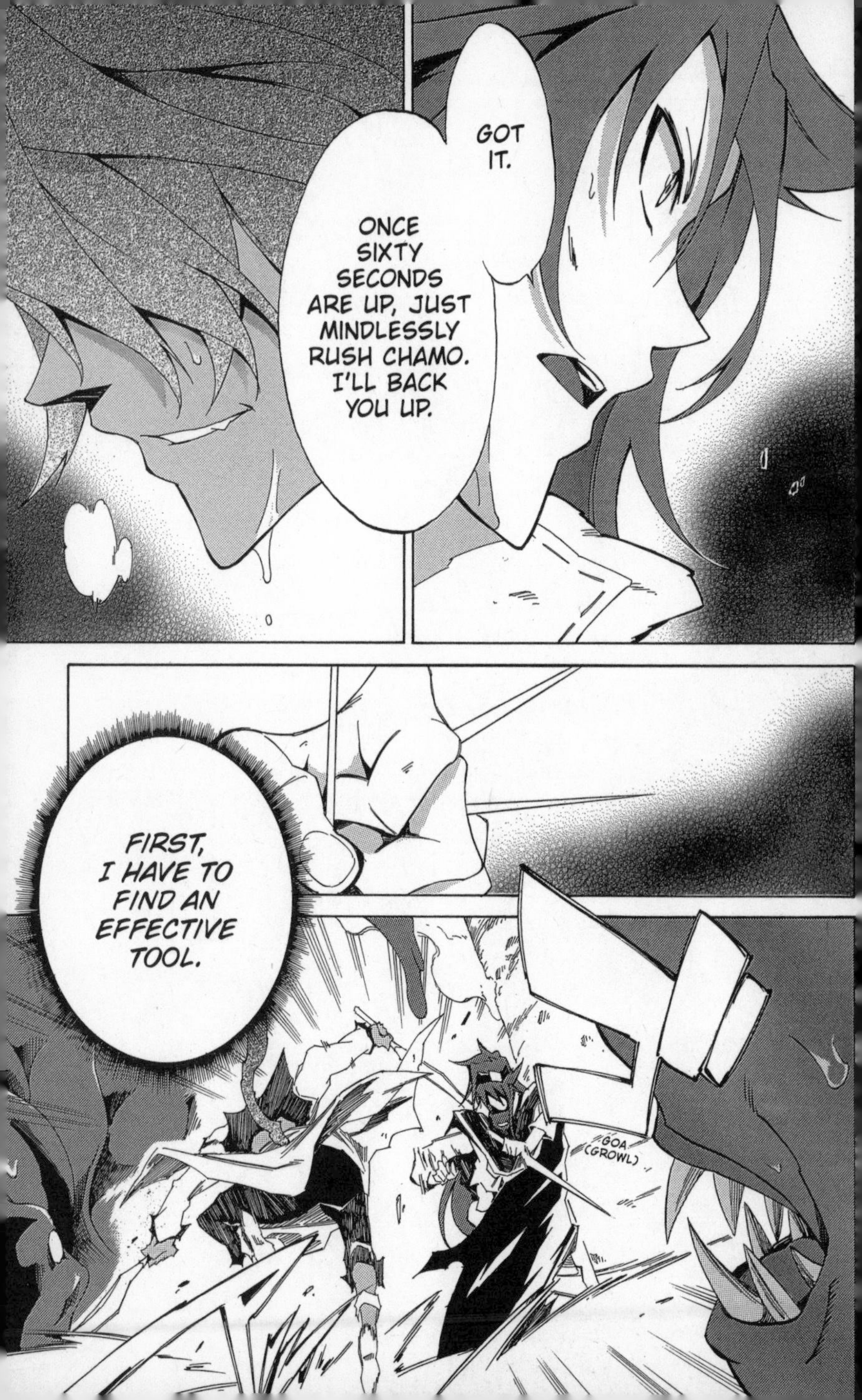
GOT IT.
ONCE SIXTY SECONDS ARE UP, JUST MINDLESSLY RUSH CHAMO. I'LL BACK YOU UP.
FIRST, I HAVE TO FIND AN EFFECTIVE TOOL.
GOA (GROWL)

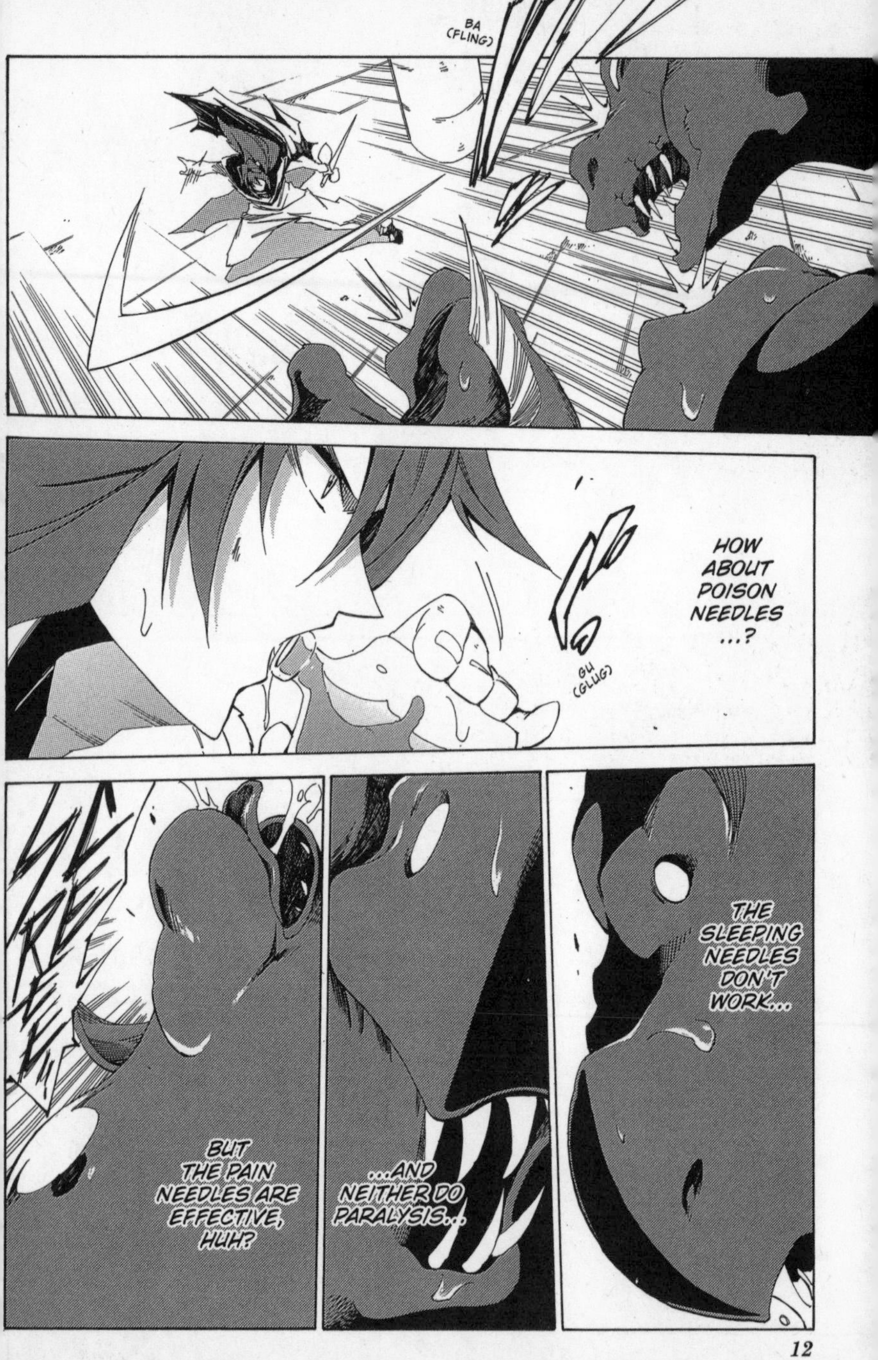
BA
(FLING)
HOW ABOUT POISON NEEDLES ...?
GU
(GLUG)
THE SLEEPING NEEDLES DON'T WORK...
...AND NEITHER DO PARALYSIS...
BUT THE PAIN NEEDLES ARE EFFECTIVE, HUH?

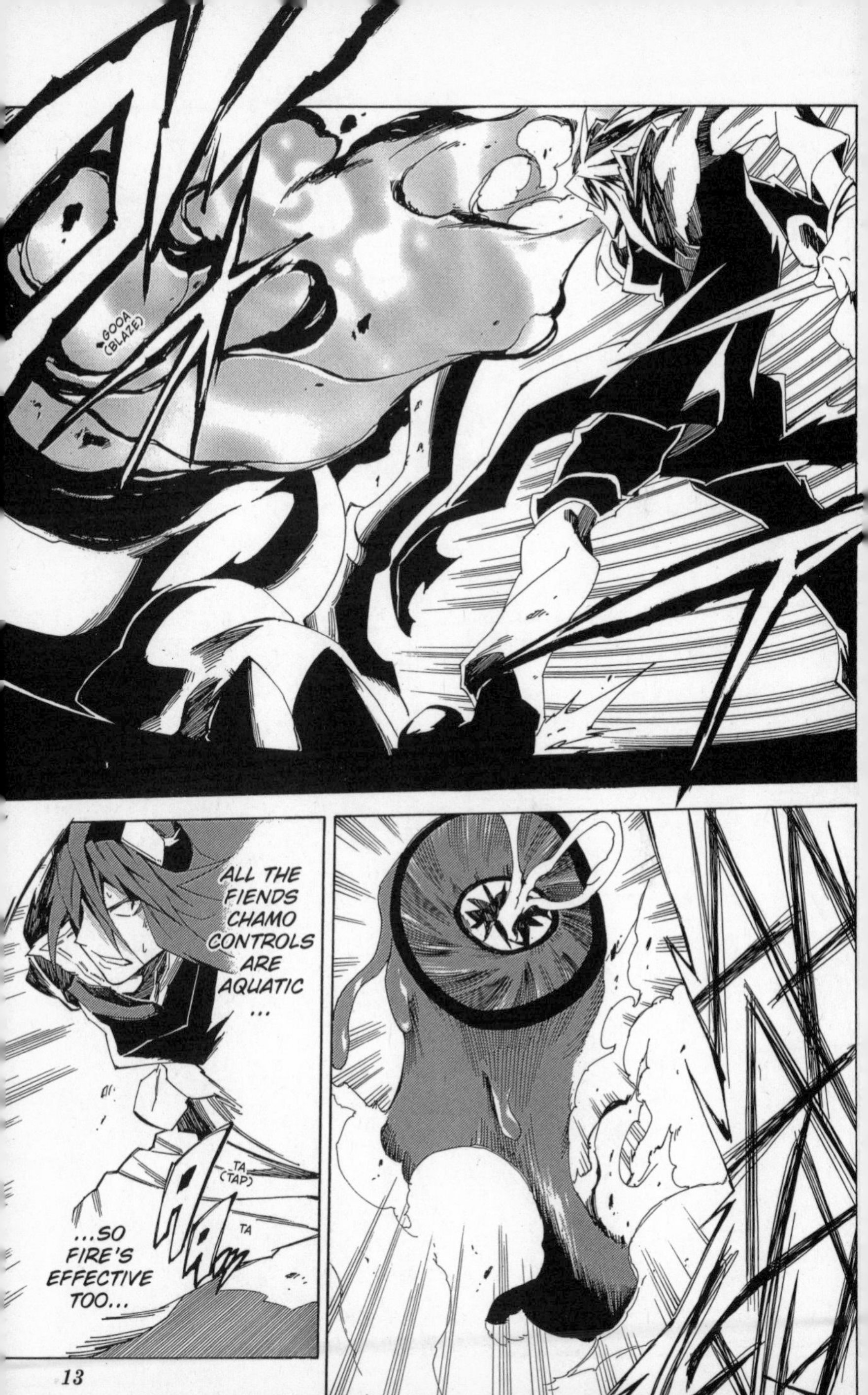
GOOA (BLAZE)
ALL THE FIENDS CHAMO CONTROLS ARE AQUATIC ...
TA (TAP)
TA
...SO FIRE'S EFFECTIVE TOO...

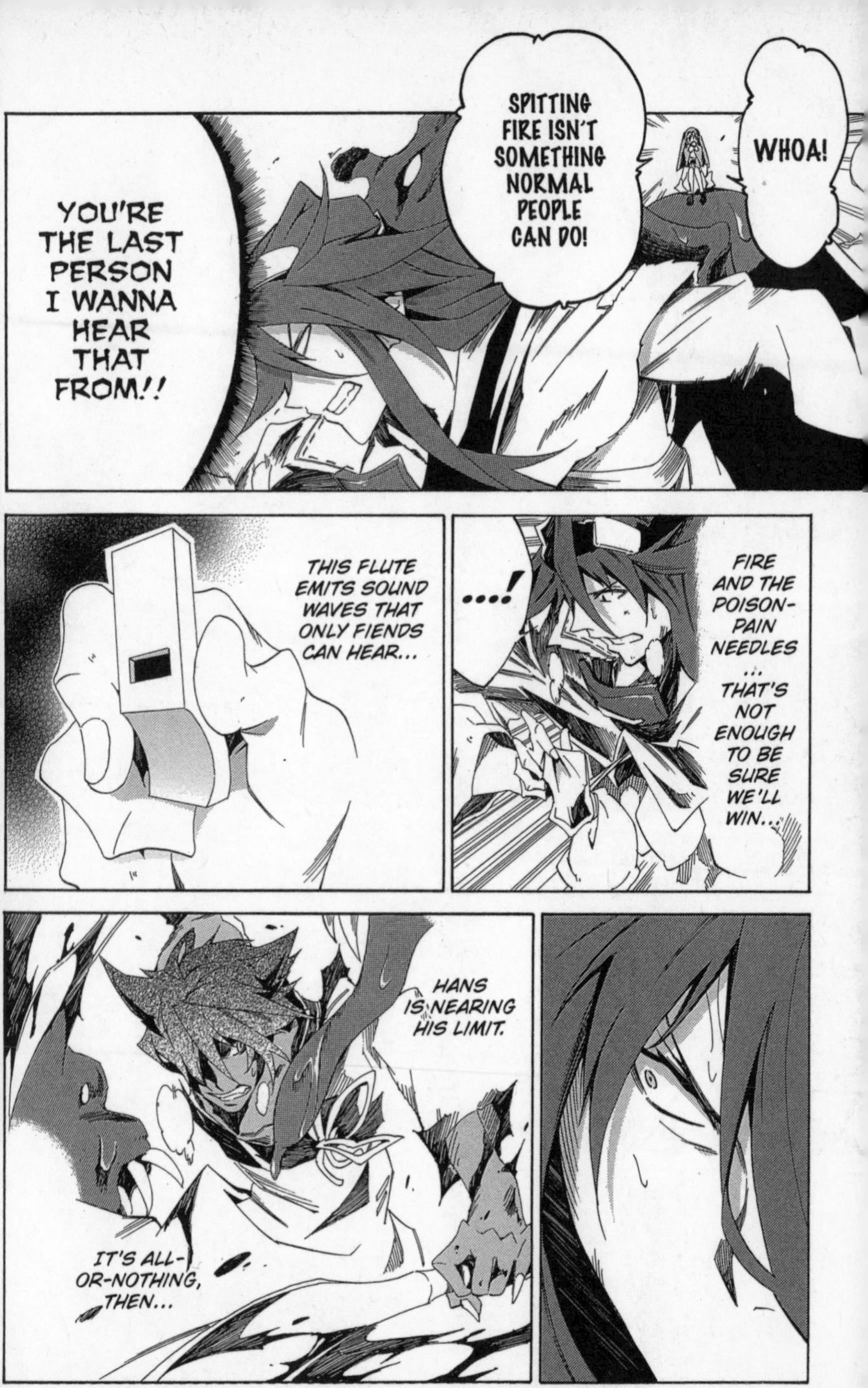
WHOA!
SPITTING FIRE ISN'T SOMETHING NORMAL PEOPLE CAN DO!
YOU'RE THE LAST PERSON I WANNA HEAR THAT FROM!!
FIRE AND THE POISON-PAIN NEEDLES... THAT'S NOT ENOUGH TO BE SURE WE'LL WIN...
...!
THIS FLUTE EMITS SOUND WAVES THAT ONLY FIENDS CAN HEAR...
HANS IS NEARING HIS LIMIT.
IT'S ALL-OR-NOTHING, THEN...

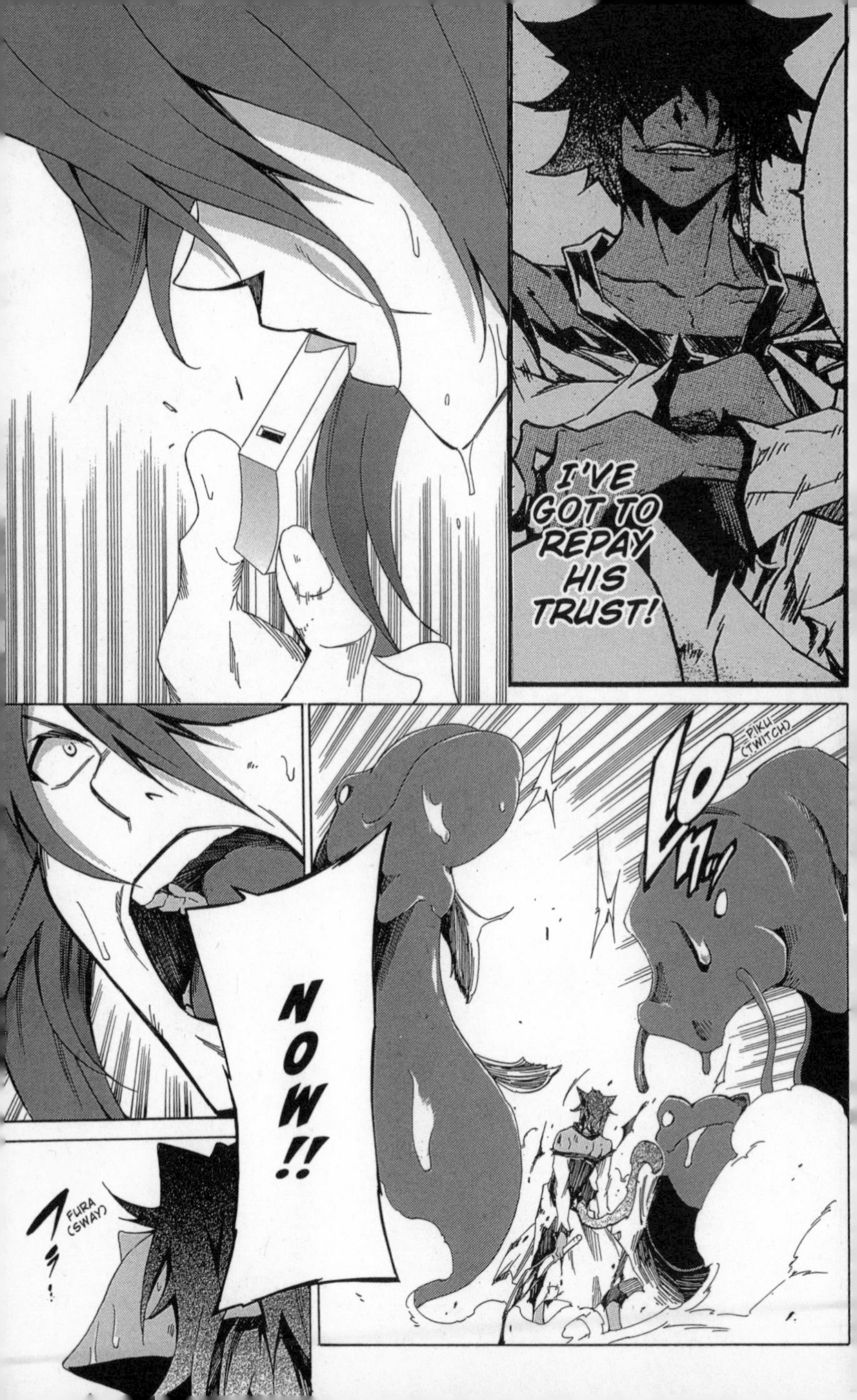
I'VE GOT TO REPAY HIS TRUST!
PIKU (TWITCH)
NOW!!
FURA (SWAY)

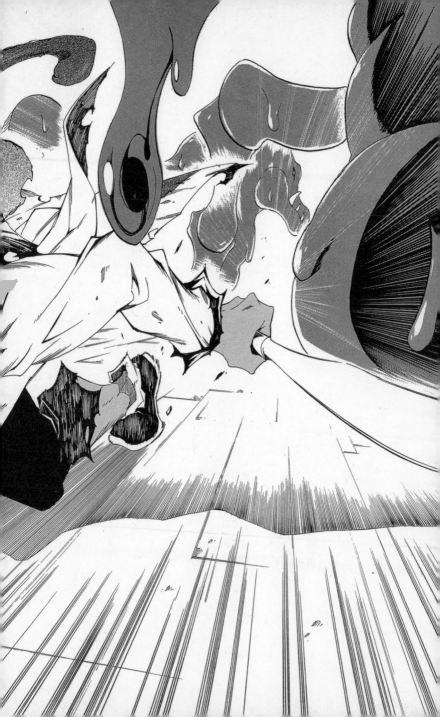

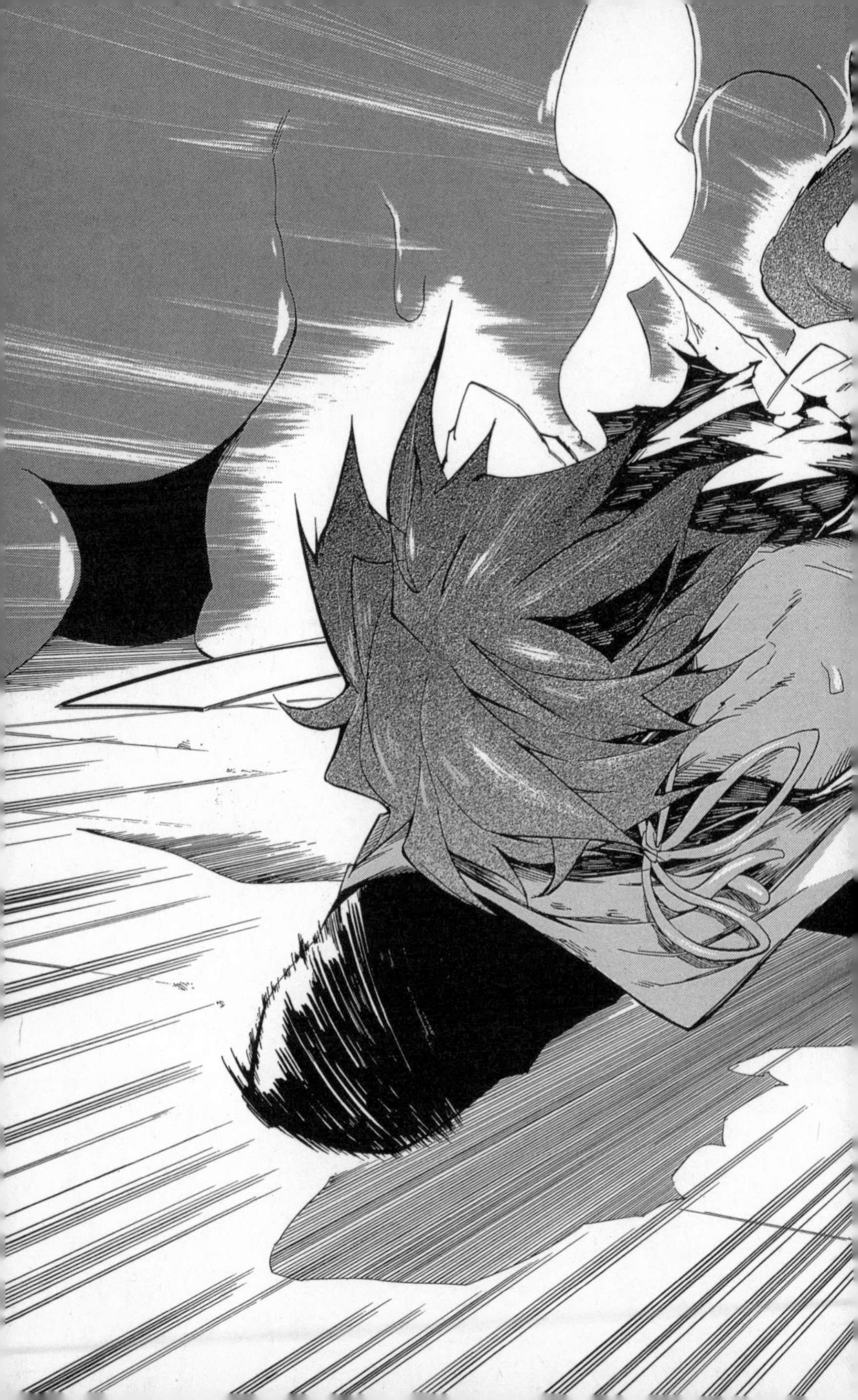

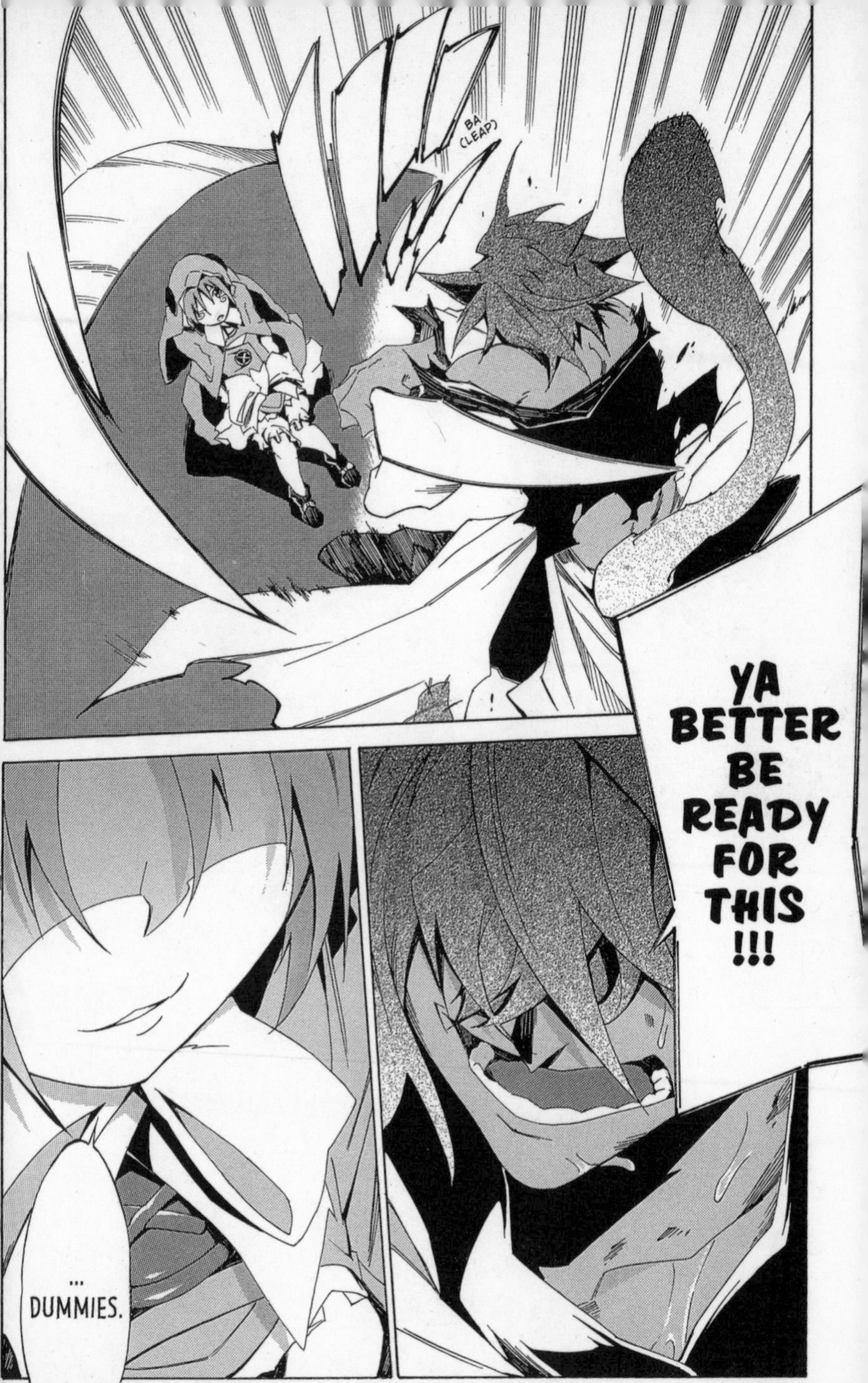
BA (LEAP)
YA BETTER BE READY FOR THIS!!!
...DUMMIES.

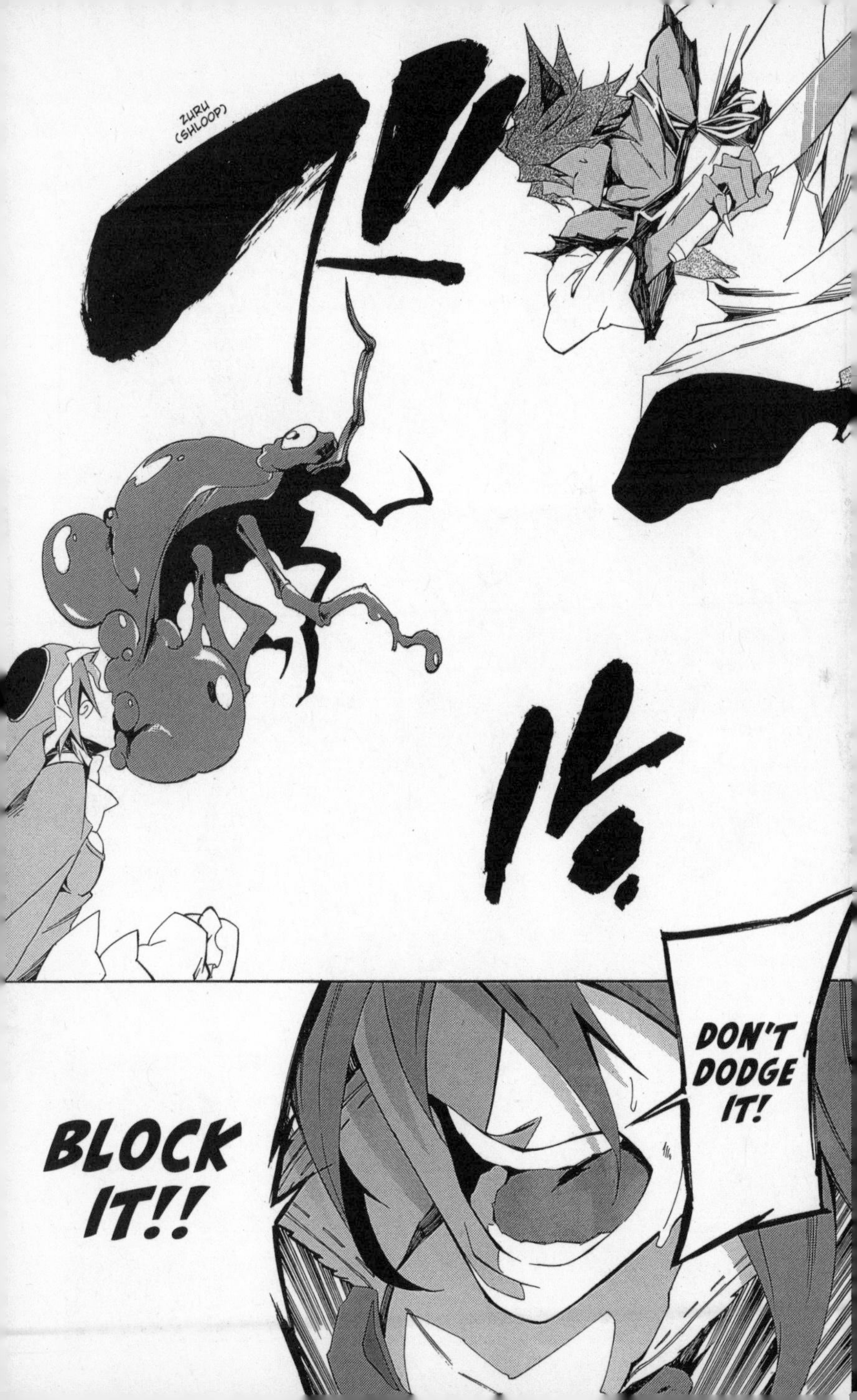
ZURU (SHLOOP)
DON'T DODGE IT!
BLOCK IT!!

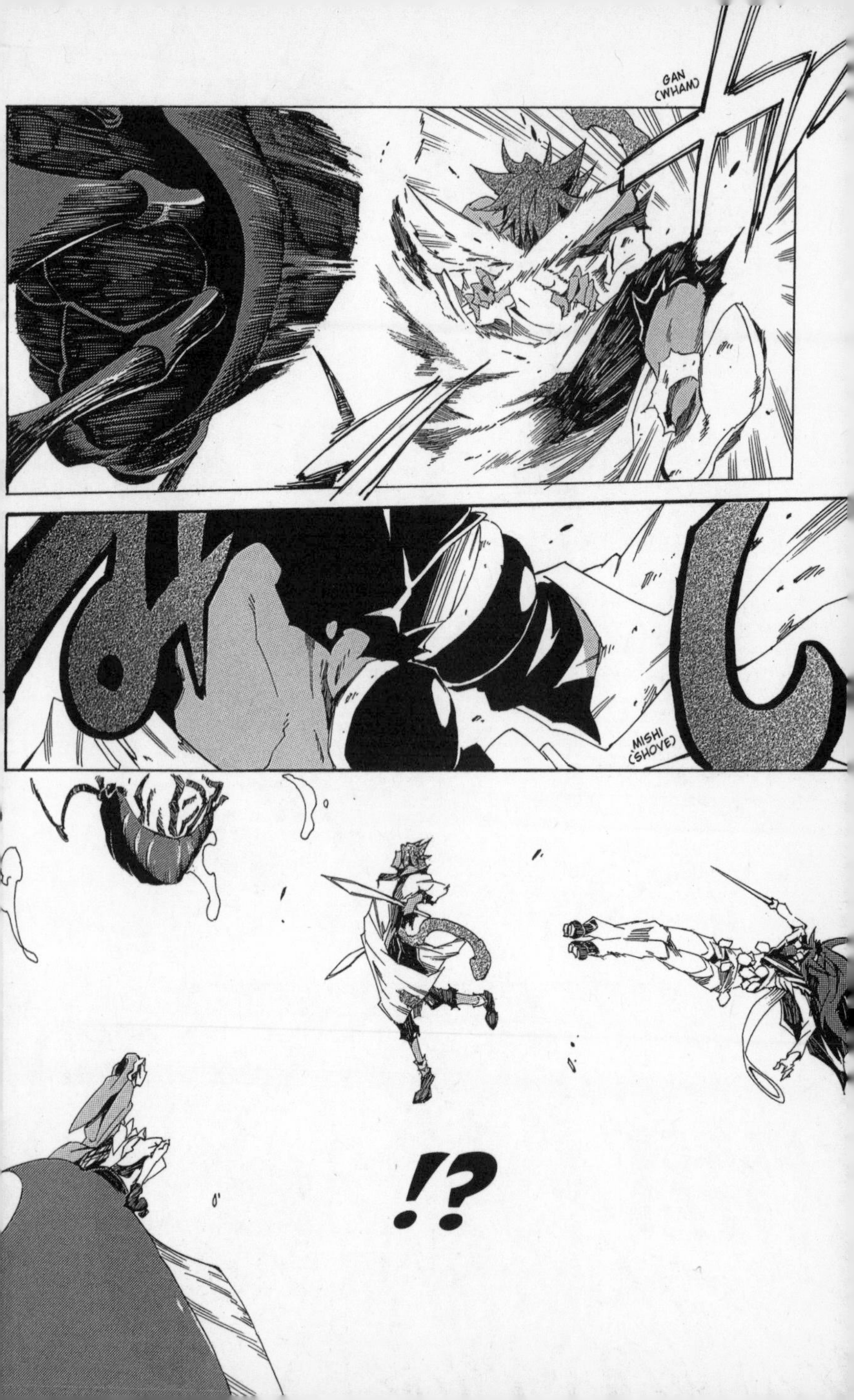
GAN (WHAM)
MISHI (SHOVE)
!?

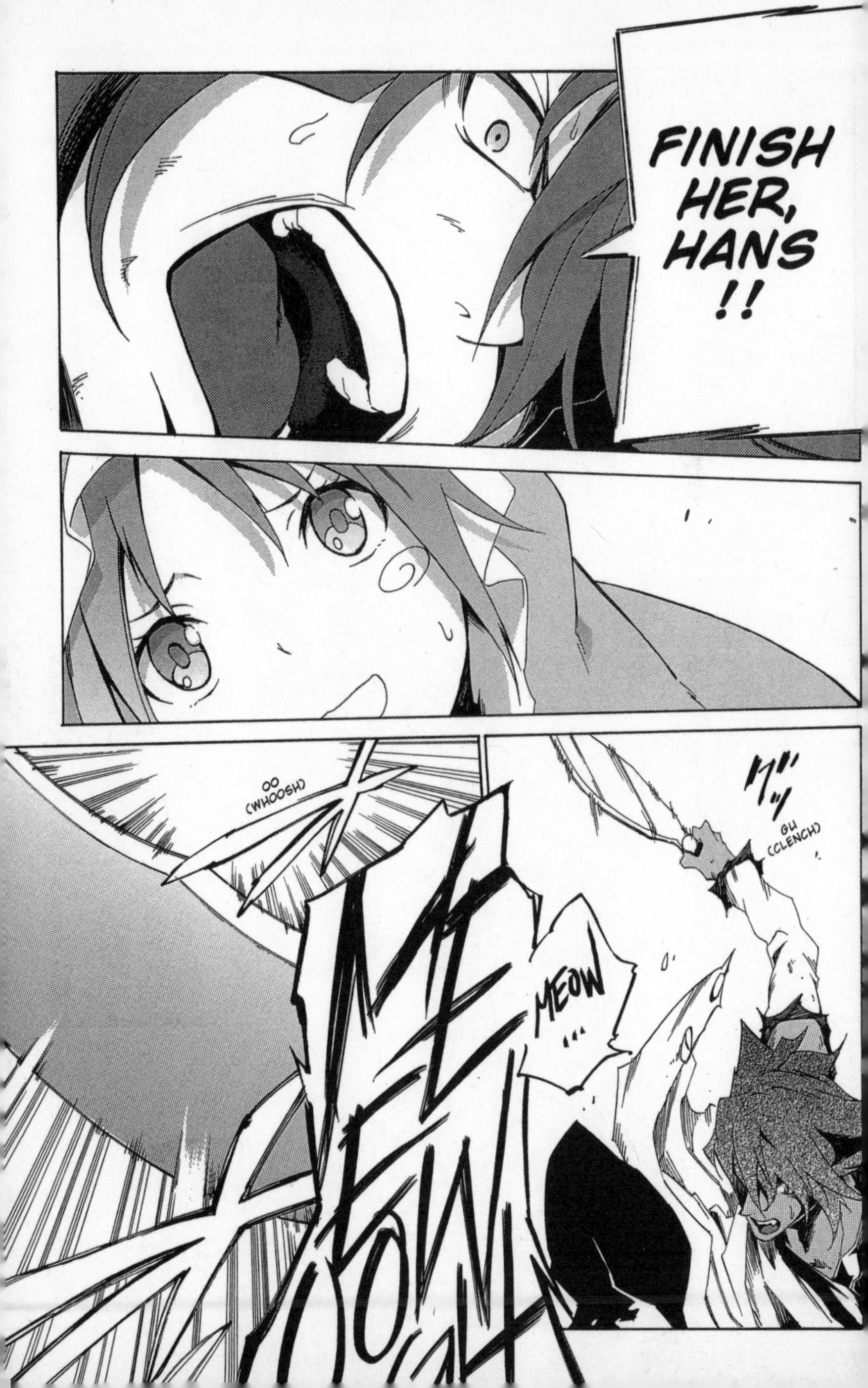
FINISH HER, HANS!!
GU (CLENCH)
MEOW...
OO (WHOOSH)

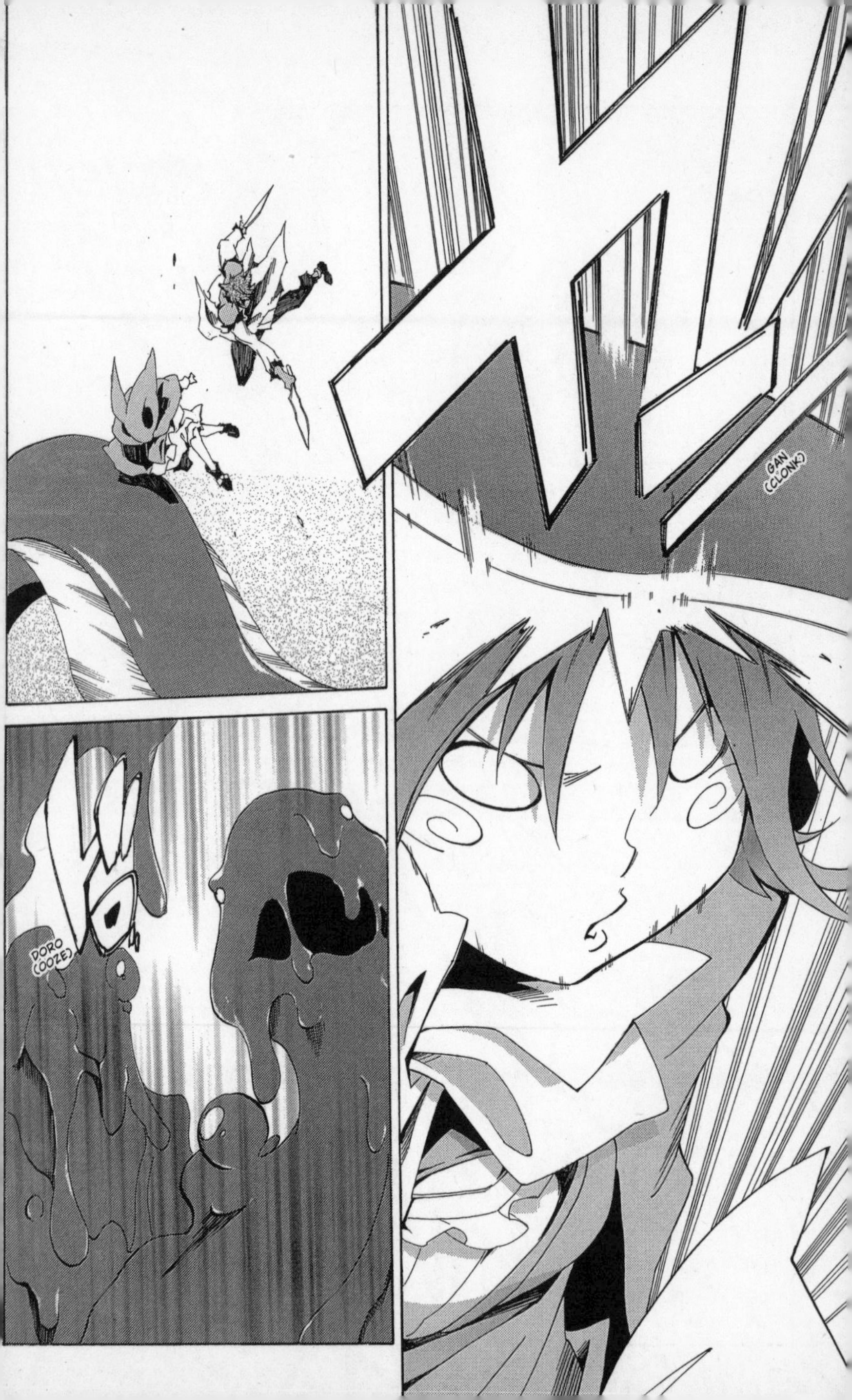
GAN (CLONK)
DORO (OOZE)

JURURURURU
(SHLOOP)

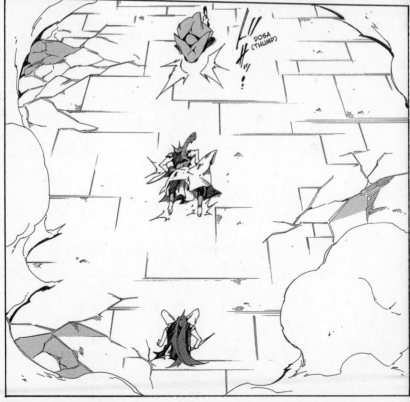

DOSA
(THUMP)

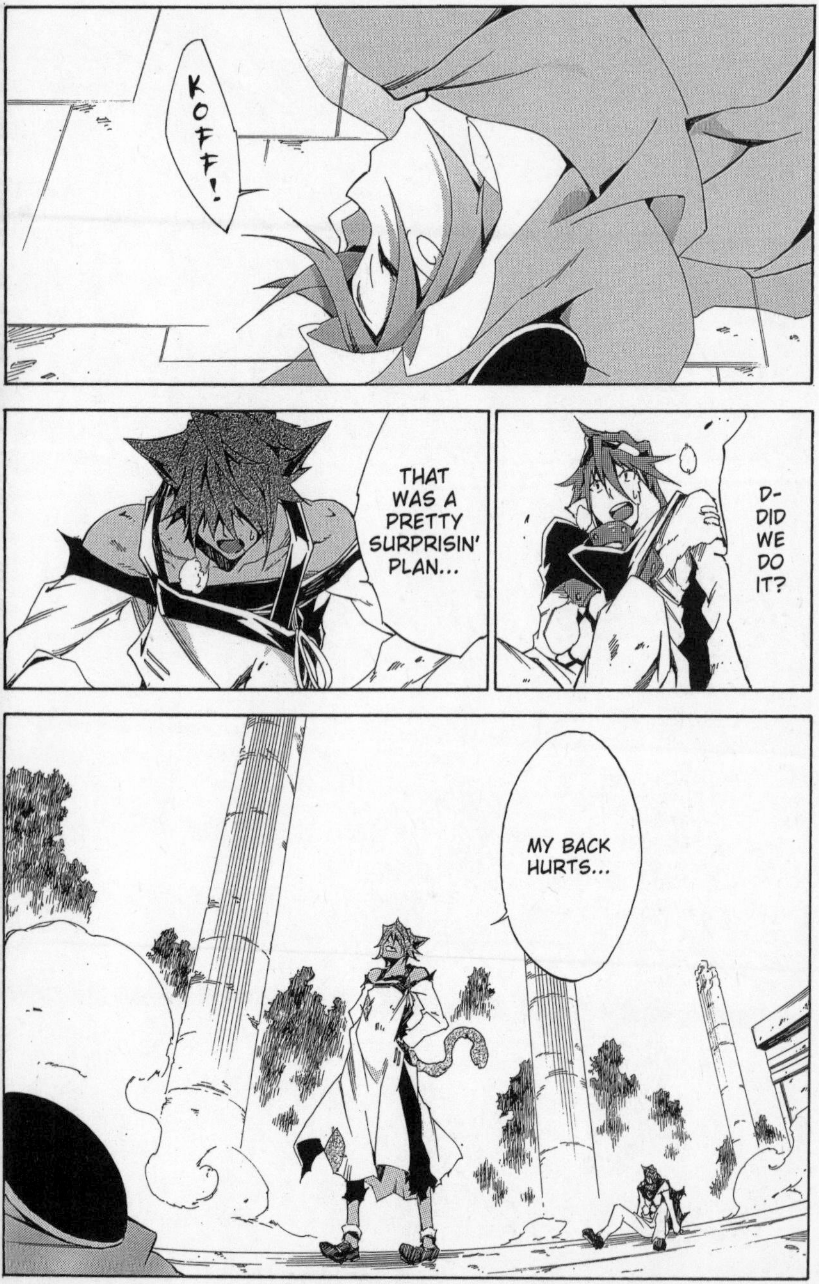
KOFF!
D-DID WE DO IT?
THAT WAS A PRETTY SURPRISIN' PLAN...
MY BACK HURTS...

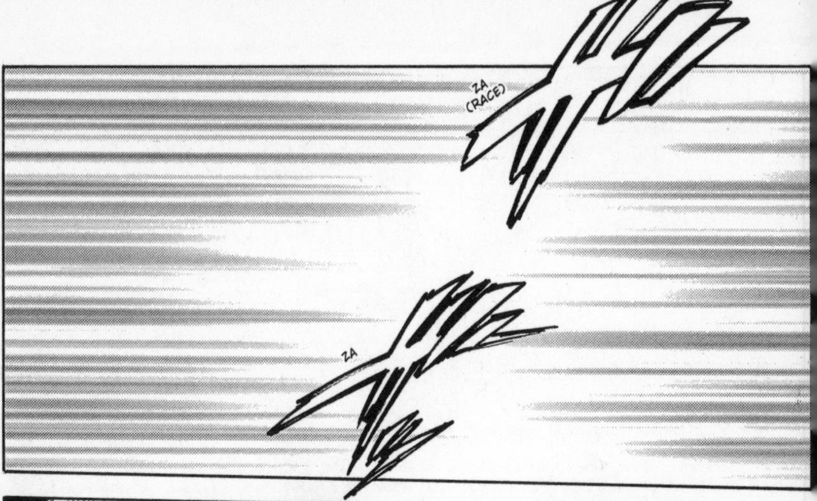
ZA
(RACE)
ZA
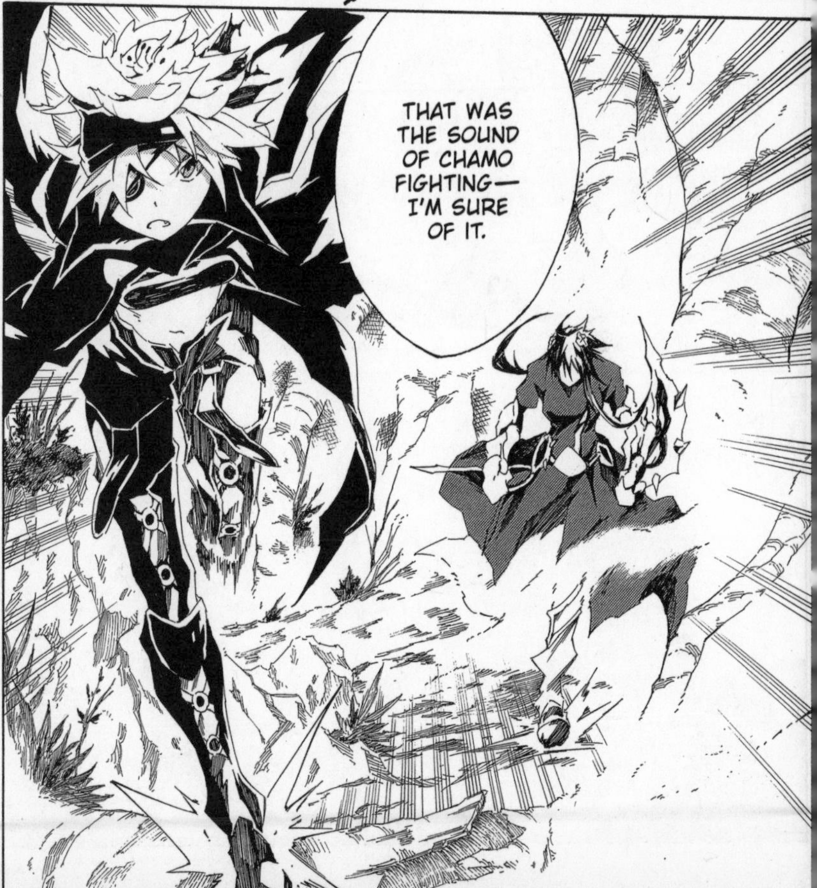
THAT WAS THE SOUND OF CHAMO FIGHTING— I'M SURE OF IT.

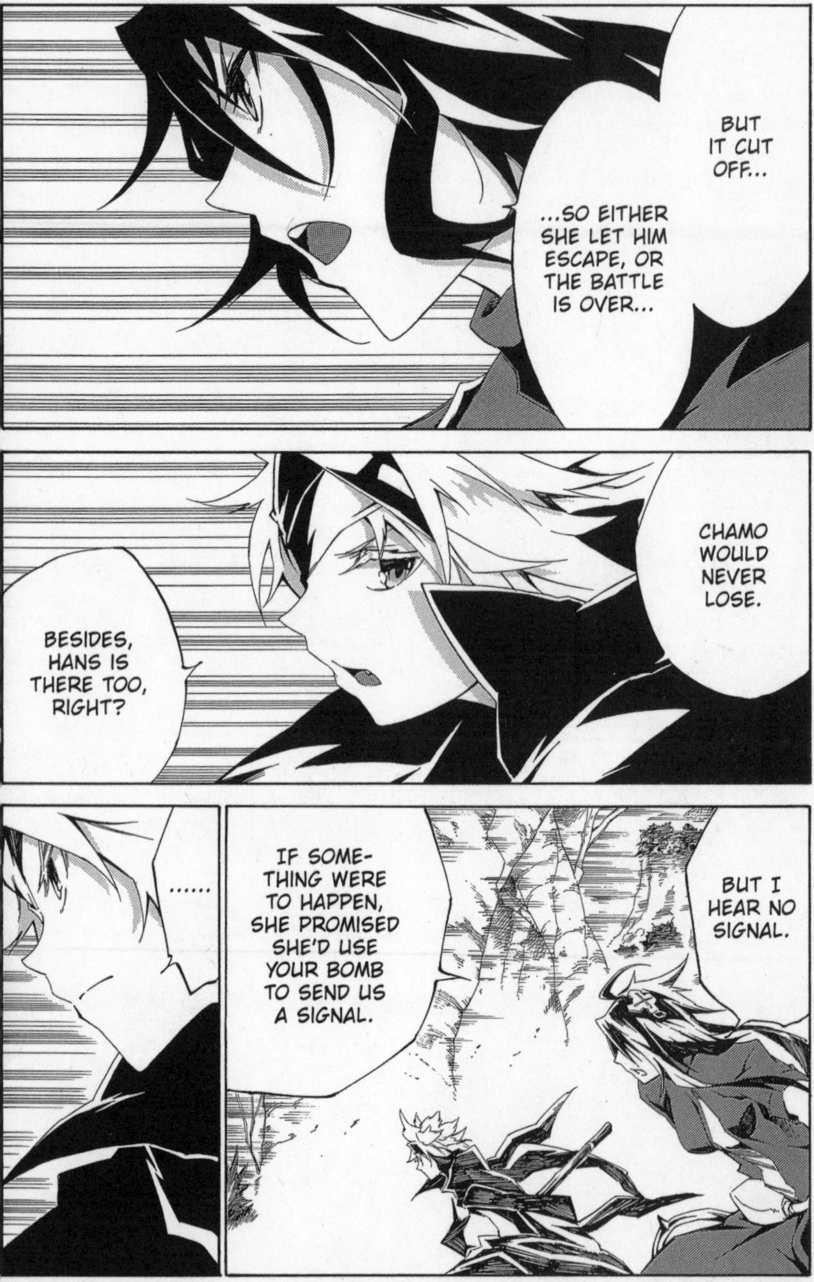
BUT IT CUT OFF...
...SO EITHER SHE LET HIM ESCAPE, OR THE BATTLE IS OVER...
CHAMO WOULD NEVER LOSE.
BESIDES, HANS IS THERE TOO, RIGHT?
BUT I HEAR NO SIGNAL.
IF SOME-THING WERE TO HAPPEN, SHE PROMISED SHE'D USE YOUR BOMB TO SEND US A SIGNAL.
......

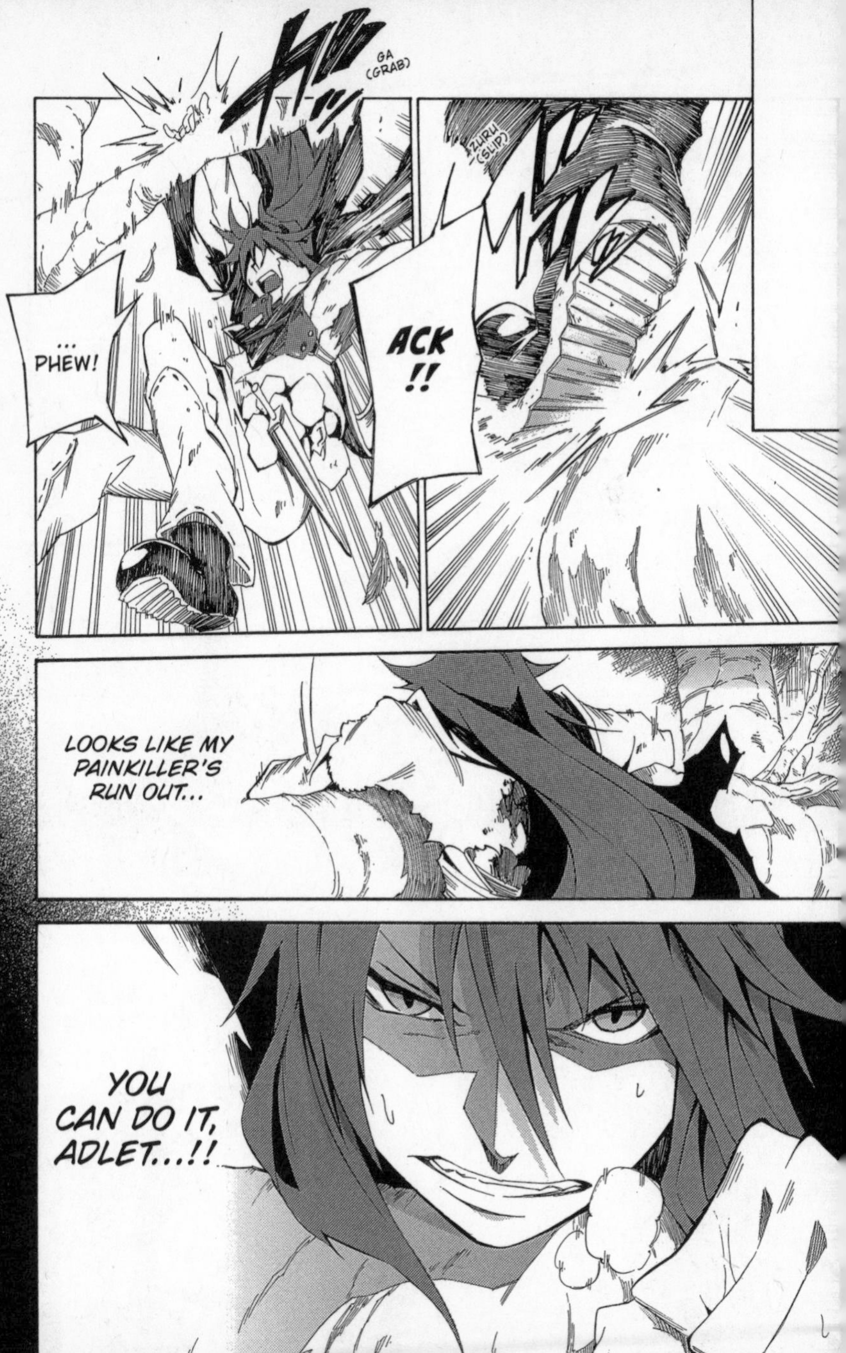

ZURU (SLIP)
ACK !!
GA (GRAB)
... PHEW!
LOOKS LIKE MY PAINKILLER'S RUN OUT...
YOU CAN DO IT, ADLET...!!

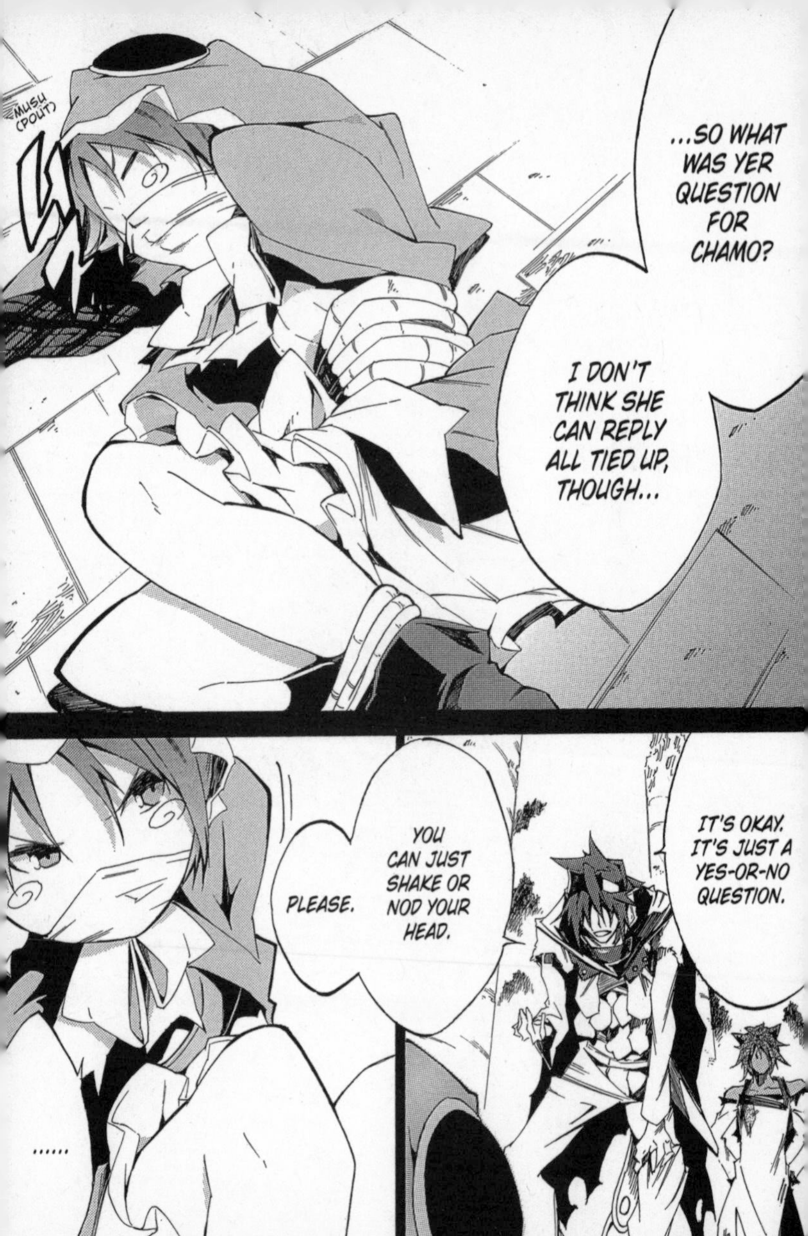
...SO WHAT WAS YER QUESTION FOR CHAMO?
I DON'T THINK SHE CAN REPLY ALL TIED UP, THOUGH...
MUSU (POUT)
IT'S OKAY. IT'S JUST A YES-OR-NO QUESTION.
YOU CAN JUST SHAKE OR NOD YOUR HEAD.
PLEASE.
......

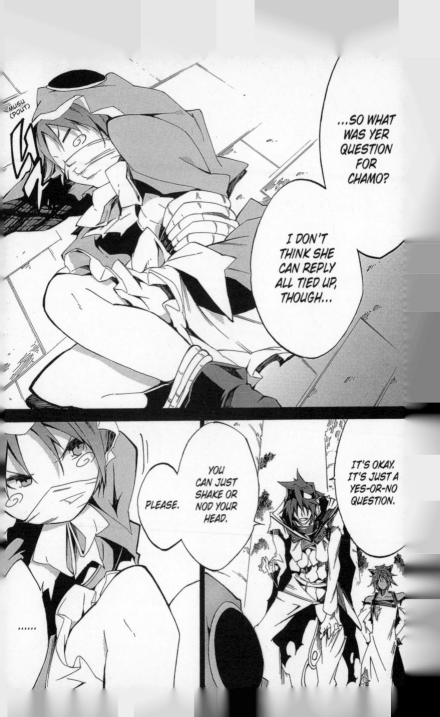

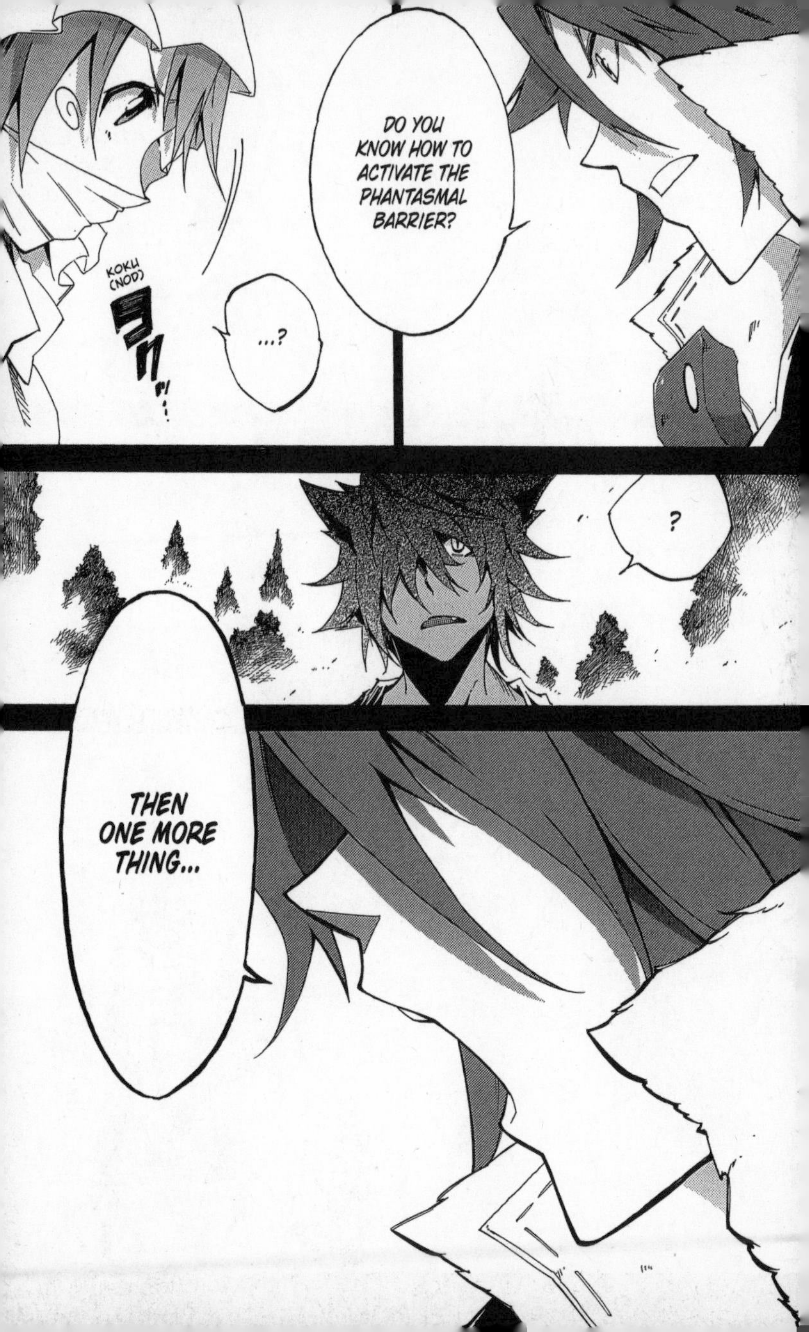
DO YOU KNOW HOW TO ACTIVATE THE PHANTASMAL BARRIER?
...?
KOKU (NOD)
?
THEN ONE MORE THING...

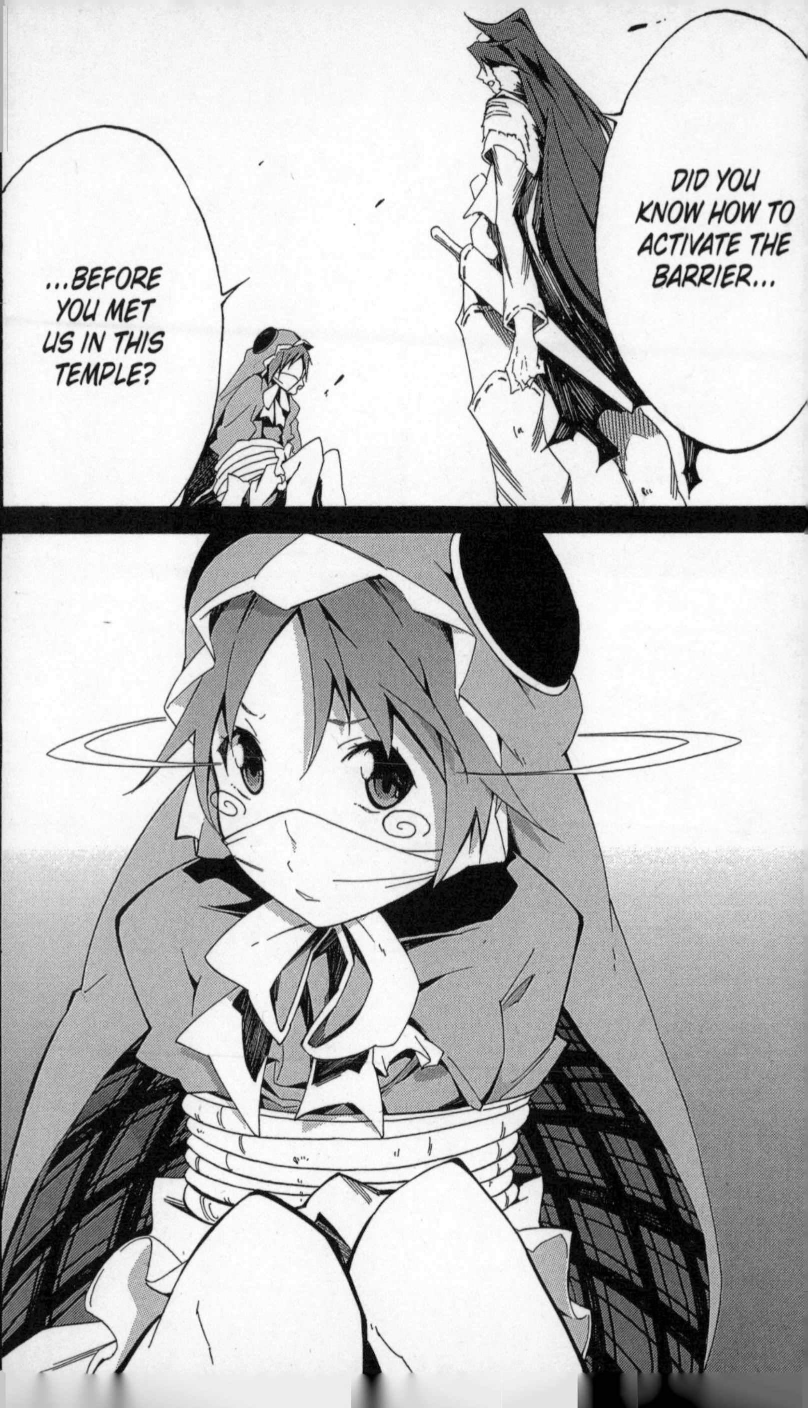
DID YOU KNOW HOW TO ACTIVATE THE BARRIER...
...BEFORE YOU MET US IN THIS TEMPLE?

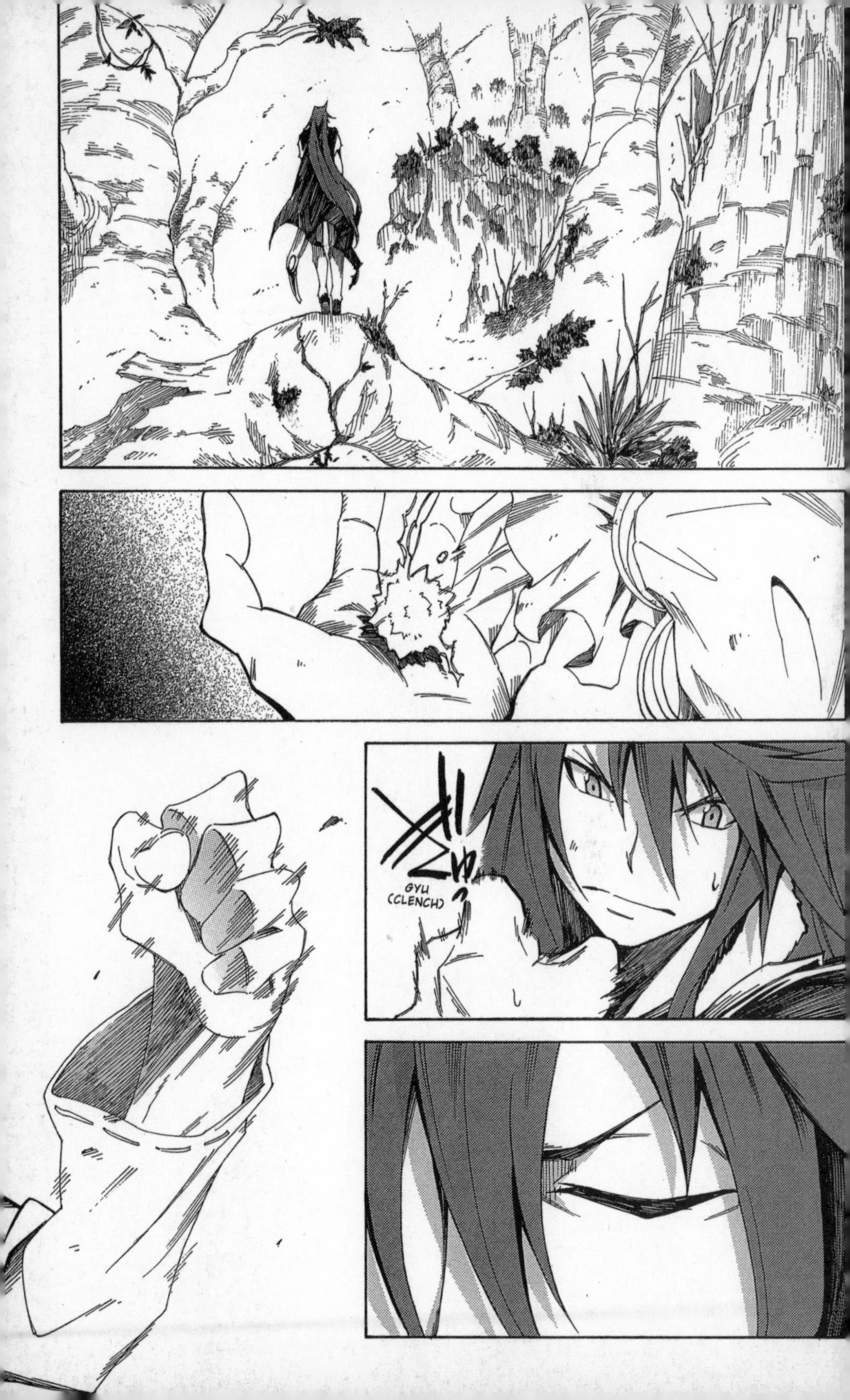
ぎゅっ
GYU
(CLENCH)

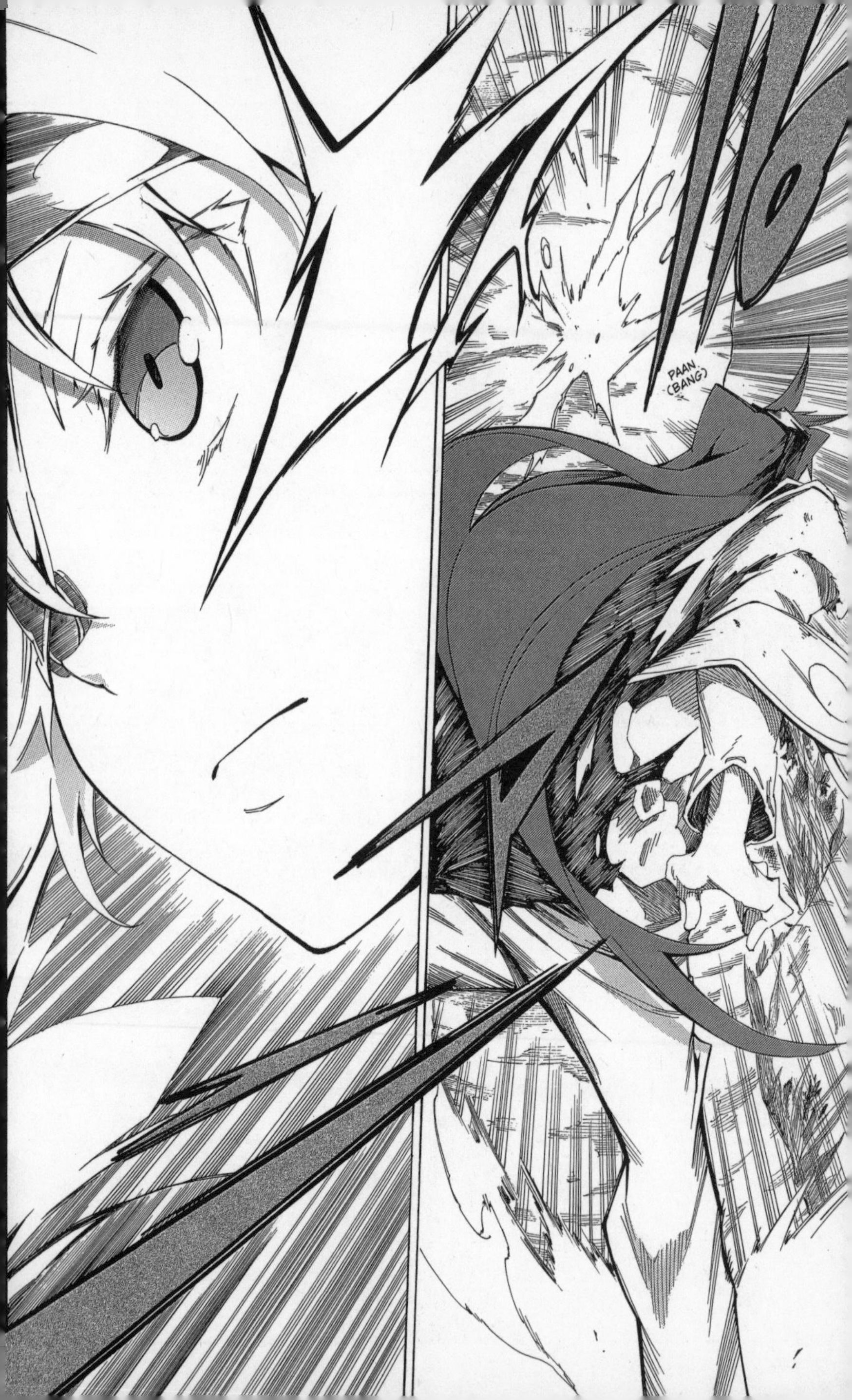
PAAN
(BANG)

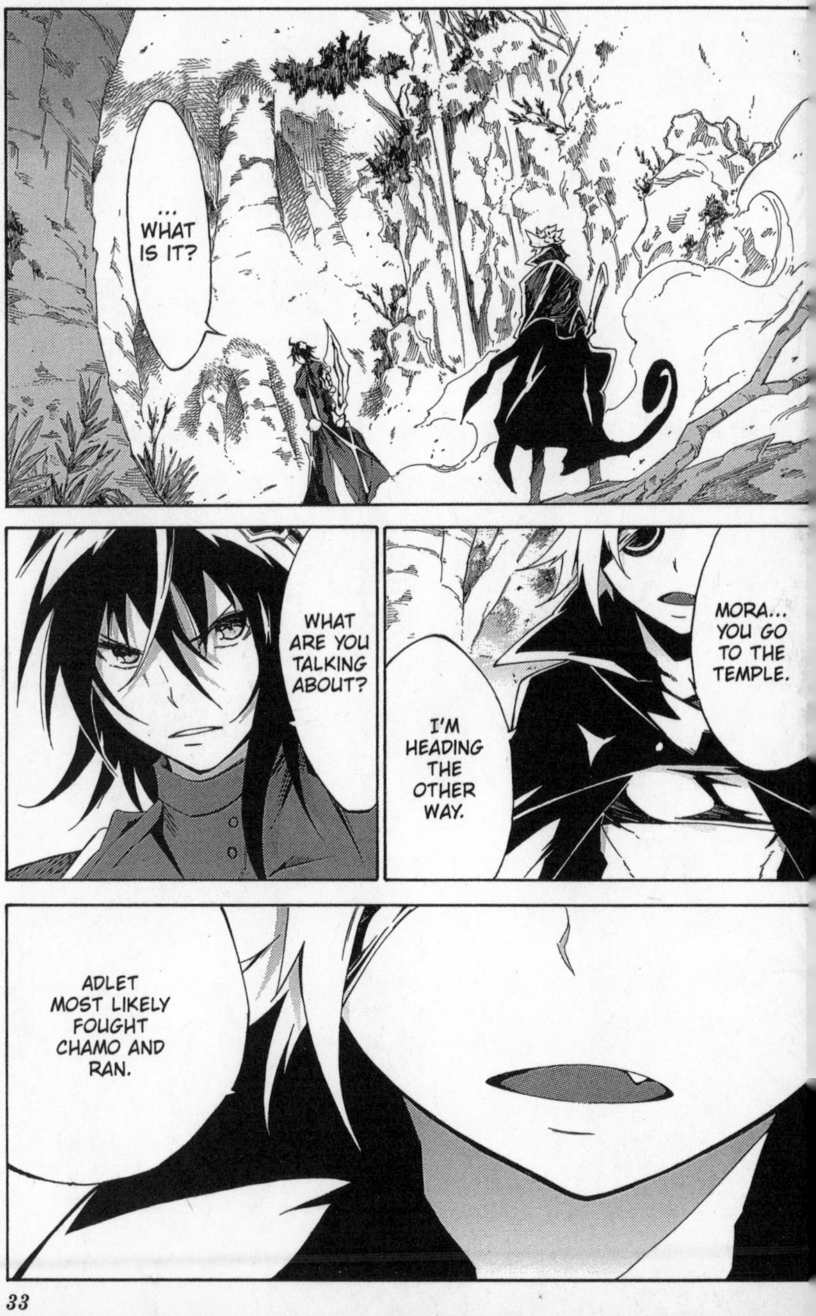
... WHAT IS IT?
MORA... YOU GO TO THE TEMPLE.
I'M HEADING THE OTHER WAY.
WHAT ARE YOU TALKING ABOUT?
ADLET MOST LIKELY FOUGHT CHAMO AND RAN.

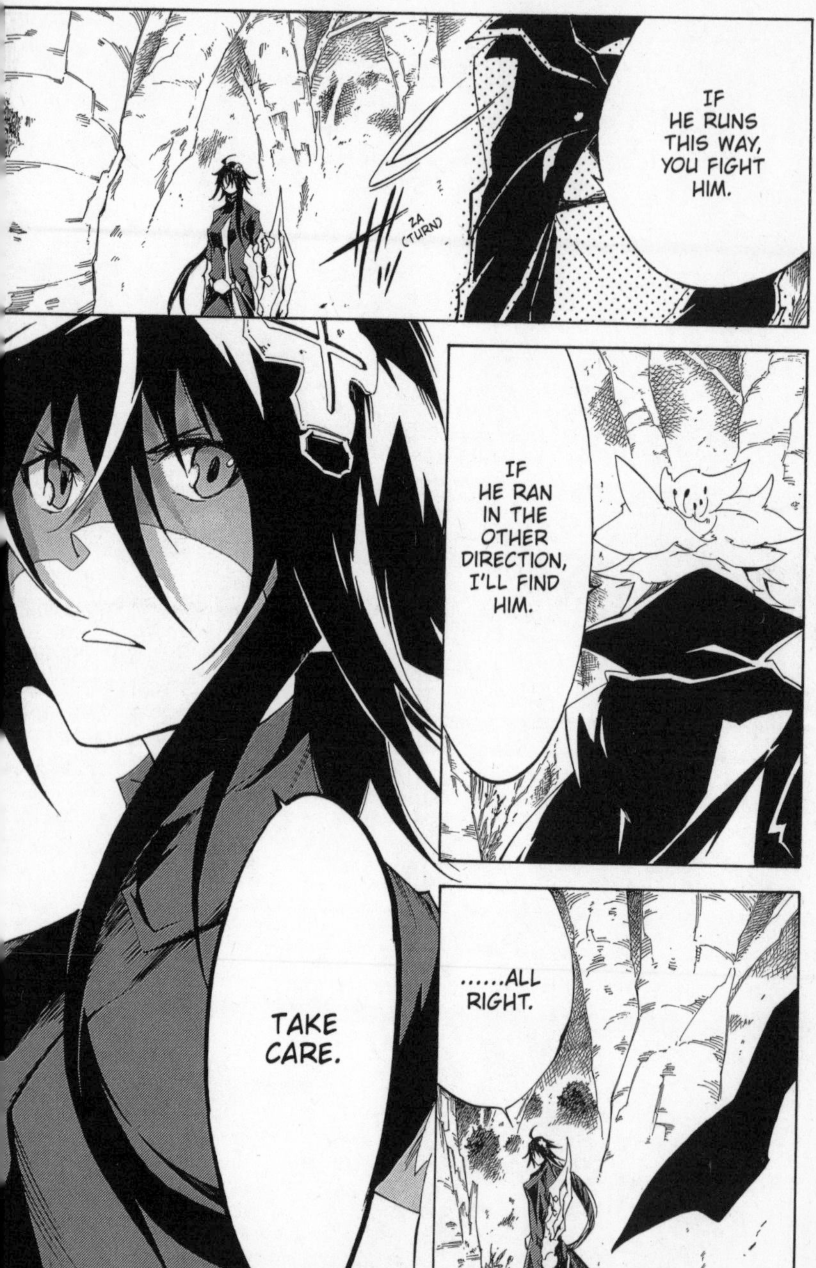
IF HE RUNS THIS WAY, YOU FIGHT HIM.
ZA (TURN)
IF HE RAN IN THE OTHER DIRECTION, I'LL FIND HIM.
......ALL RIGHT.
TAKE CARE.

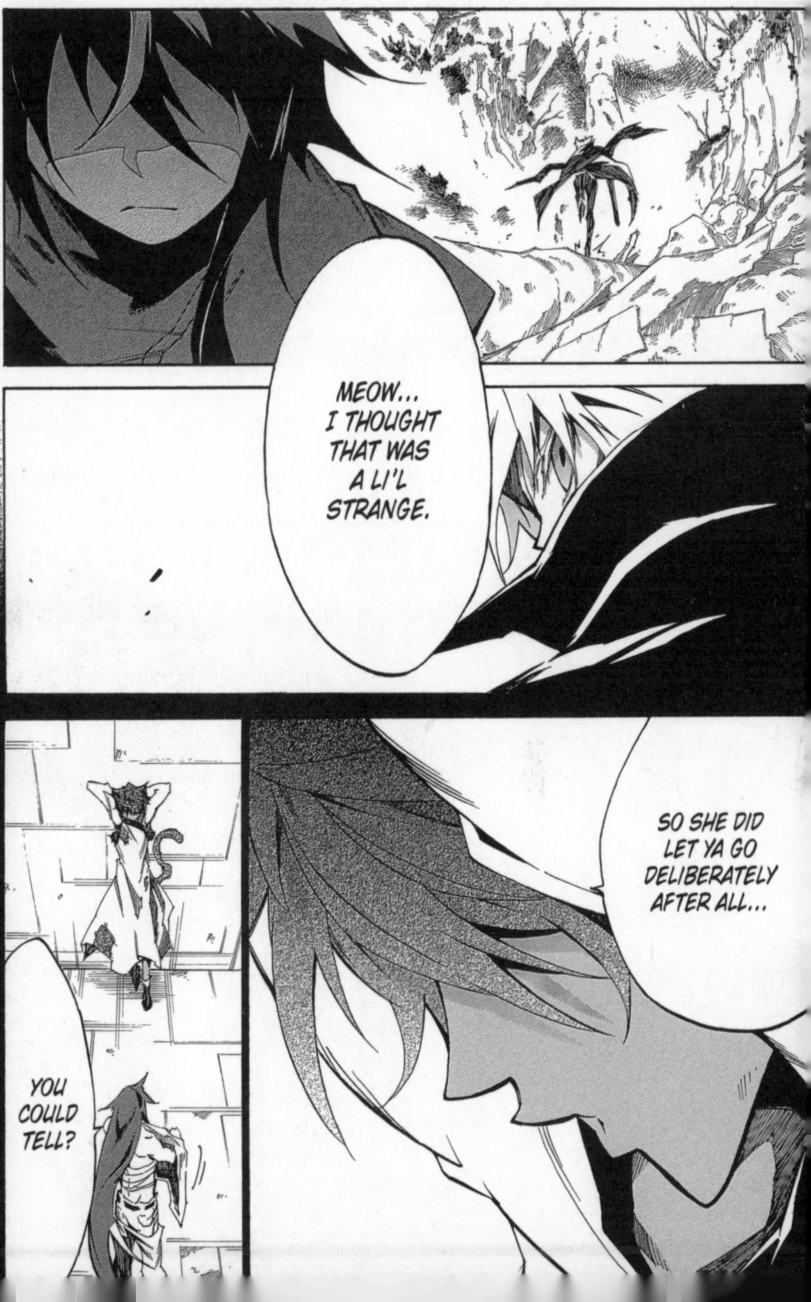
MEOW... I THOUGHT THAT WAS A LI'L STRANGE.
SO SHE DID LET YA GO DELIBERATELY AFTER ALL...
YOU COULD TELL?

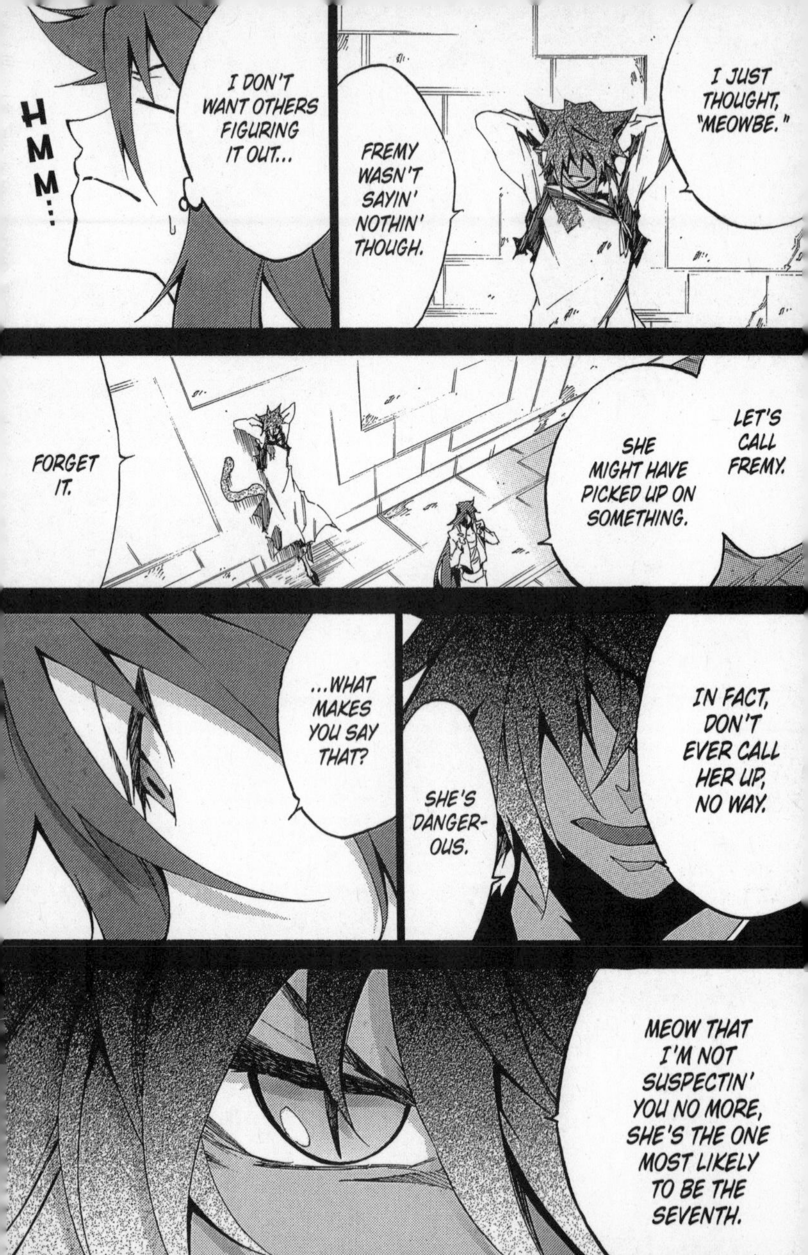
I JUST THOUGHT, "MEOWBE."
FREMY WASN'T SAYIN' NOTHIN' THOUGH.
I DON'T WANT OTHERS FIGURING IT OUT...
HMM...
LET'S CALL FREMY.
SHE MIGHT HAVE PICKED UP ON SOMETHING.
FORGET IT.
IN FACT, DON'T EVER CALL HER UP, NO WAY.
SHE'S DANGER-OUS.
...WHAT MAKES YOU SAY THAT?
MEOW THAT I'M NOT SUSPECTIN' YOU NO MORE, SHE'S THE ONE MOST LIKELY TO BE THE SEVENTH.

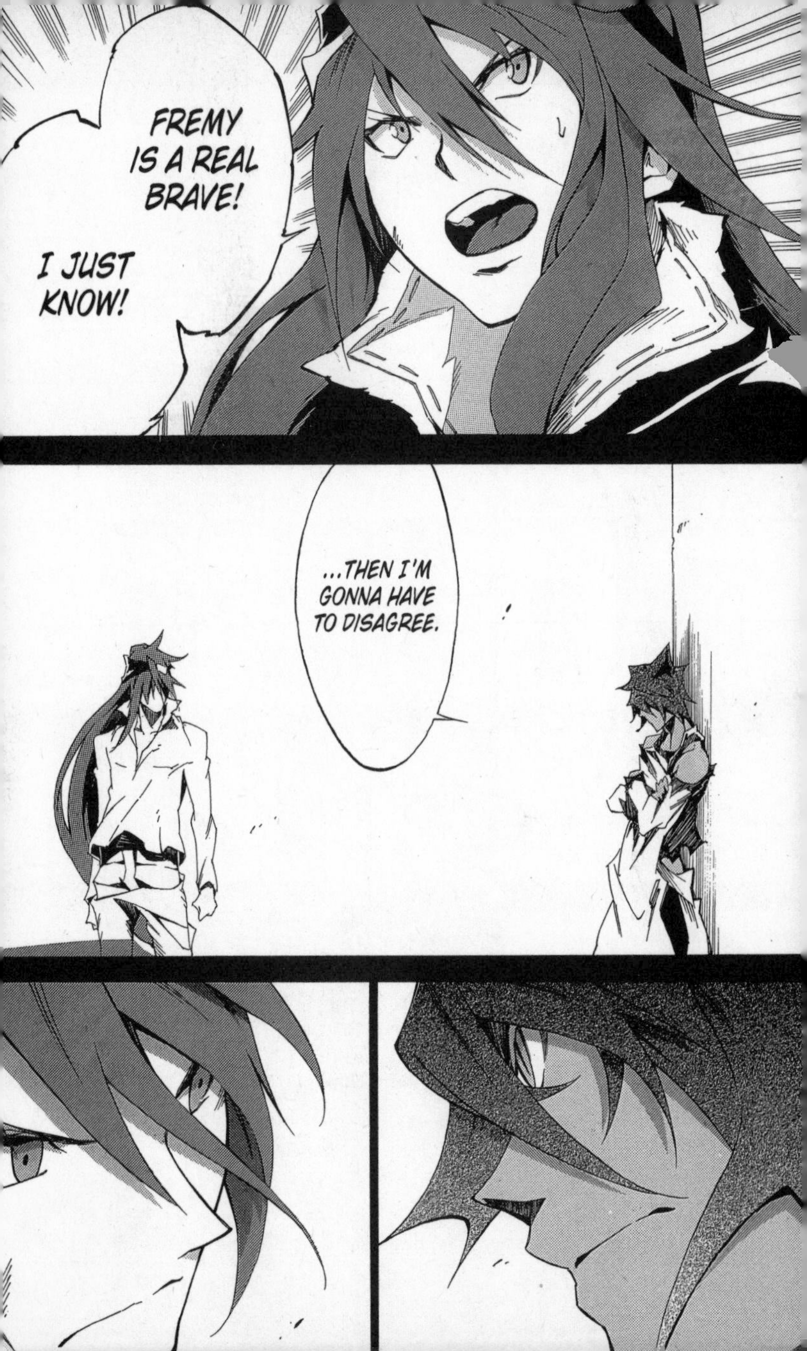
FREMY IS A REAL BRAVE!
I JUST KNOW!
...THEN I'M GONNA HAVE TO DISAGREE.

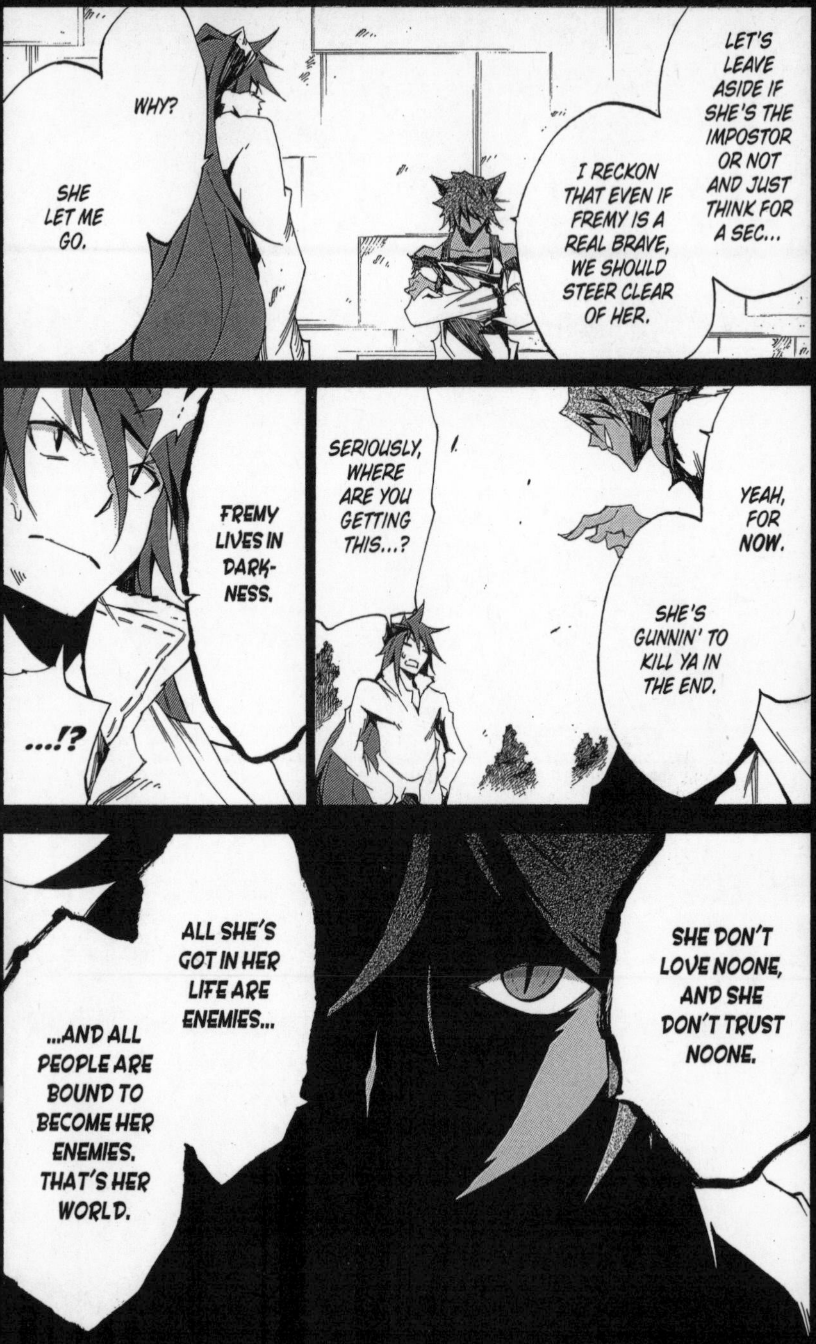
LET'S LEAVE ASIDE IF SHE'S THE IMPOSTOR OR NOT AND JUST THINK FOR A SEC...
I RECKON THAT EVEN IF FREMY IS A REAL BRAVE, WE SHOULD STEER CLEAR OF HER.
WHY?
SHE LET ME GO.
YEAH, FOR NOW.
SHE'S GUNNIN' TO KILL YA IN THE END.
SERIOUSLY, WHERE ARE YOU GETTING THIS...?
FREMY LIVES IN DARKNESS.
...!?
SHE DON'T LOVE NOONE, AND SHE DON'T TRUST NOONE.
ALL SHE'S GOT IN HER LIFE ARE ENEMIES...
...AND ALL PEOPLE ARE BOUND TO BECOME HER ENEMIES. THAT'S HER WORLD.

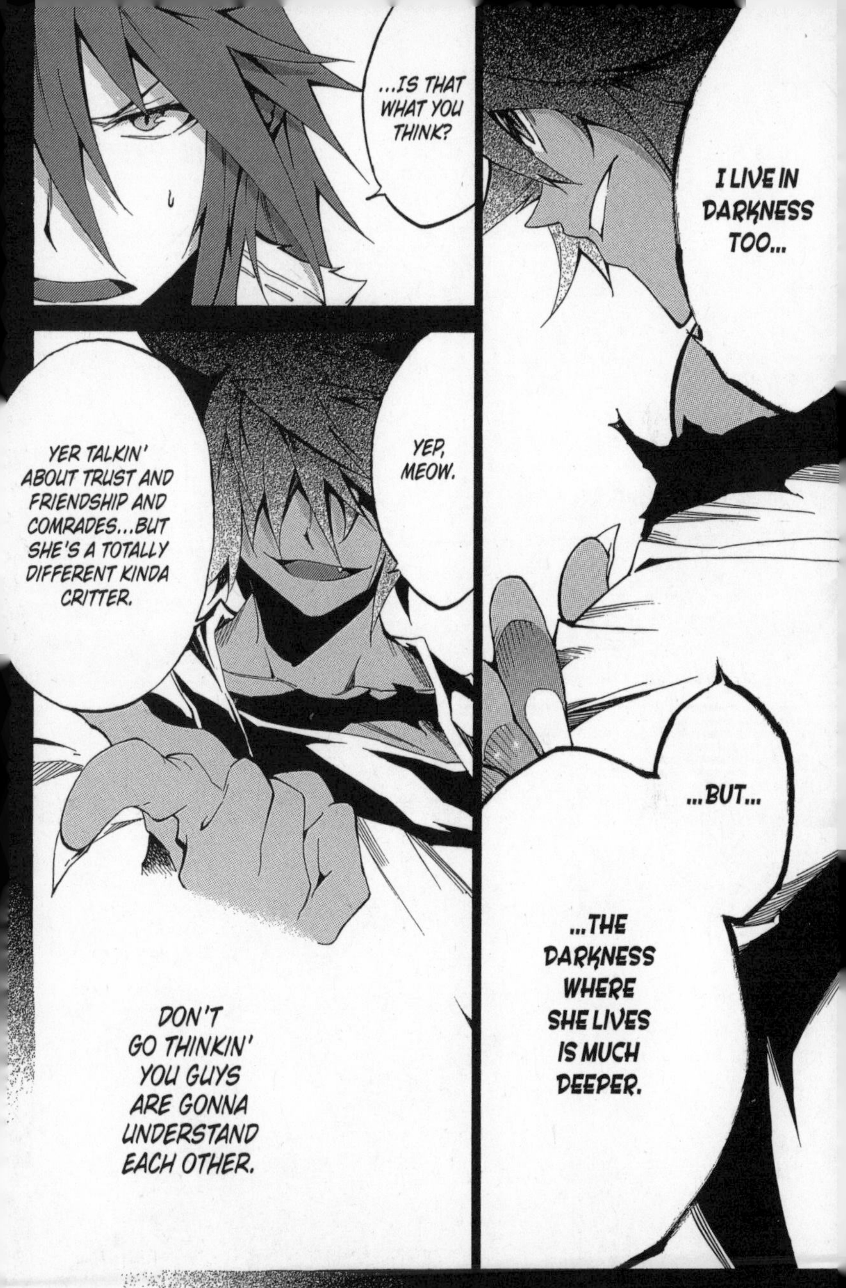
I LIVE IN DARKNESS TOO...
...BUT...
...THE DARKNESS WHERE SHE LIVES IS MUCH DEEPER.
...IS THAT WHAT YOU THINK?
YEP, MEOW.
YER TALKIN' ABOUT TRUST AND FRIENDSHIP AND COMRADES...BUT SHE'S A TOTALLY DIFFERENT KINDA CRITTER.
DON'T GO THINKIN' YOU GUYS ARE GONNA UNDERSTAND EACH OTHER.

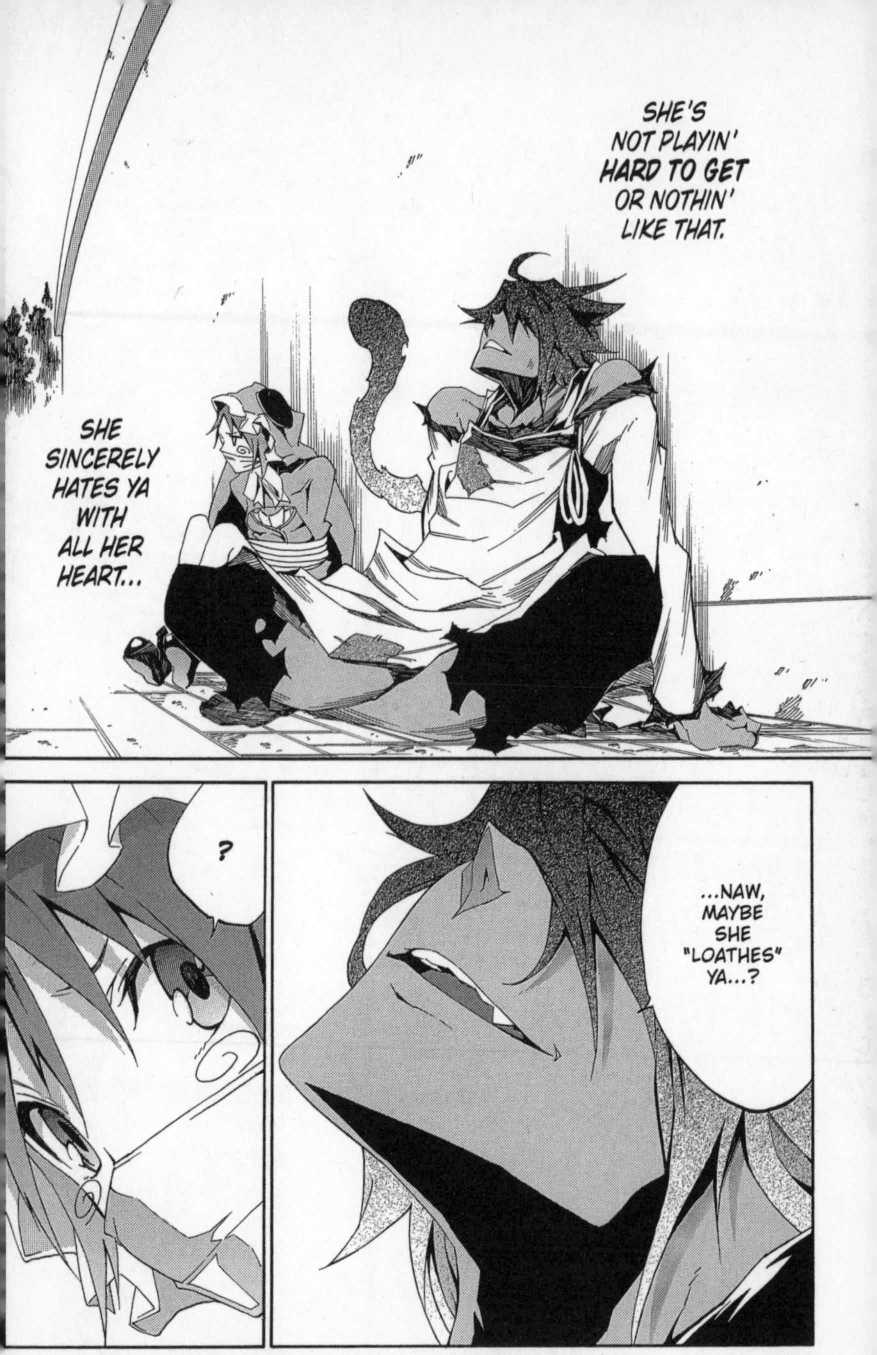
SHE'S NOT PLAYIN' HARD TO GET OR NOTHIN' LIKE THAT.
SHE SINCERELY HATES YA WITH ALL HER HEART...
...NAW, MAYBE SHE "LOATHES" YA...?
?

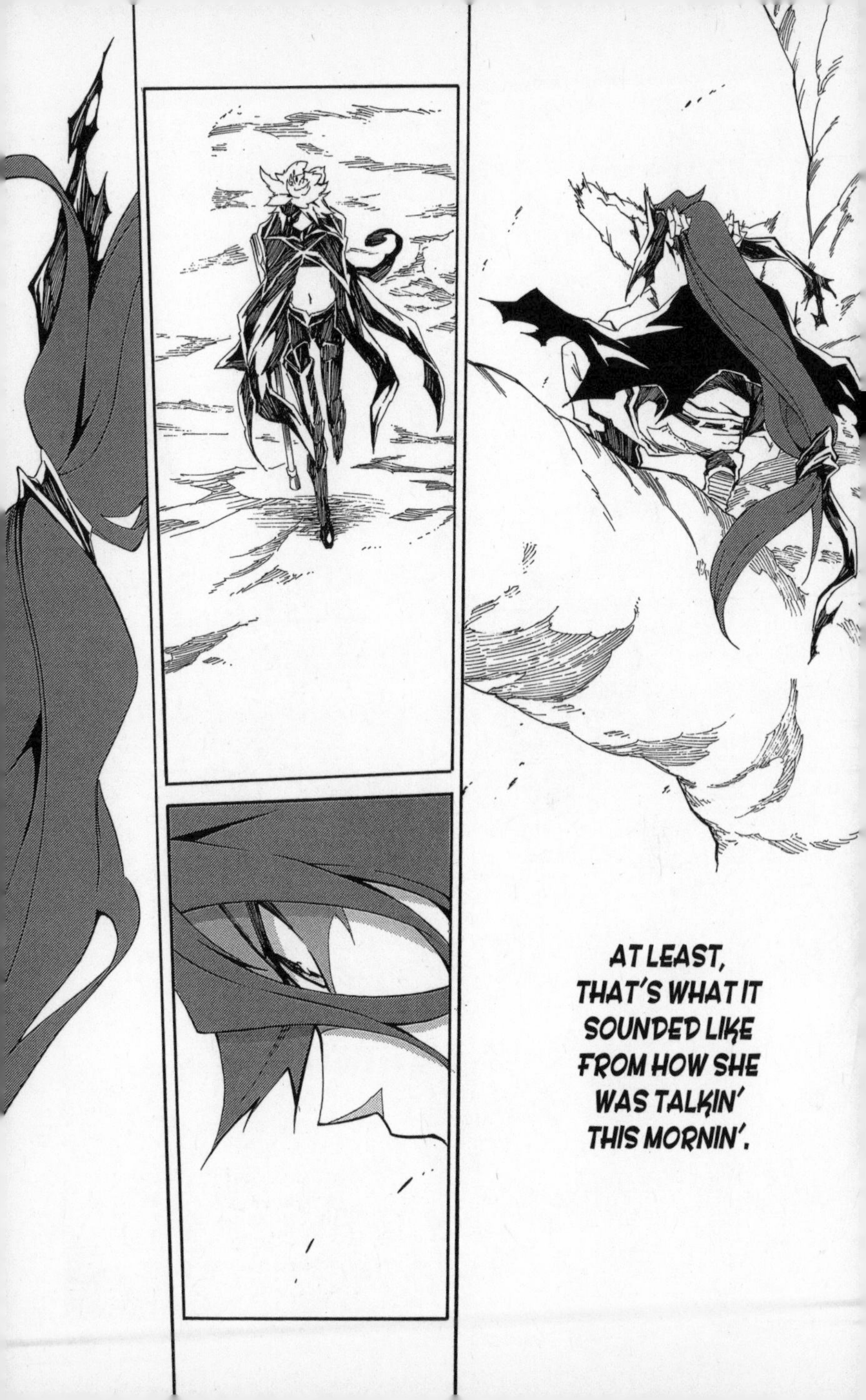
AT LEAST, THAT'S WHAT IT SOUNDED LIKE FROM HOW SHE WAS TALKIN' THIS MORNIN'.

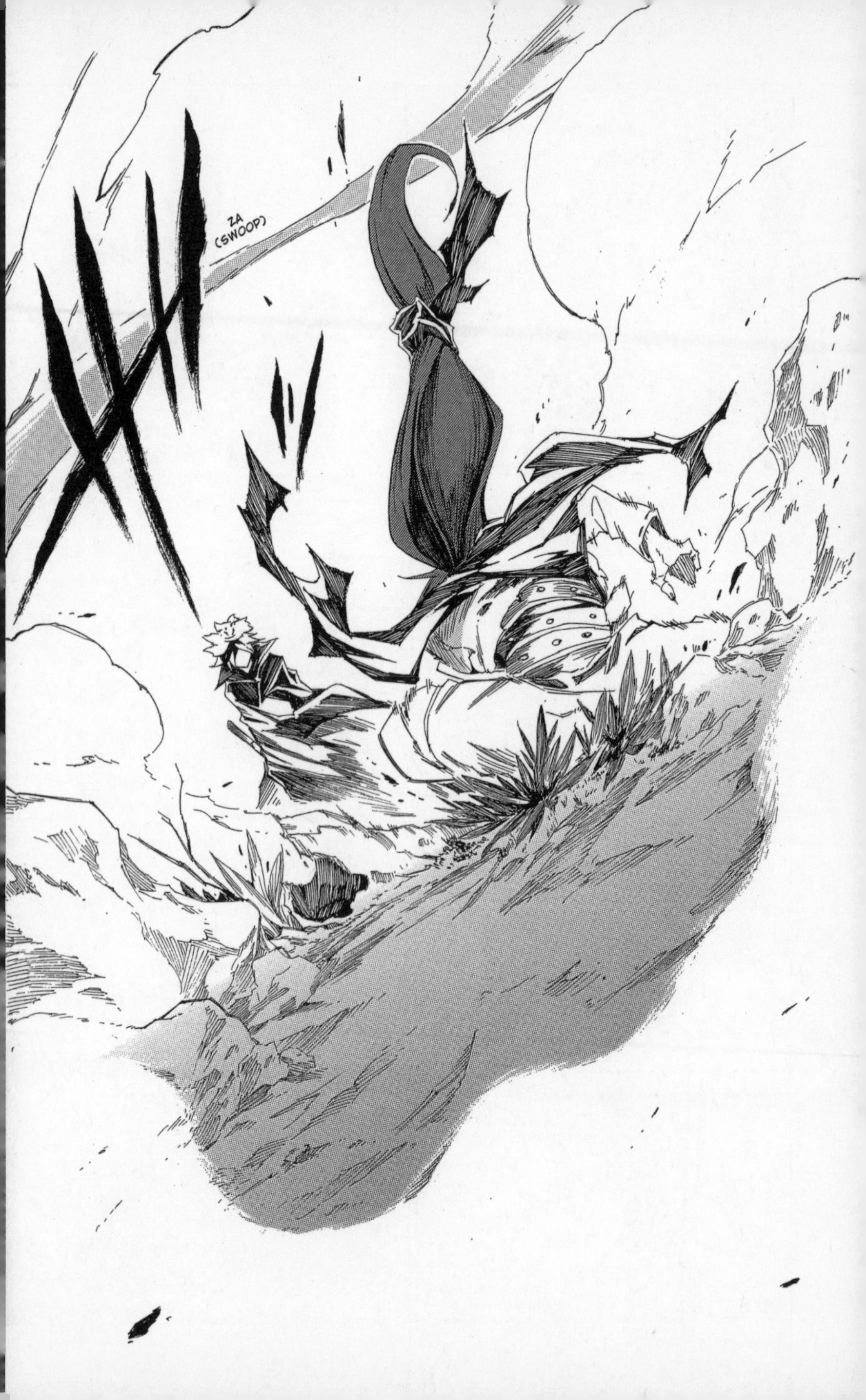
ZA
(SWOOP)

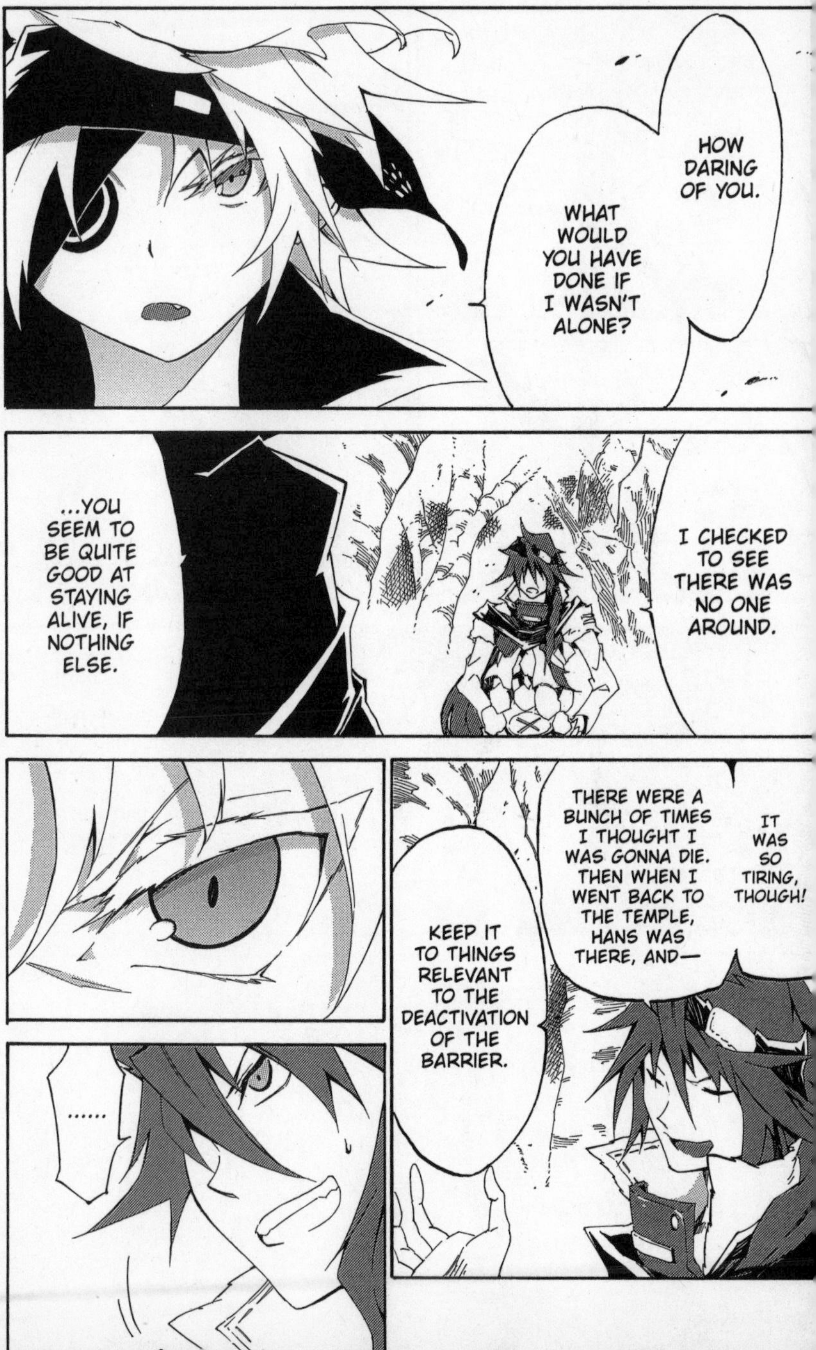
HOW DARING OF YOU.
WHAT WOULD YOU HAVE DONE IF I WASN'T ALONE?
I CHECKED TO SEE THERE WAS NO ONE AROUND.
...YOU SEEM TO BE QUITE GOOD AT STAYING ALIVE, IF NOTHING ELSE.
IT WAS SO TIRING, THOUGH!
THERE WERE A BUNCH OF TIMES I THOUGHT I WAS GONNA DIE. THEN WHEN I WENT BACK TO THE TEMPLE, HANS WAS THERE, AND—
KEEP IT TO THINGS RELEVANT TO THE DEACTIVATION OF THE BARRIER.
......

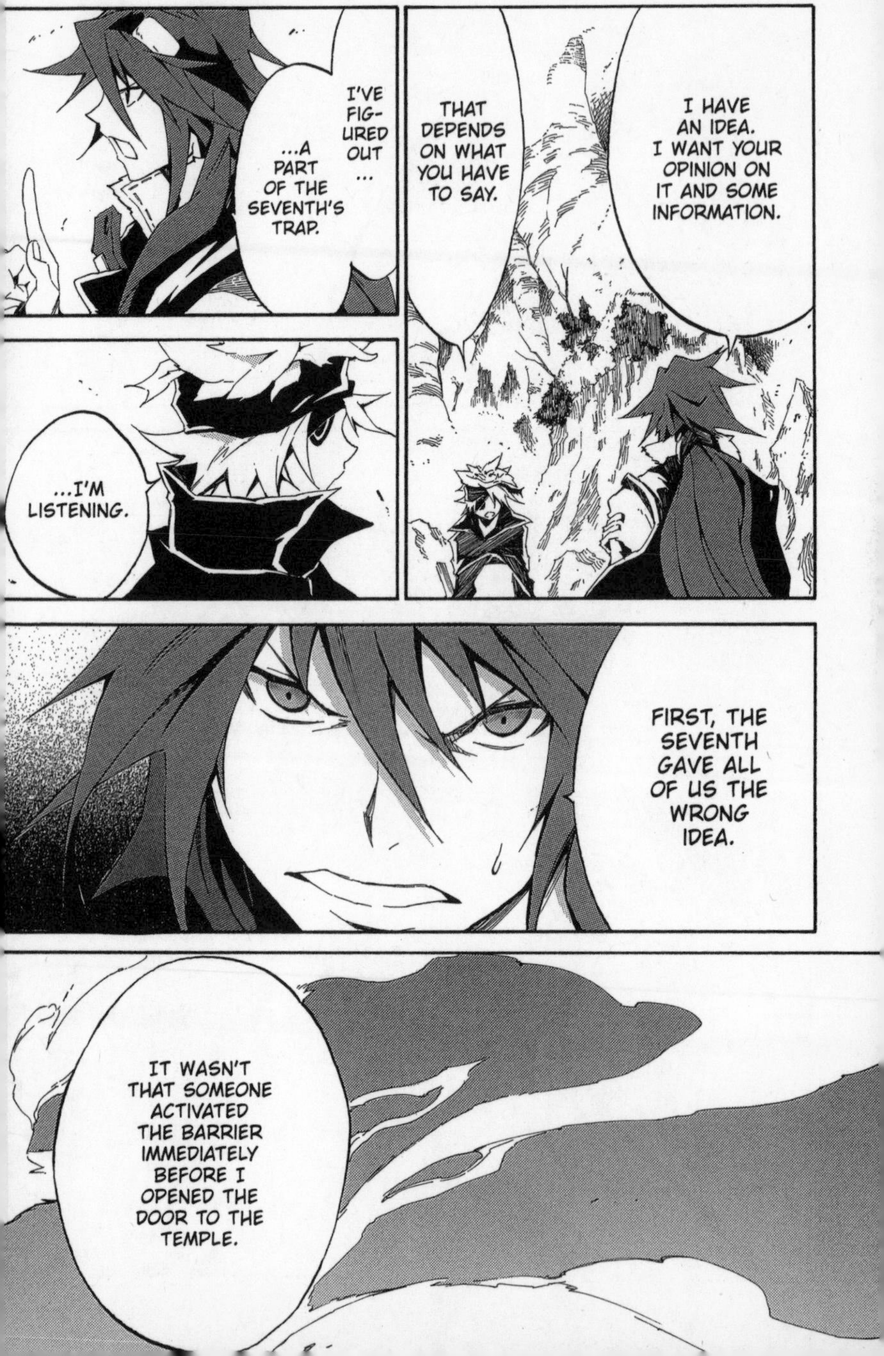

I HAVE AN IDEA. I WANT YOUR OPINION ON IT AND SOME INFORMATION.
THAT DEPENDS ON WHAT YOU HAVE TO SAY.
I'VE FIG-URED OUT...
...A PART OF THE SEVENTH'S TRAP.
...I'M LISTENING.
FIRST, THE SEVENTH GAVE ALL OF US THE WRONG IDEA.
IT WASN'T THAT SOMEONE ACTIVATED THE BARRIER IMMEDIATELY BEFORE I OPENED THE DOOR TO THE TEMPLE.

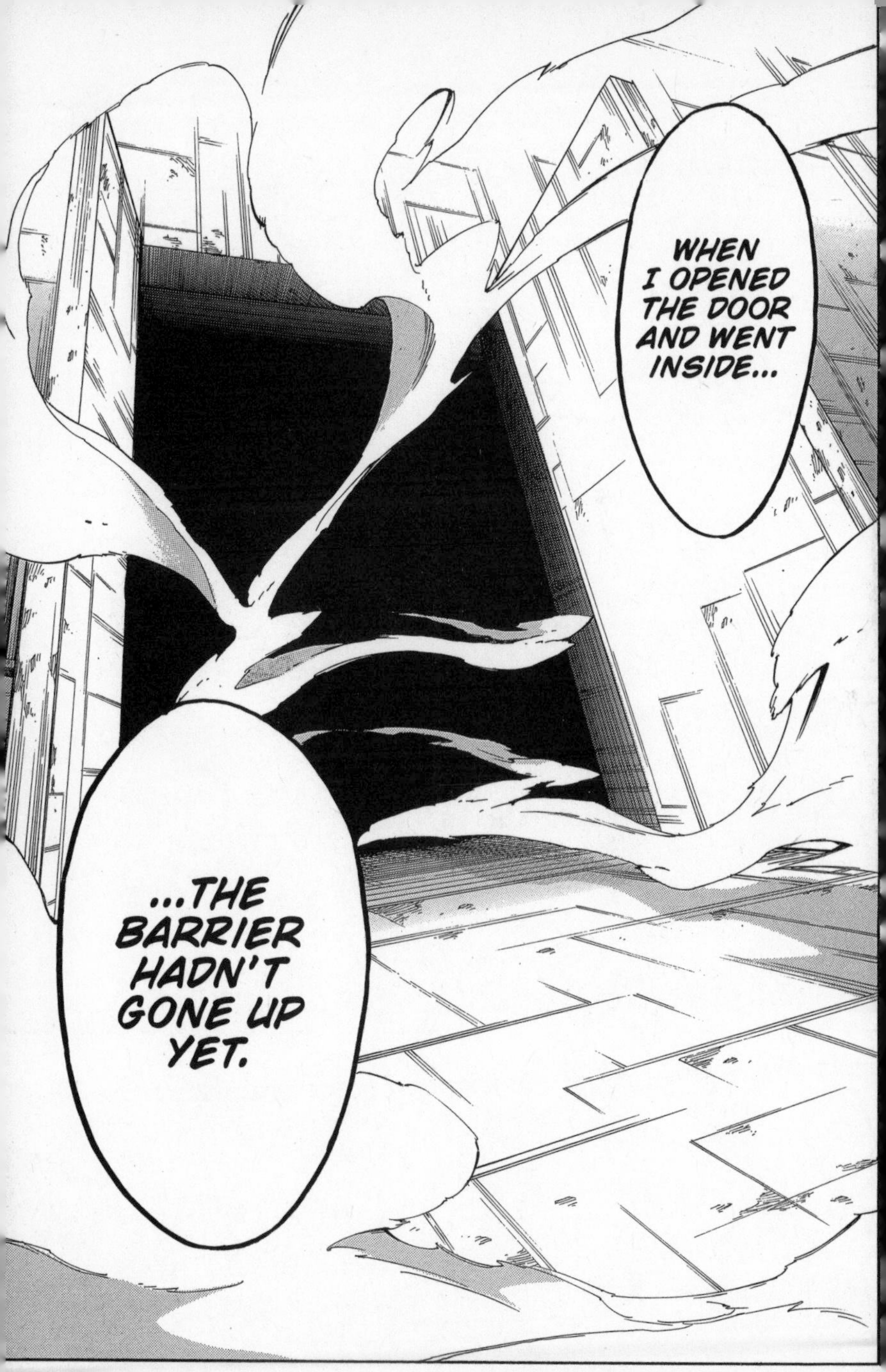
WHEN I OPENED THE DOOR AND WENT INSIDE...
...THE BARRIER HADN'T GONE UP YET.

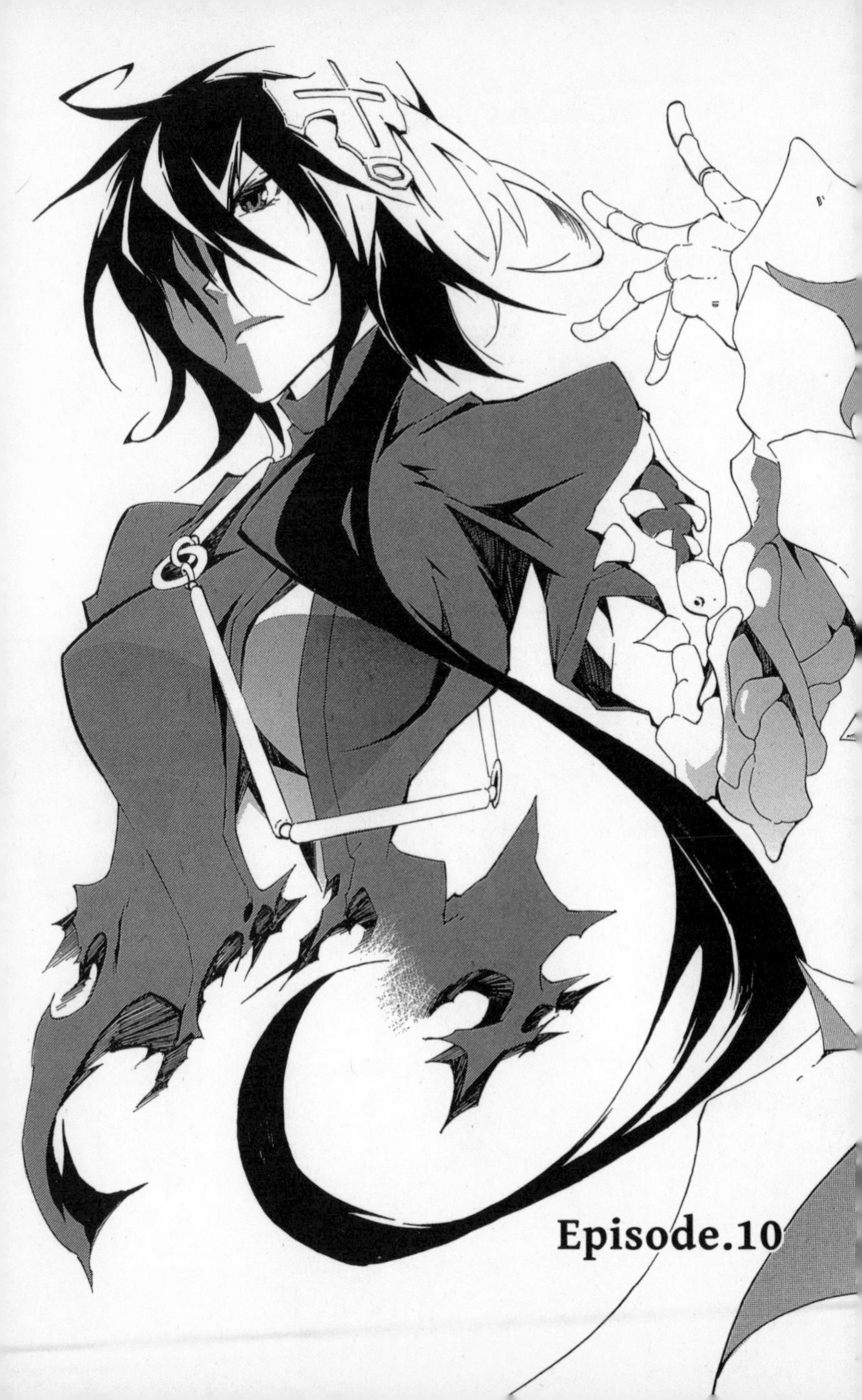

Episode.10

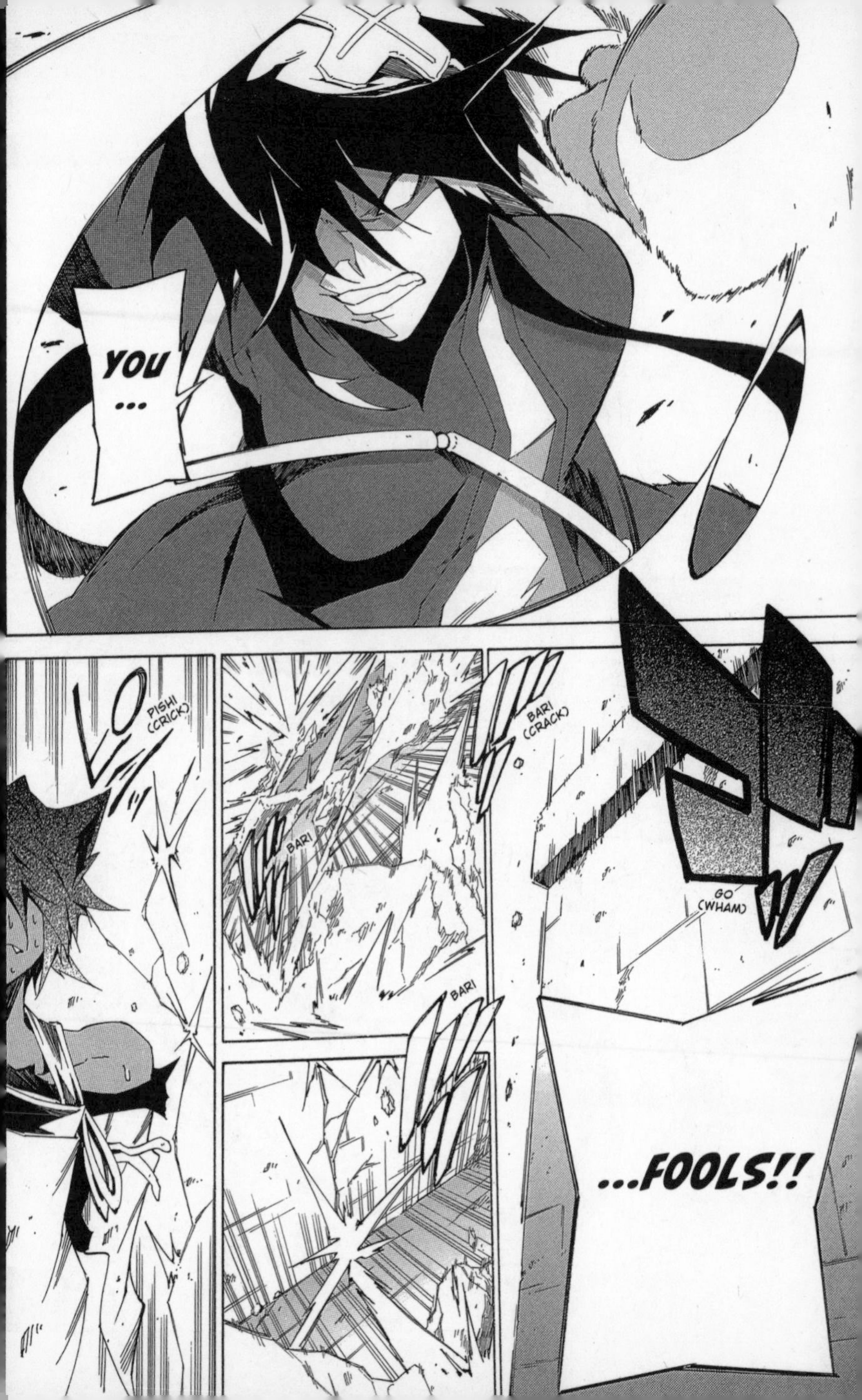
YOU ...
BARI (CRACK)
GO (WHAM)
...FOOLS!!
BARI
BARI
PISHI (CRICK)

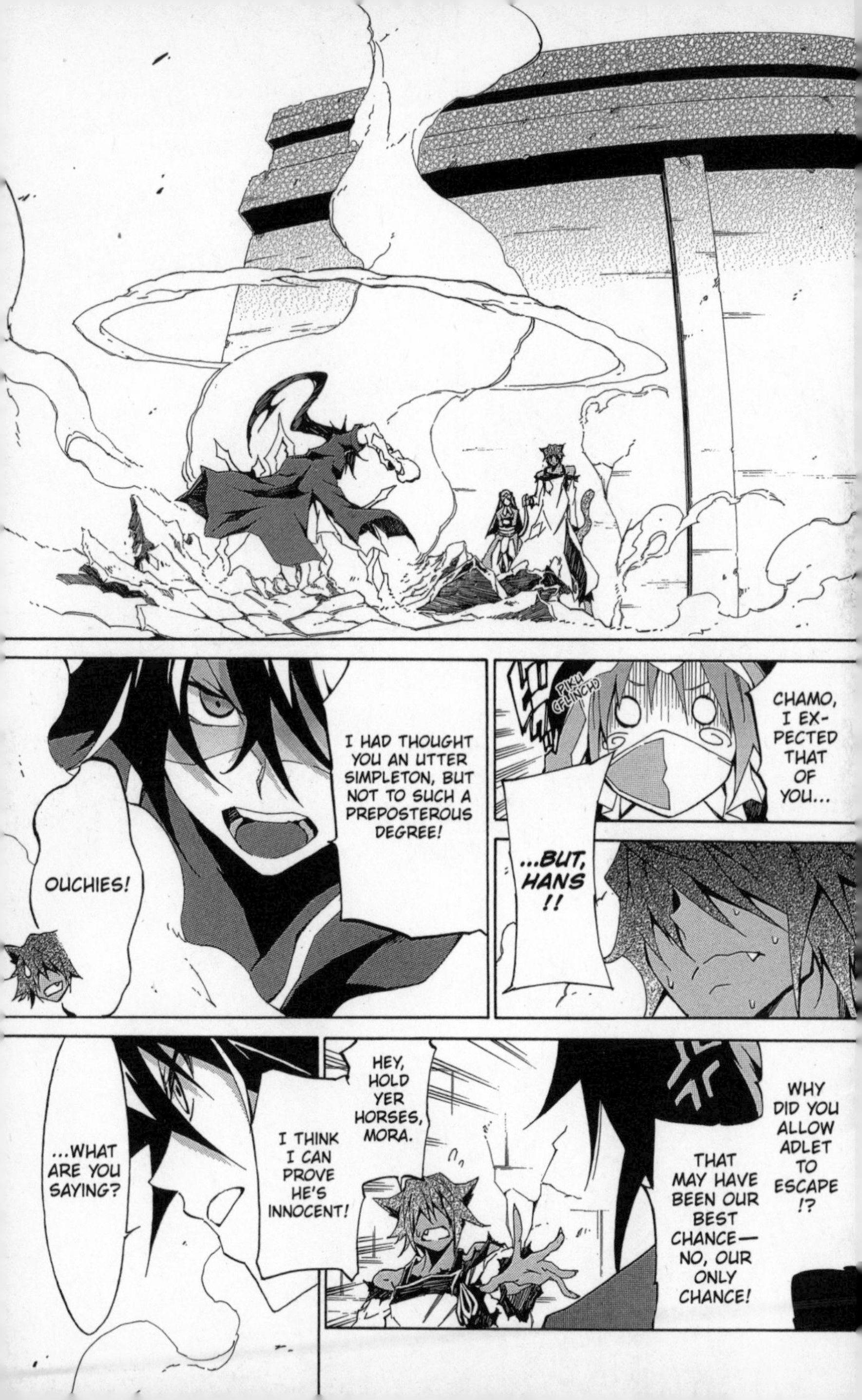
PIKU (FLINCH)
CHAMO, I EXPECTED THAT OF YOU...
...BUT, HANS!!
I HAD THOUGHT YOU AN UTTER SIMPLETON, BUT NOT TO SUCH A PREPOSTEROUS DEGREE!
OUCHIES!
WHY DID YOU ALLOW ADLET TO ESCAPE!?
THAT MAY HAVE BEEN OUR BEST CHANCE—NO, OUR ONLY CHANCE!
HEY, HOLD YER HORSES, MORA.
I THINK I CAN PROVE HE'S INNOCENT!
...WHAT ARE YOU SAYING?

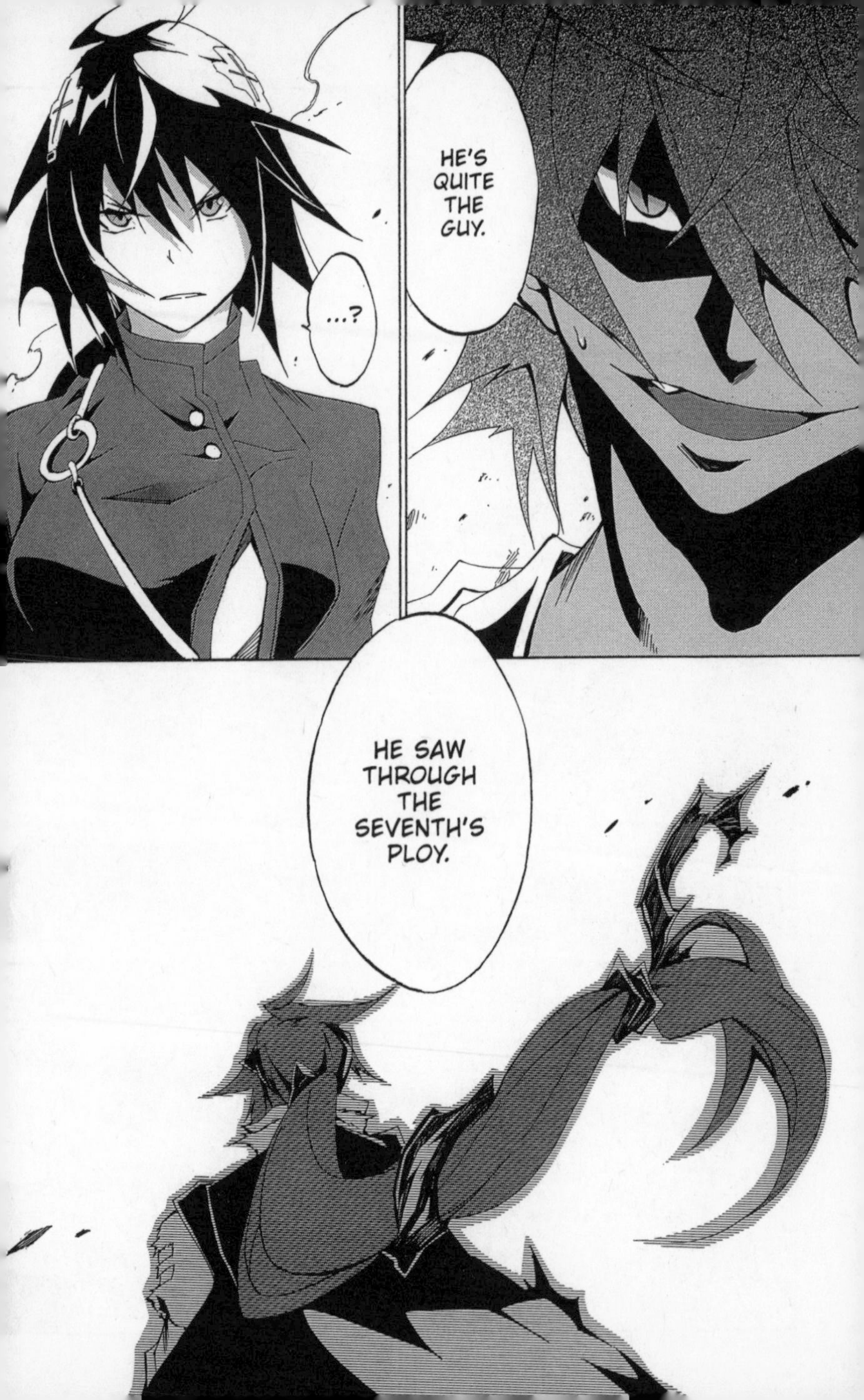
HE'S QUITE THE GUY.
...?
HE SAW THROUGH THE SEVENTH'S PLOY.

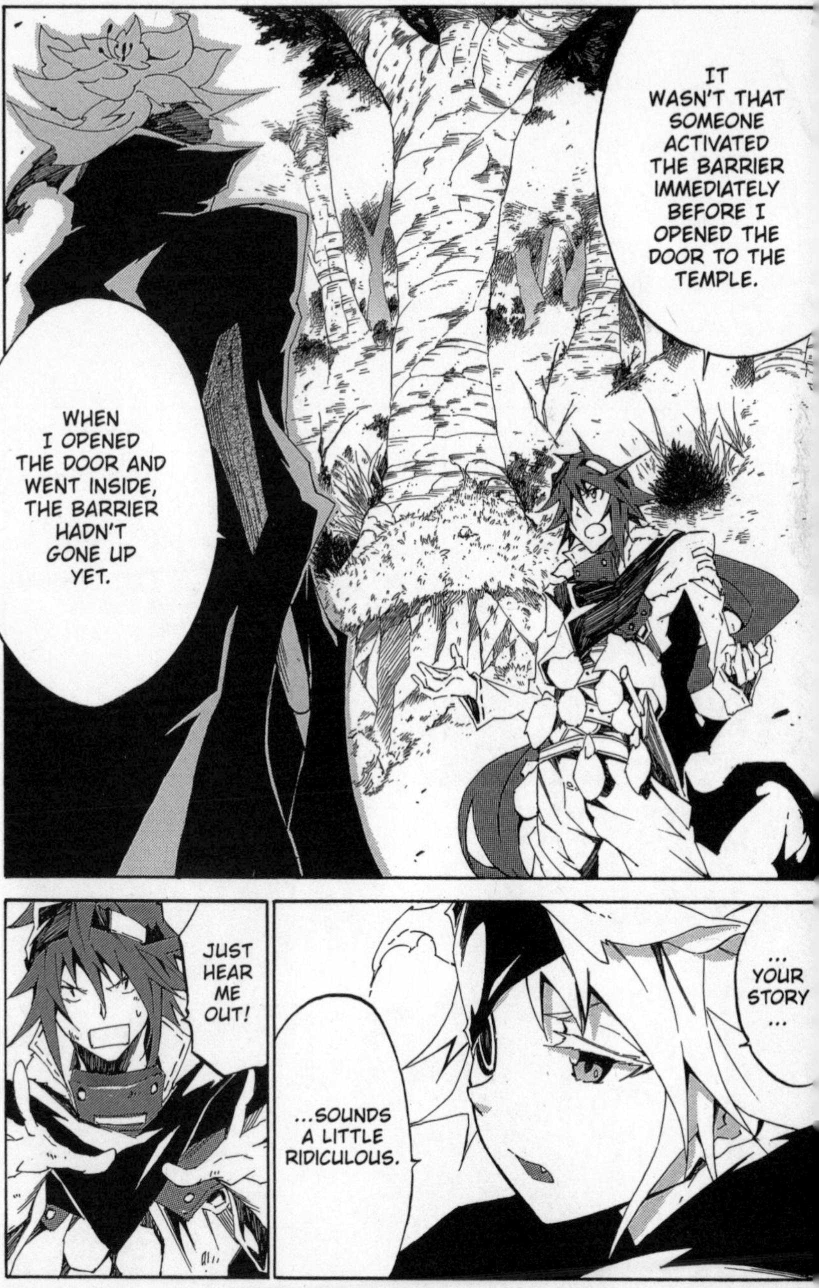
IT WASN'T THAT SOMEONE ACTIVATED THE BARRIER IMMEDIATELY BEFORE I OPENED THE DOOR TO THE TEMPLE.
WHEN I OPENED THE DOOR AND WENT INSIDE, THE BARRIER HADN'T GONE UP YET.
...YOUR STORY...
...SOUNDS A LITTLE RIDICULOUS.
JUST HEAR ME OUT!

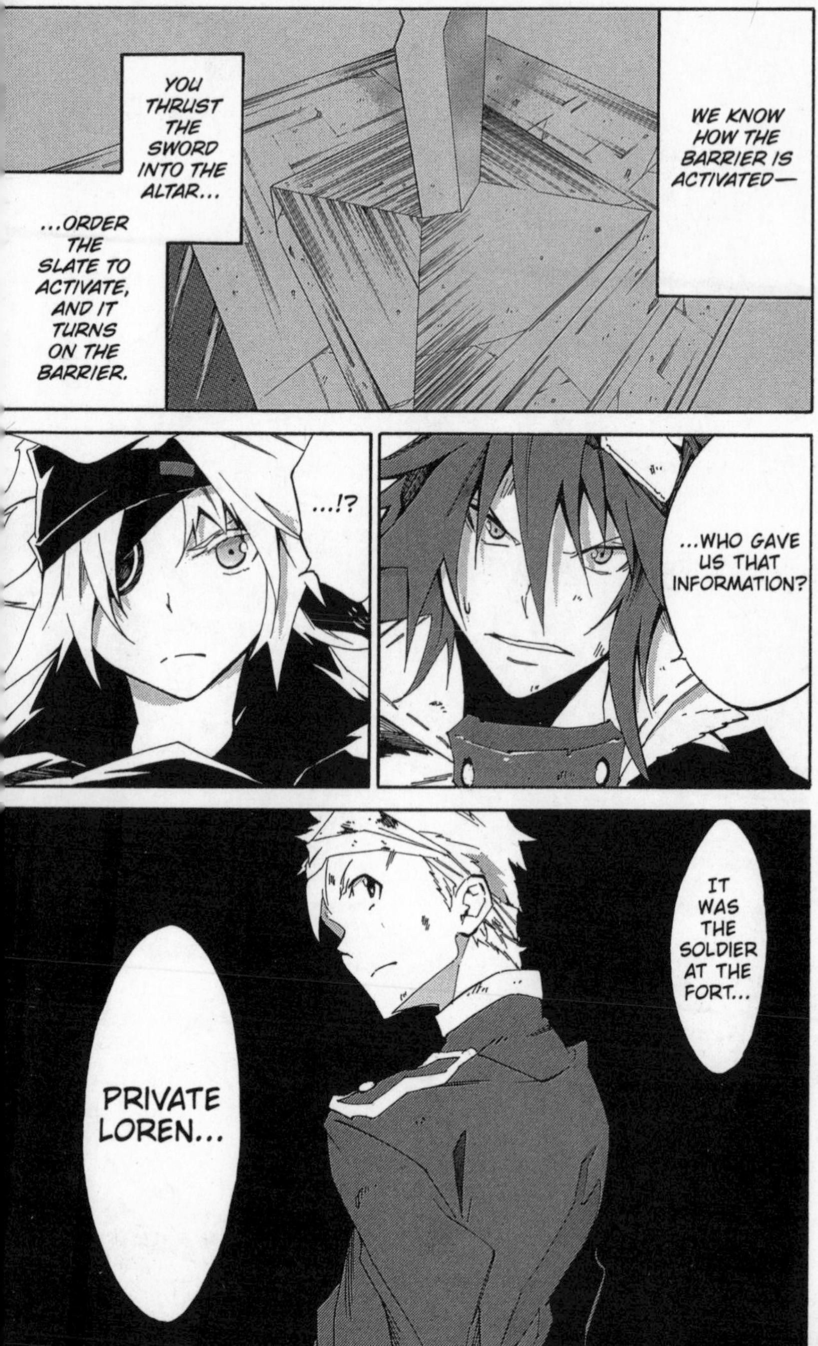
WE KNOW HOW THE BARRIER IS ACTIVATED—
YOU THRUST THE SWORD INTO THE ALTAR...
...ORDER THE SLATE TO ACTIVATE, AND IT TURNS ON THE BARRIER.
...WHO GAVE US THAT INFORMATION?
...!?
IT WAS THE SOLDIER AT THE FORT...
PRIVATE LOREN...

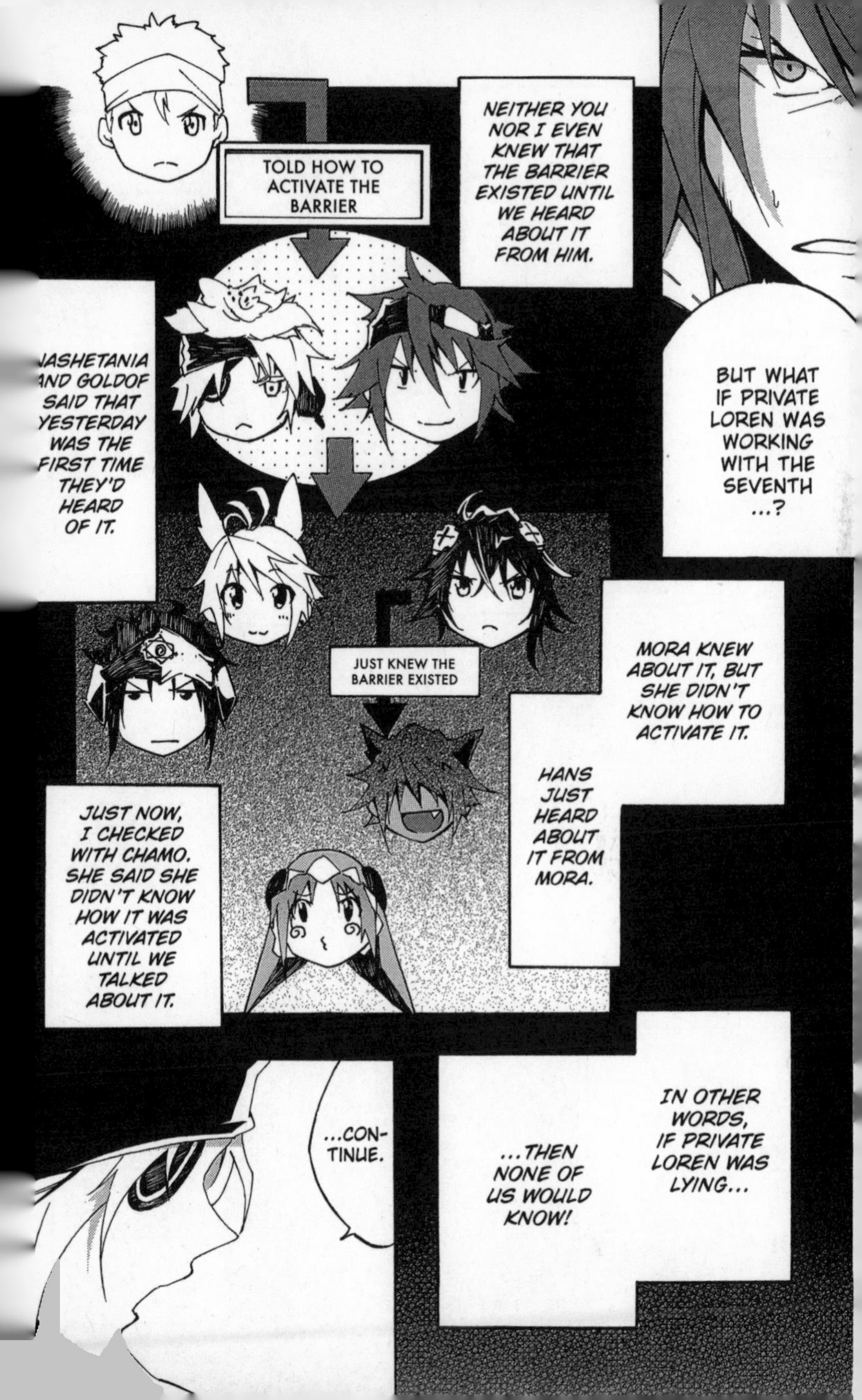
NEITHER YOU NOR I EVEN KNEW THAT THE BARRIER EXISTED UNTIL WE HEARD ABOUT IT FROM HIM.
TOLD HOW TO ACTIVATE THE BARRIER
NASHETANIA AND GOLDOF SAID THAT YESTERDAY WAS THE FIRST TIME THEY'D HEARD OF IT.
JUST KNEW THE BARRIER EXISTED
MORA KNEW ABOUT IT, BUT SHE DIDN'T KNOW HOW TO ACTIVATE IT.
HANS JUST HEARD ABOUT IT FROM MORA.
JUST NOW, I CHECKED WITH CHAMO. SHE SAID SHE DIDN'T KNOW HOW IT WAS ACTIVATED UNTIL WE TALKED ABOUT IT.
BUT WHAT IF PRIVATE LOREN WAS WORKING WITH THE SEVENTH ...?
IN OTHER WORDS, IF PRIVATE LOREN WAS LYING...
...THEN NONE OF US WOULD KNOW!
...CON-TINUE.

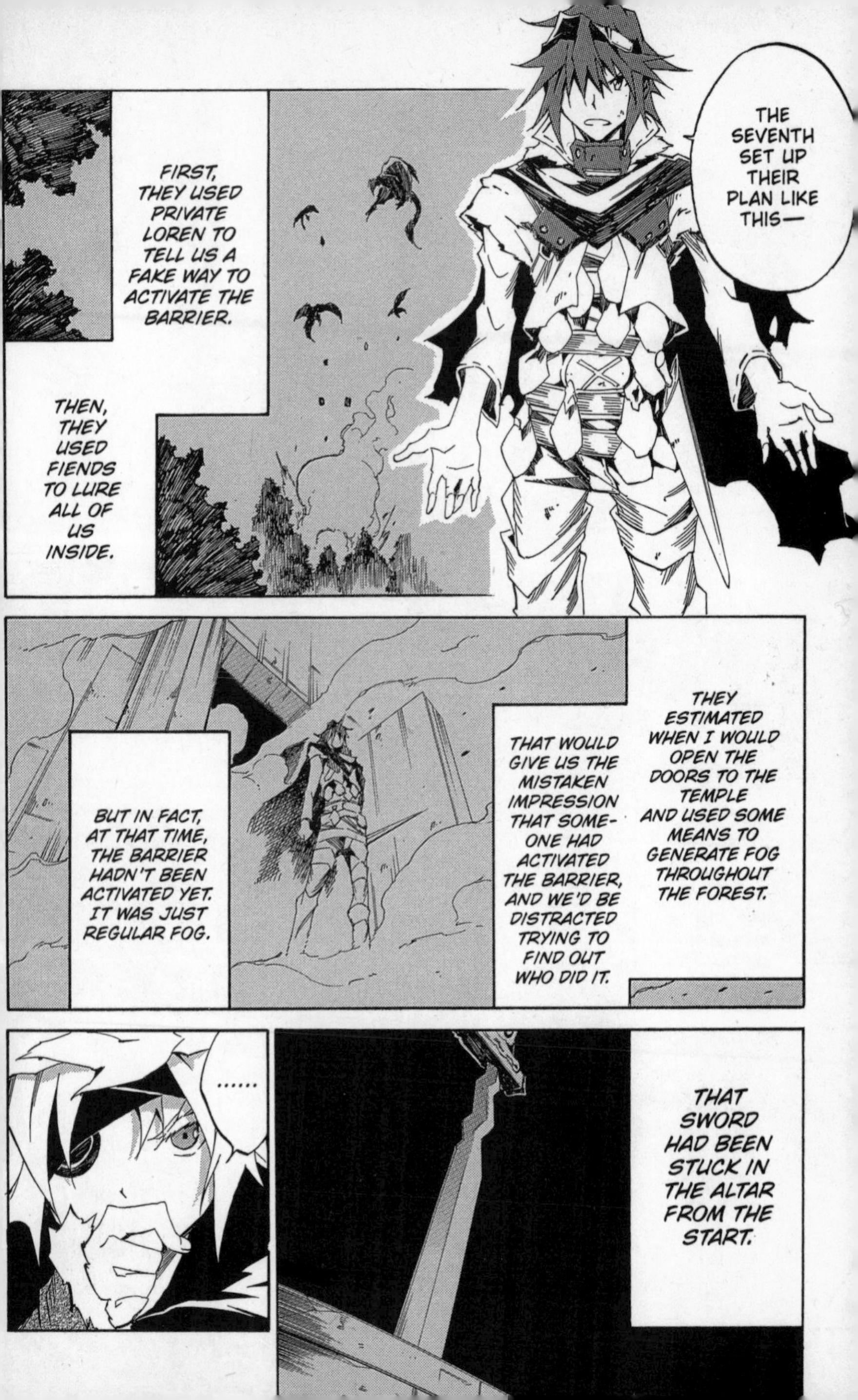
THE SEVENTH SET UP THEIR PLAN LIKE THIS—
FIRST, THEY USED PRIVATE LOREN TO TELL US A FAKE WAY TO ACTIVATE THE BARRIER.
THEN, THEY USED FIENDS TO LURE ALL OF US INSIDE.
THEY ESTIMATED WHEN I WOULD OPEN THE DOORS TO THE TEMPLE AND USED SOME MEANS TO GENERATE FOG THROUGHOUT THE FOREST.
THAT WOULD GIVE US THE MISTAKEN IMPRESSION THAT SOME-ONE HAD ACTIVATED THE BARRIER, AND WE'D BE DISTRACTED TRYING TO FIND OUT WHO DID IT.
BUT IN FACT, AT THAT TIME, THE BARRIER HADN'T BEEN ACTIVATED YET. IT WAS JUST REGULAR FOG.
THAT SWORD HAD BEEN STUCK IN THE ALTAR FROM THE START.
......

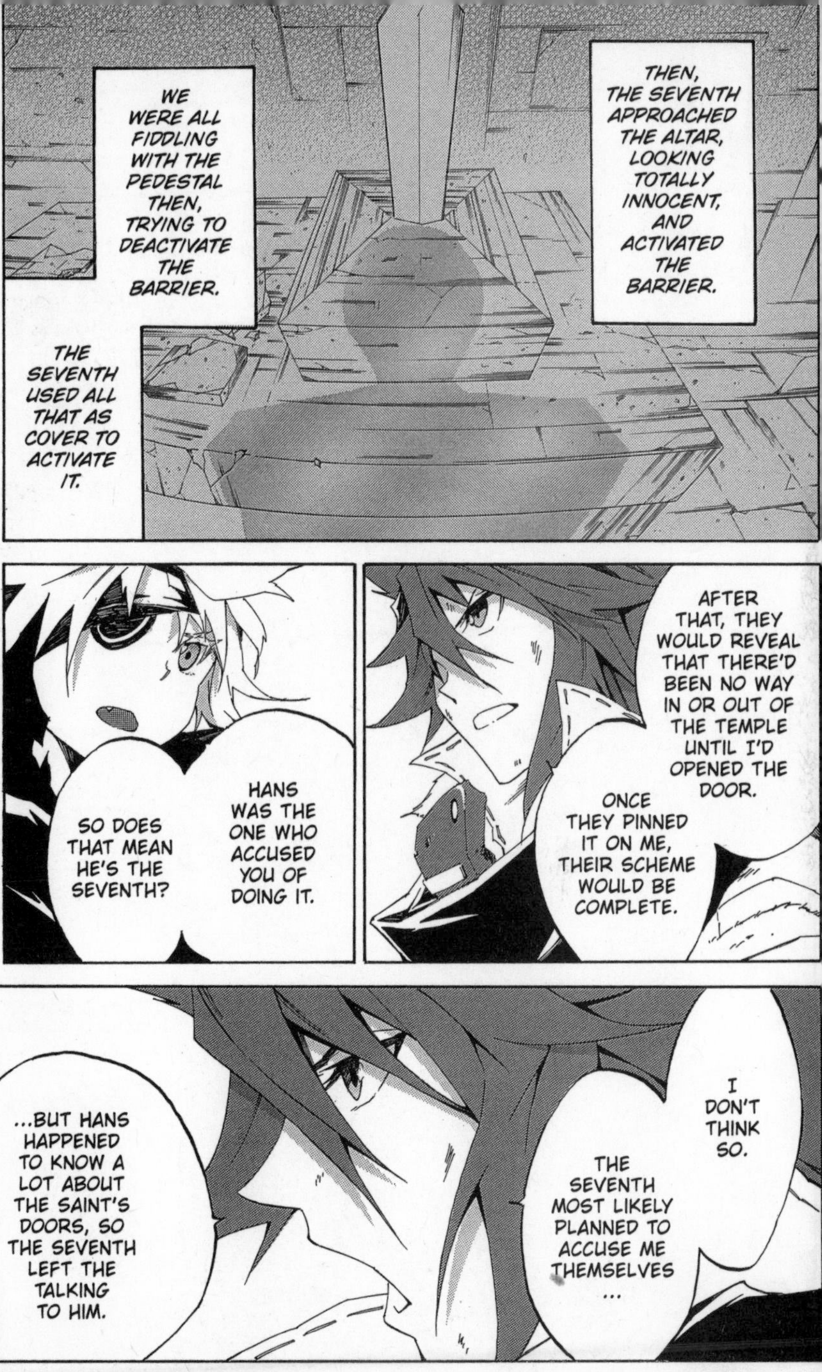
THEN, THE SEVENTH APPROACHED THE ALTAR, LOOKING TOTALLY INNOCENT, AND ACTIVATED THE BARRIER.
WE WERE ALL FIDDLING WITH THE PEDESTAL THEN, TRYING TO DEACTIVATE THE BARRIER.
THE SEVENTH USED ALL THAT AS COVER TO ACTIVATE IT.
AFTER THAT, THEY WOULD REVEAL THAT THERE'D BEEN NO WAY IN OR OUT OF THE TEMPLE UNTIL I'D OPENED THE DOOR.
ONCE THEY PINNED IT ON ME, THEIR SCHEME WOULD BE COMPLETE.
HANS WAS THE ONE WHO ACCUSED YOU OF DOING IT.
SO DOES THAT MEAN HE'S THE SEVENTH?
I DON'T THINK SO.
THE SEVENTH MOST LIKELY PLANNED TO ACCUSE ME THEMSELVES ...
...BUT HANS HAPPENED TO KNOW A LOT ABOUT THE SAINT'S DOORS, SO THE SEVENTH LEFT THE TALKING TO HIM.

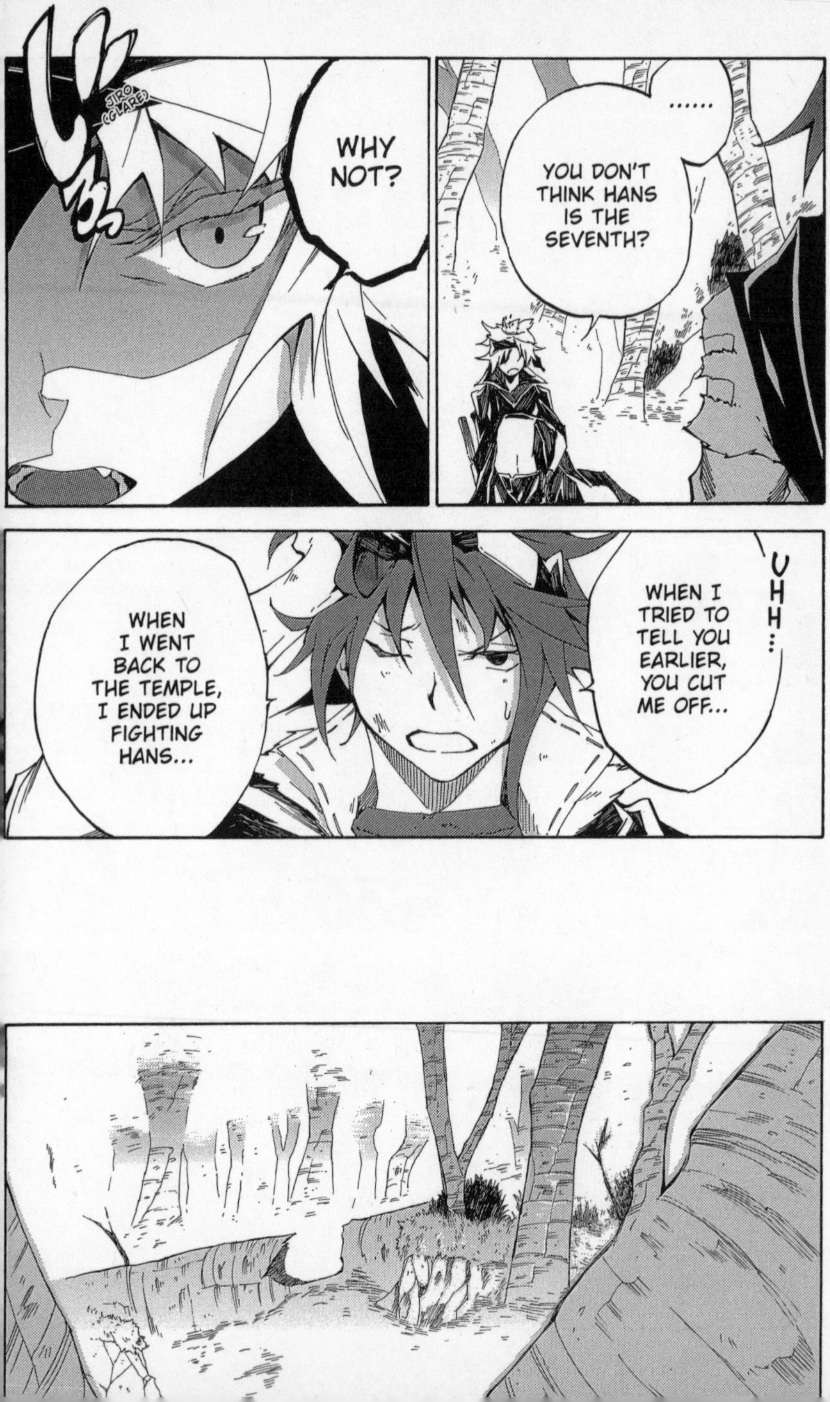
......
YOU DON'T THINK HANS IS THE SEVENTH?
JIRO (GLARE)
WHY NOT?
UHH...
WHEN I TRIED TO TELL YOU EARLIER, YOU CUT ME OFF...
WHEN I WENT BACK TO THE TEMPLE, I ENDED UP FIGHTING HANS...

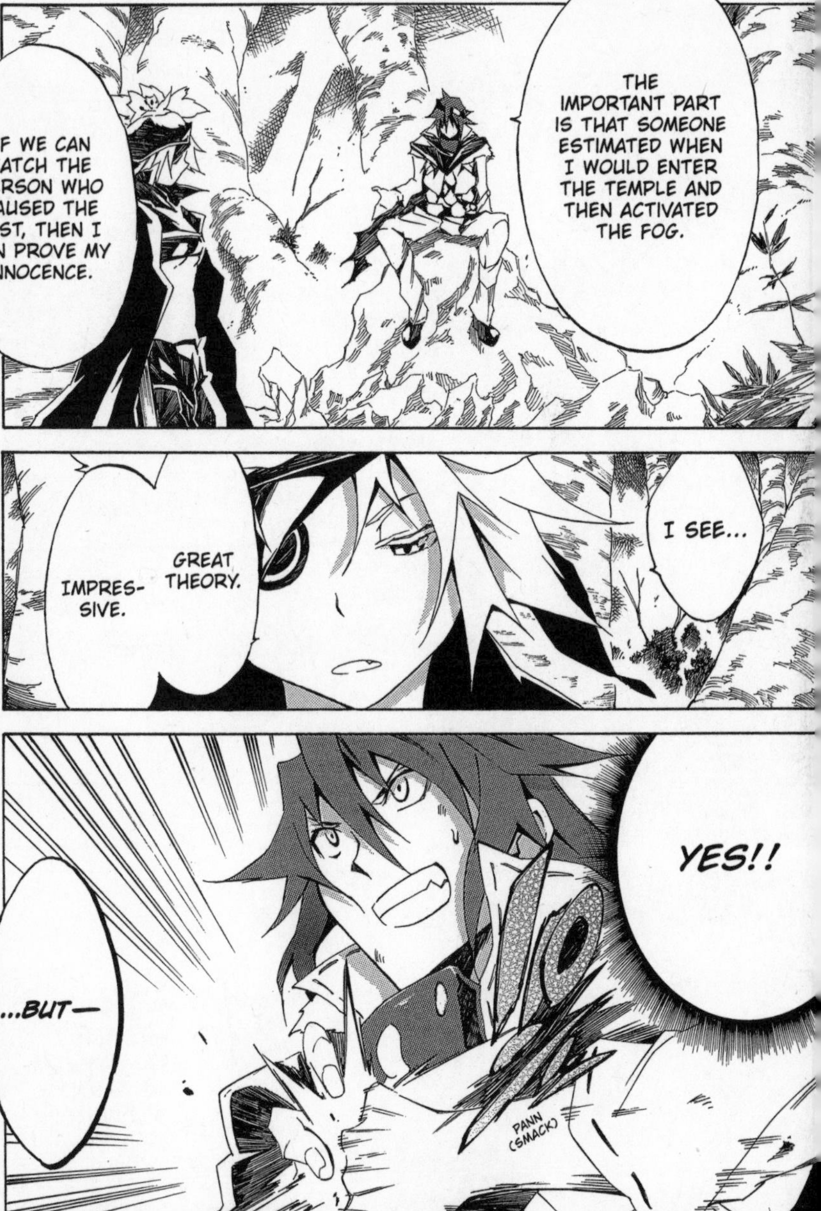
THE IMPORTANT PART IS THAT SOMEONE ESTIMATED WHEN I WOULD ENTER THE TEMPLE AND THEN ACTIVATED THE FOG.
IF WE CAN CATCH THE PERSON WHO CAUSED THE MIST, THEN I CAN PROVE MY INNOCENCE.
I SEE...
GREAT THEORY.
IMPRES- SIVE.
YES!!
...BUT—
PANN (SMACK)

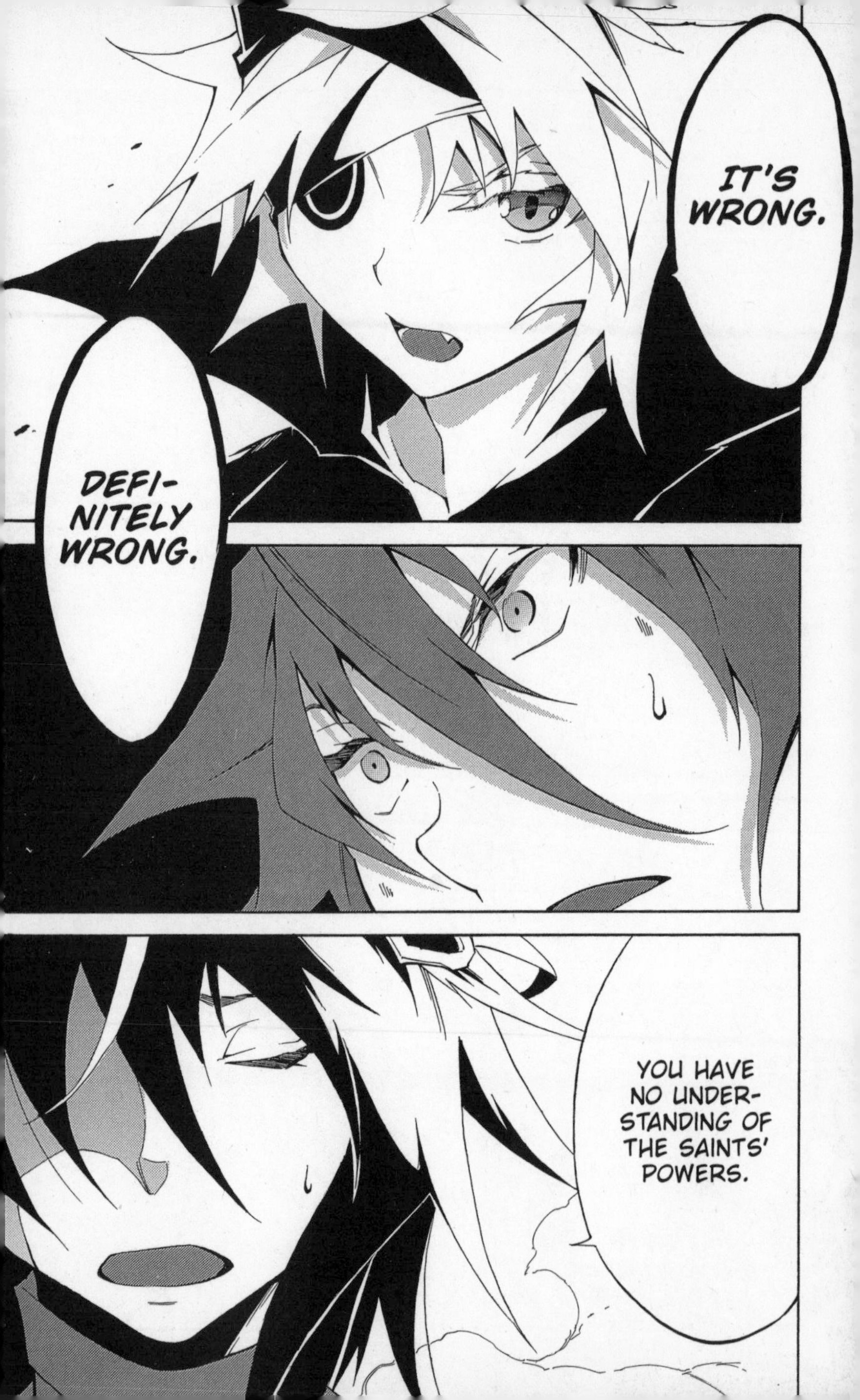
IT'S WRONG.
DEFI-NITELY WRONG.
YOU HAVE NO UNDER-STANDING OF THE SAINTS' POWERS.

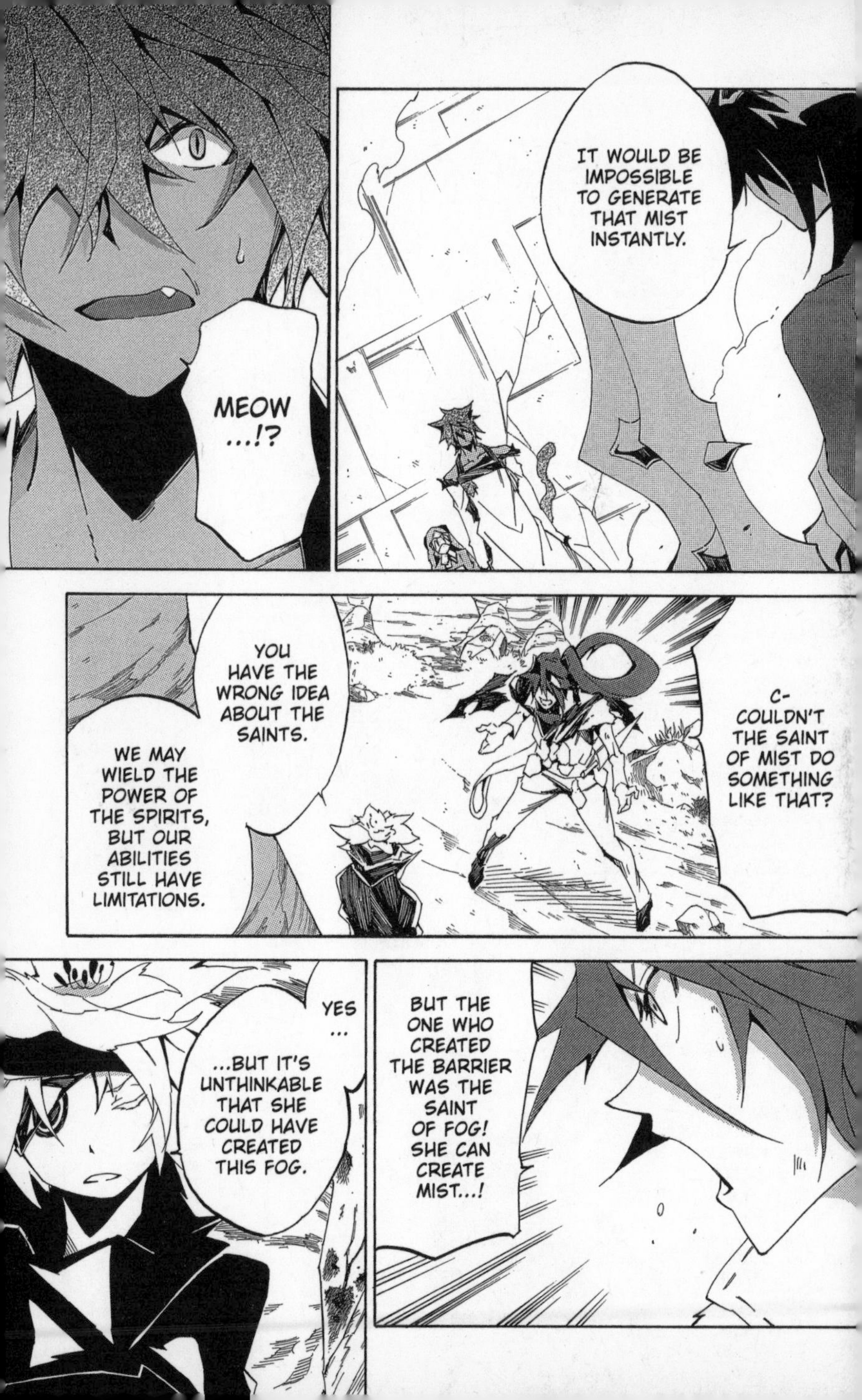
IT WOULD BE IMPOSSIBLE TO GENERATE THAT MIST INSTANTLY.
MEOW ...!?
C- COULDN'T THE SAINT OF MIST DO SOMETHING LIKE THAT?
YOU HAVE THE WRONG IDEA ABOUT THE SAINTS.
WE MAY WIELD THE POWER OF THE SPIRITS, BUT OUR ABILITIES STILL HAVE LIMITATIONS.
BUT THE ONE WHO CREATED THE BARRIER WAS THE SAINT OF FOG! SHE CAN CREATE MIST...!
YES ...
...BUT IT'S UNTHINKABLE THAT SHE COULD HAVE CREATED THIS FOG.

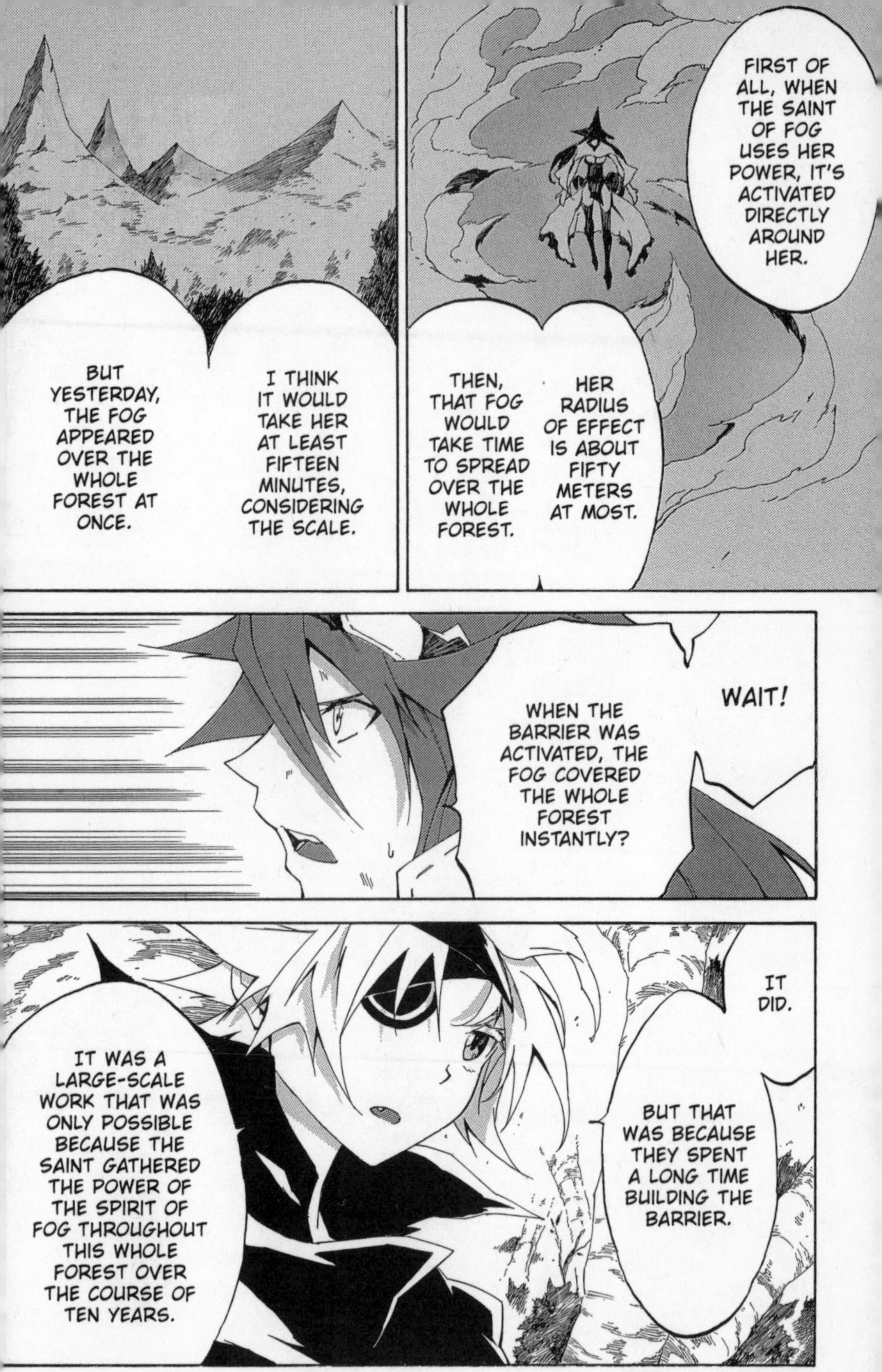
FIRST OF ALL, WHEN THE SAINT OF FOG USES HER POWER, IT'S ACTIVATED DIRECTLY AROUND HER.
HER RADIUS OF EFFECT IS ABOUT FIFTY METERS AT MOST.
THEN, THAT FOG WOULD TAKE TIME TO SPREAD OVER THE WHOLE FOREST.
I THINK IT WOULD TAKE HER AT LEAST FIFTEEN MINUTES, CONSIDERING THE SCALE.
BUT YESTERDAY, THE FOG APPEARED OVER THE WHOLE FOREST AT ONCE.
WAIT!
WHEN THE BARRIER WAS ACTIVATED, THE FOG COVERED THE WHOLE FOREST INSTANTLY?
IT DID.
BUT THAT WAS BECAUSE THEY SPENT A LONG TIME BUILDING THE BARRIER.
IT WAS A LARGE-SCALE WORK THAT WAS ONLY POSSIBLE BECAUSE THE SAINT GATHERED THE POWER OF THE SPIRIT OF FOG THROUGHOUT THIS WHOLE FOREST OVER THE COURSE OF TEN YEARS.

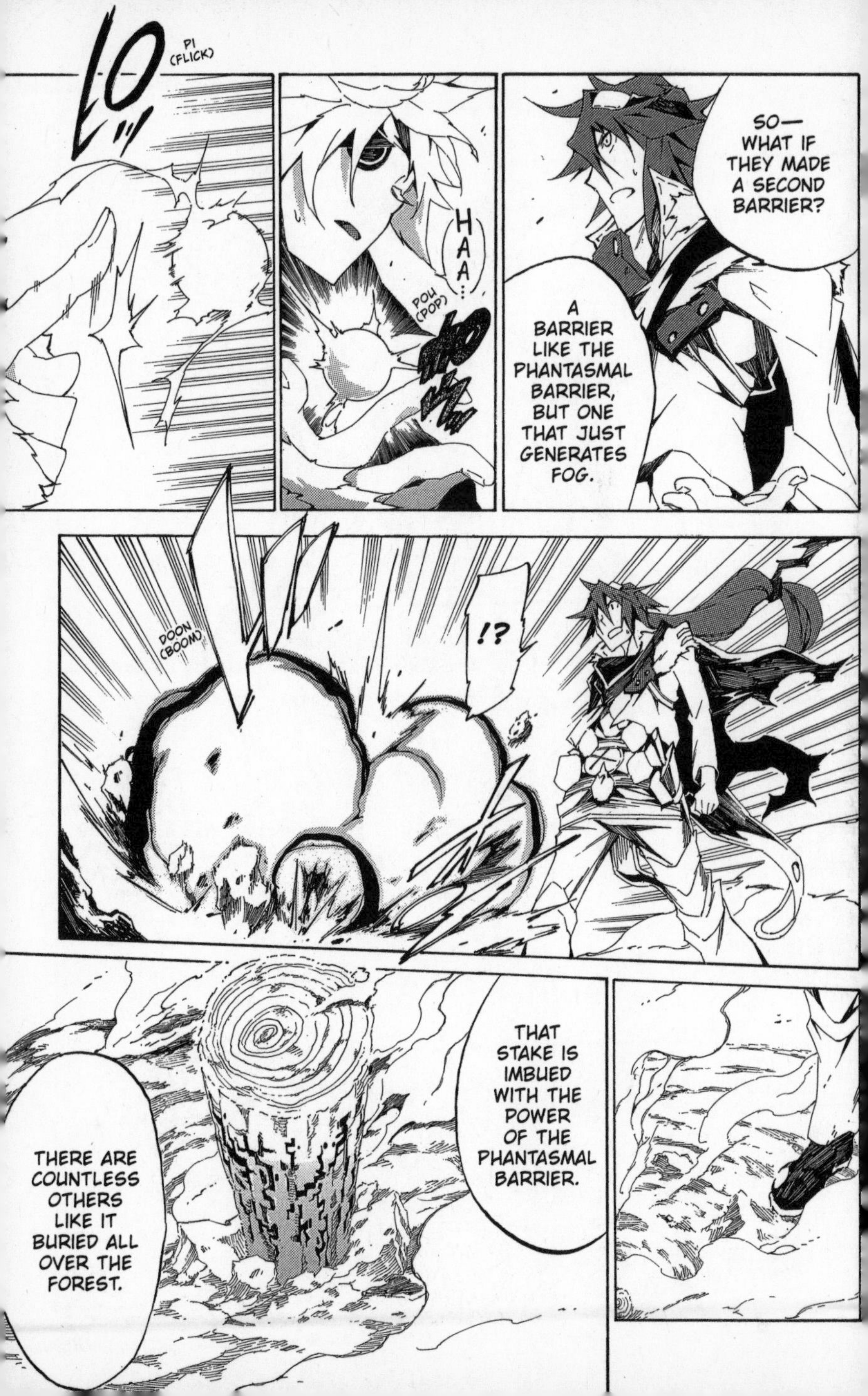
SO— WHAT IF THEY MADE A SECOND BARRIER?
A BARRIER LIKE THE PHANTASMAL BARRIER, BUT ONE THAT JUST GENERATES FOG.
HAA...
POU (POP)
PI (FLICK)
!?
DOON (BOOM)
THAT STAKE IS IMBUED WITH THE POWER OF THE PHANTASMAL BARRIER.
THERE ARE COUNTLESS OTHERS LIKE IT BURIED ALL OVER THE FOREST.

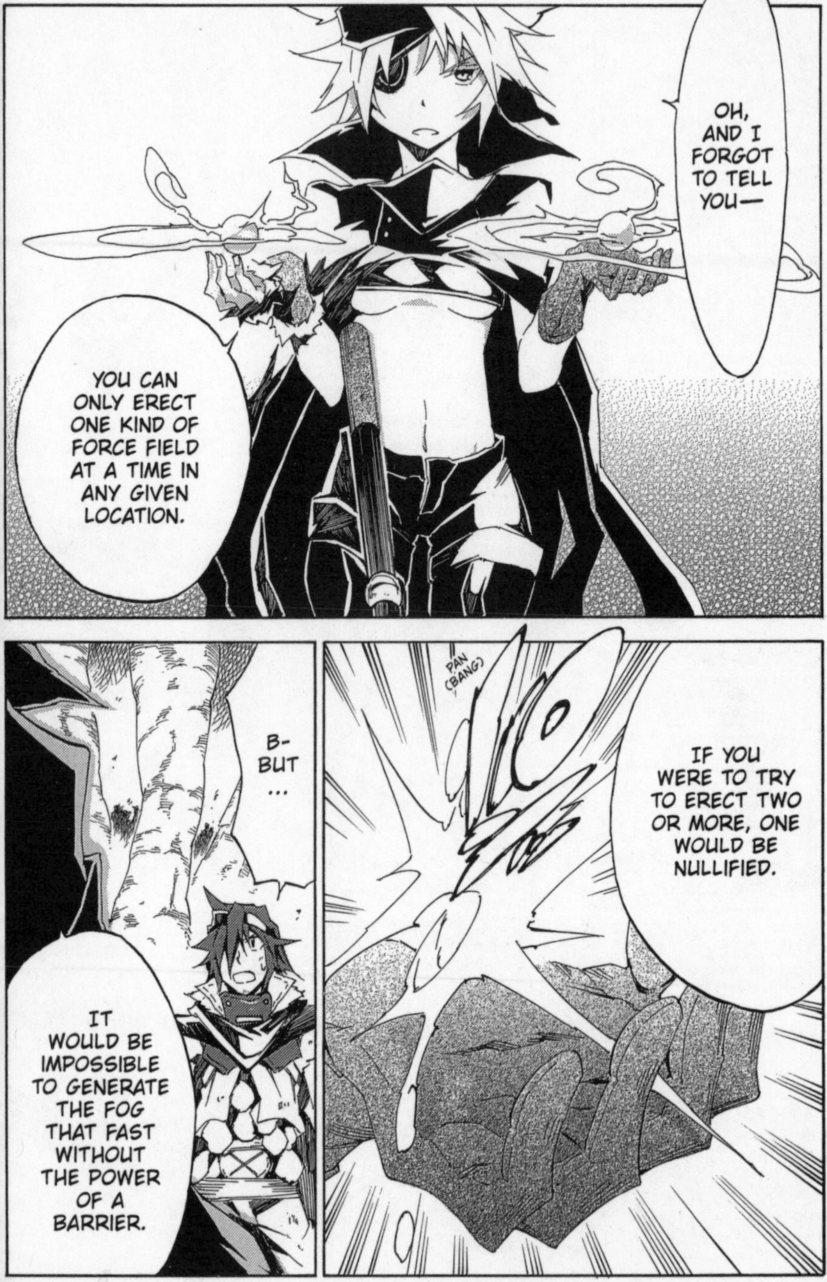
OH, AND I FORGOT TO TELL YOU—
YOU CAN ONLY ERECT ONE KIND OF FORCE FIELD AT A TIME IN ANY GIVEN LOCATION.
PAN (BANG)
IF YOU WERE TO TRY TO ERECT TWO OR MORE, ONE WOULD BE NULLIFIED.
B-BUT ...
IT WOULD BE IMPOSSIBLE TO GENERATE THE FOG THAT FAST WITHOUT THE POWER OF A BARRIER.

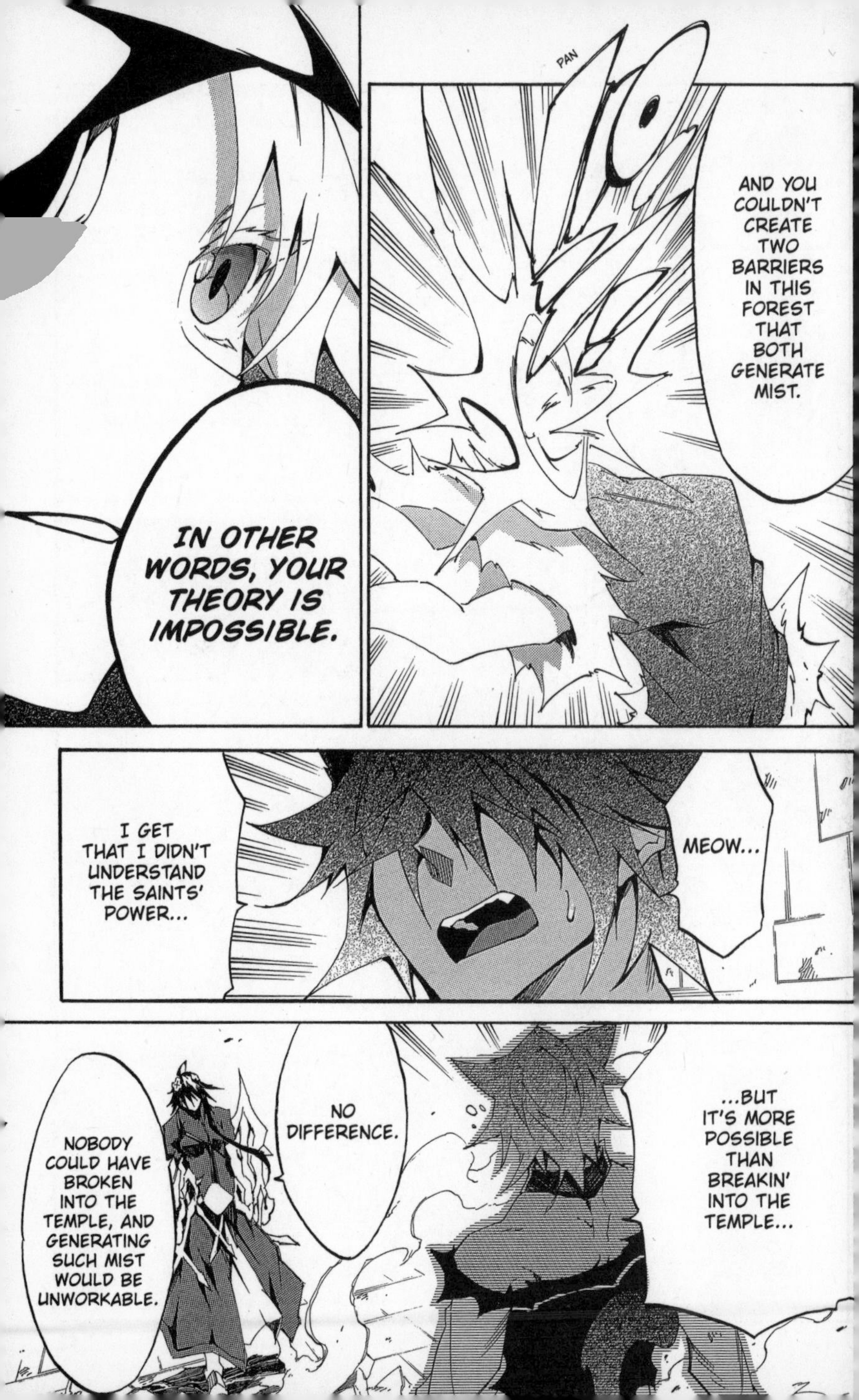
PAN
AND YOU COULDN'T CREATE TWO BARRIERS IN THIS FOREST THAT BOTH GENERATE MIST.
IN OTHER WORDS, YOUR THEORY IS IMPOSSIBLE.
MEOW...
I GET THAT I DIDN'T UNDERSTAND THE SAINTS' POWER...
...BUT IT'S MORE POSSIBLE THAN BREAKIN' INTO THE TEMPLE...
NO DIFFERENCE.
NOBODY COULD HAVE BROKEN INTO THE TEMPLE, AND GENERATING SUCH MIST WOULD BE UNWORKABLE.

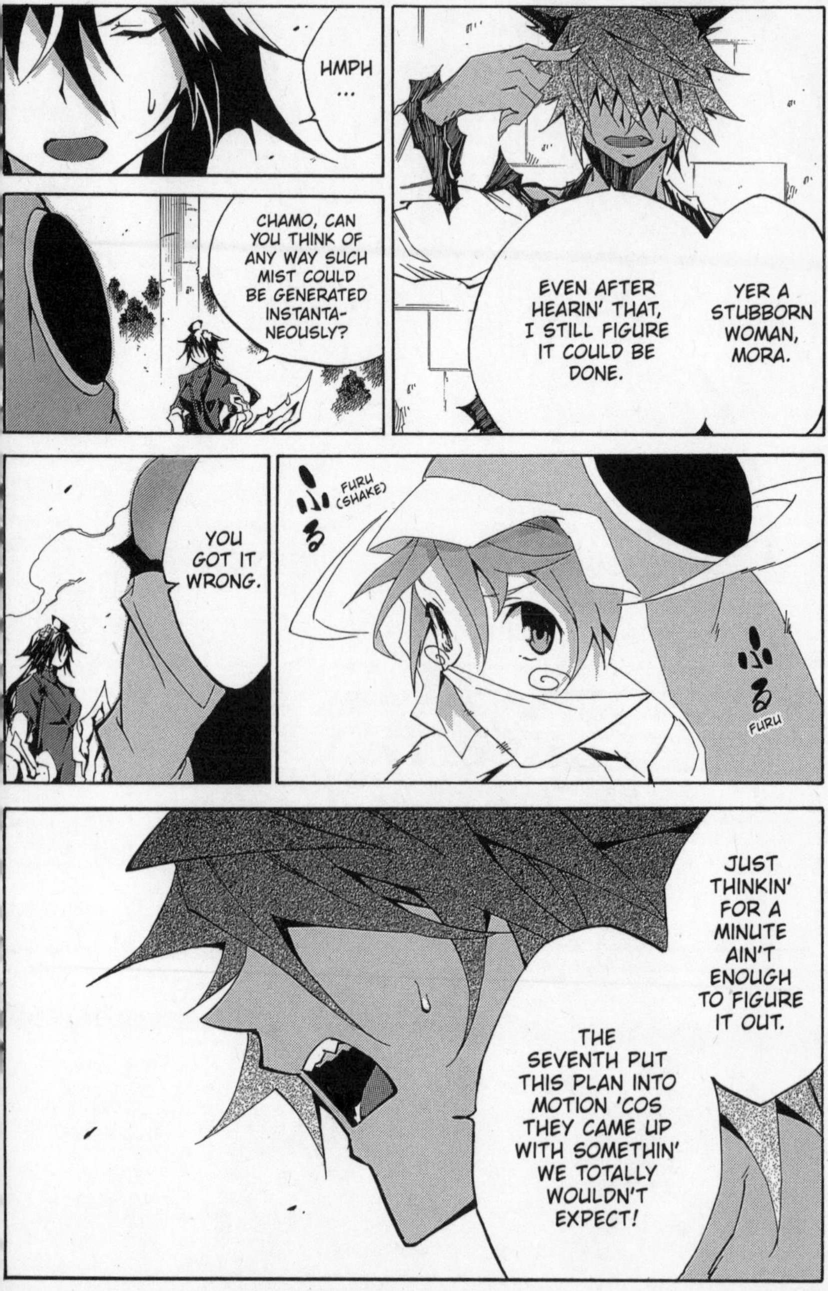
YER A STUBBORN WOMAN, MORA.
EVEN AFTER HEARIN' THAT, I STILL FIGURE IT COULD BE DONE.
HMPH ...
CHAMO, CAN YOU THINK OF ANY WAY SUCH MIST COULD BE GENERATED INSTANTANEOUSLY?
ふる
FURU (SHAKE)
ふる
FURU
YOU GOT IT WRONG.
JUST THINKIN' FOR A MINUTE AIN'T ENOUGH TO FIGURE IT OUT.
THE SEVENTH PUT THIS PLAN INTO MOTION 'COS THEY CAME UP WITH SOMETHIN' WE TOTALLY WOULDN'T EXPECT!

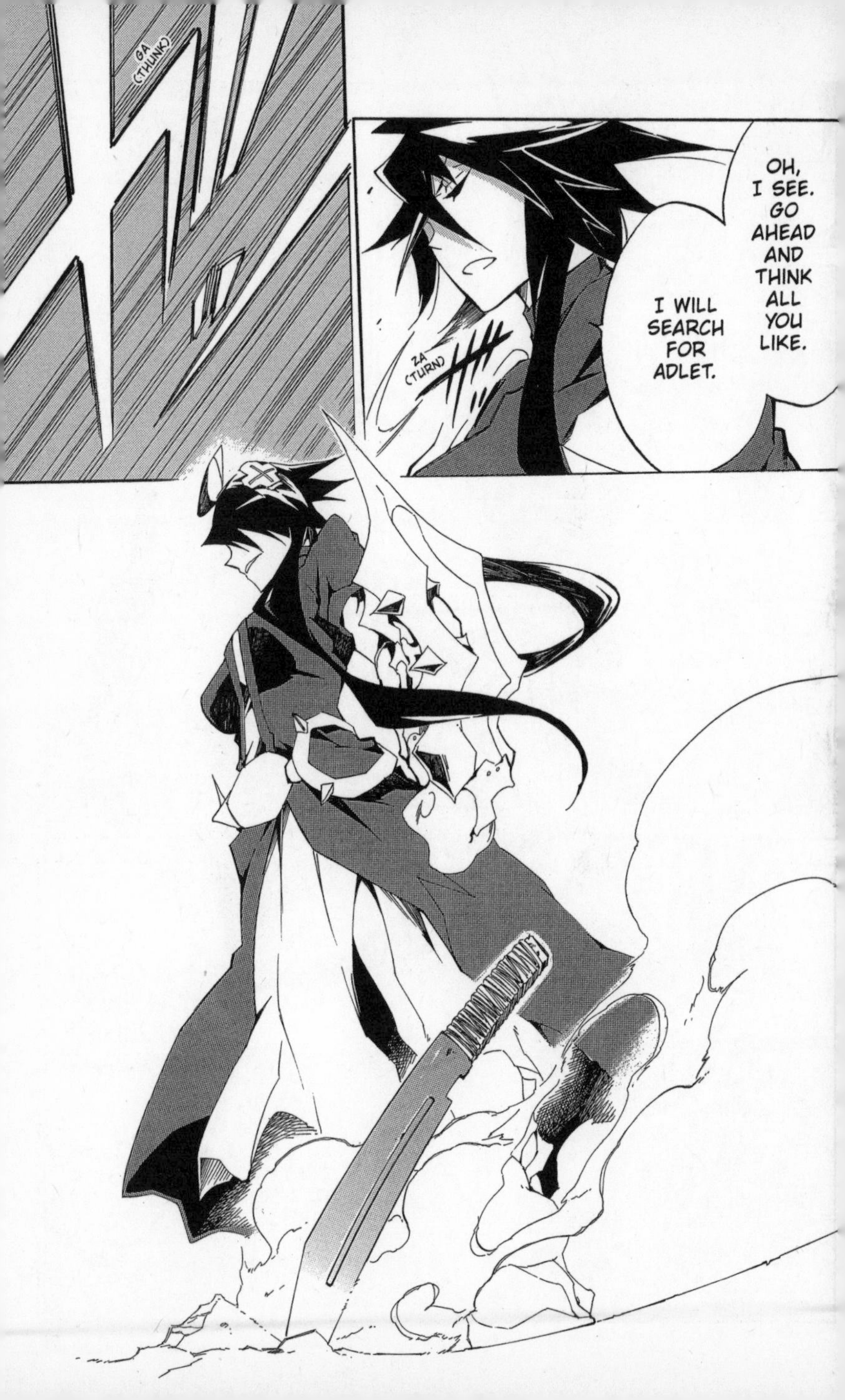
OH, I SEE. GO AHEAD AND THINK ALL YOU LIKE.
I WILL SEARCH FOR ADLET.
ZA (TURN)
GA (THUNK)

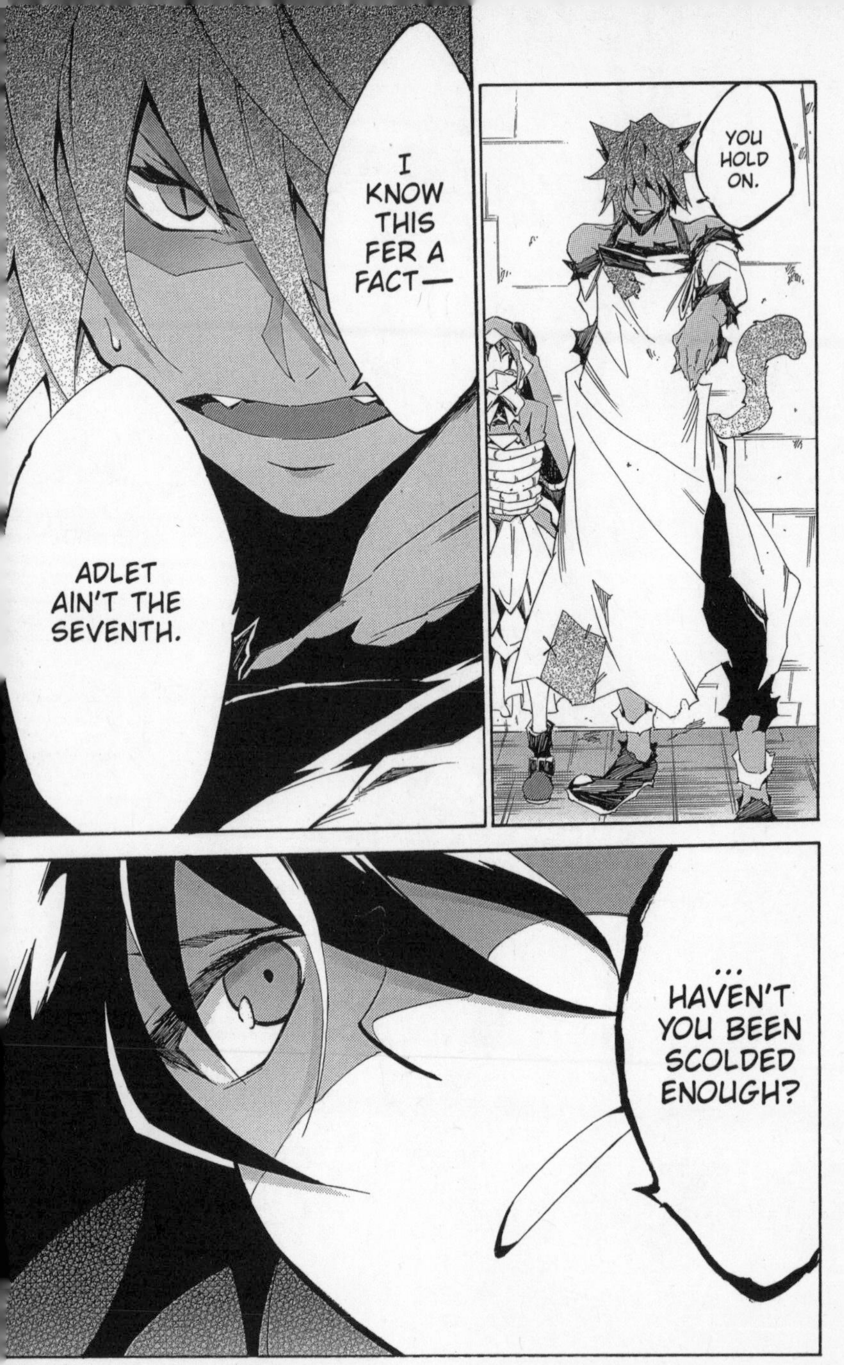
YOU HOLD ON.
I KNOW THIS FER A FACT—
ADLET AIN'T THE SEVENTH.
... HAVEN'T YOU BEEN SCOLDED ENOUGH?

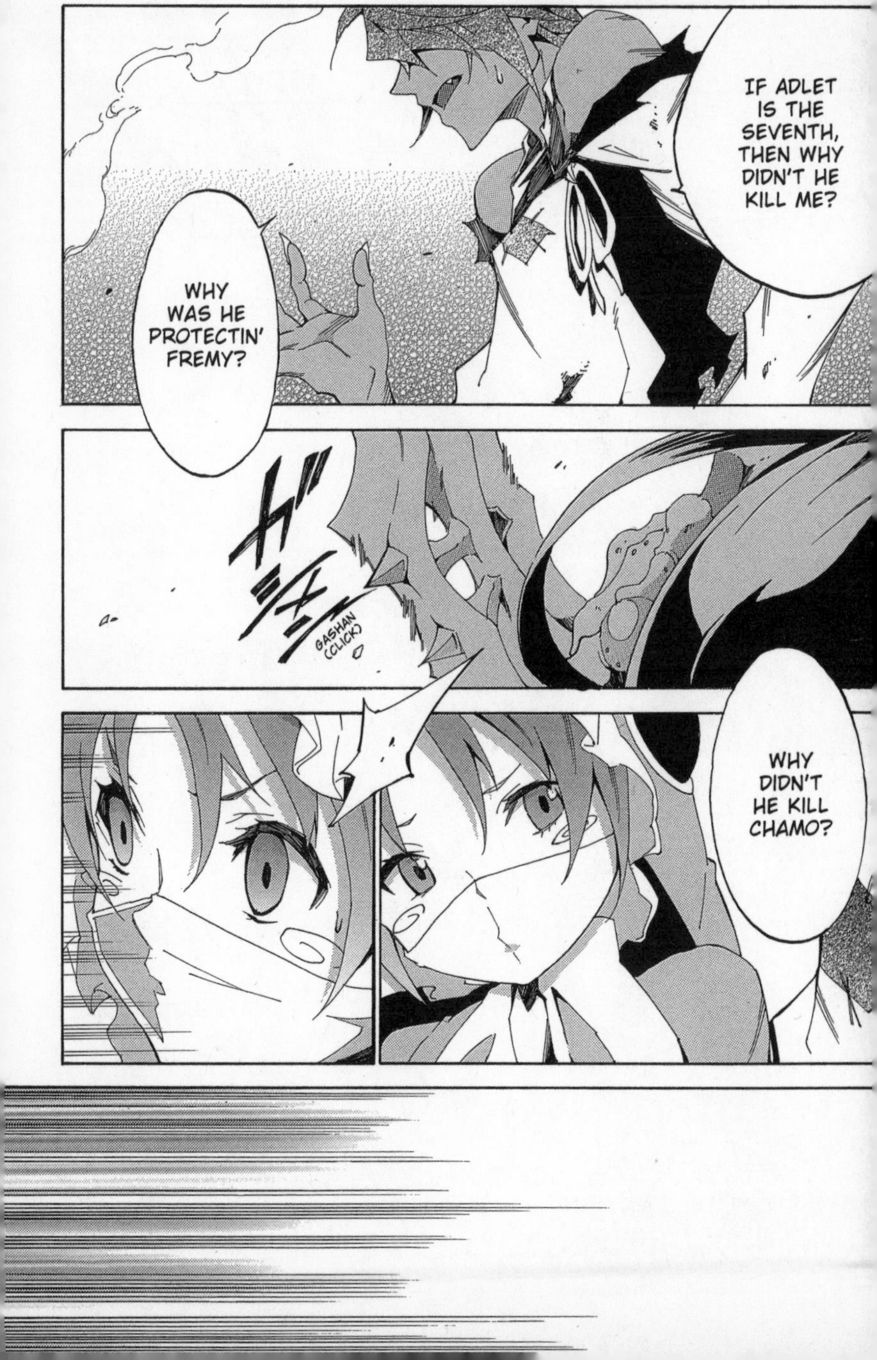
IF ADLET IS THE SEVENTH, THEN WHY DIDN'T HE KILL ME?
WHY WAS HE PROTECTIN' FREMY?
GASHAN (CLICK)
WHY DIDN'T HE KILL CHAMO?

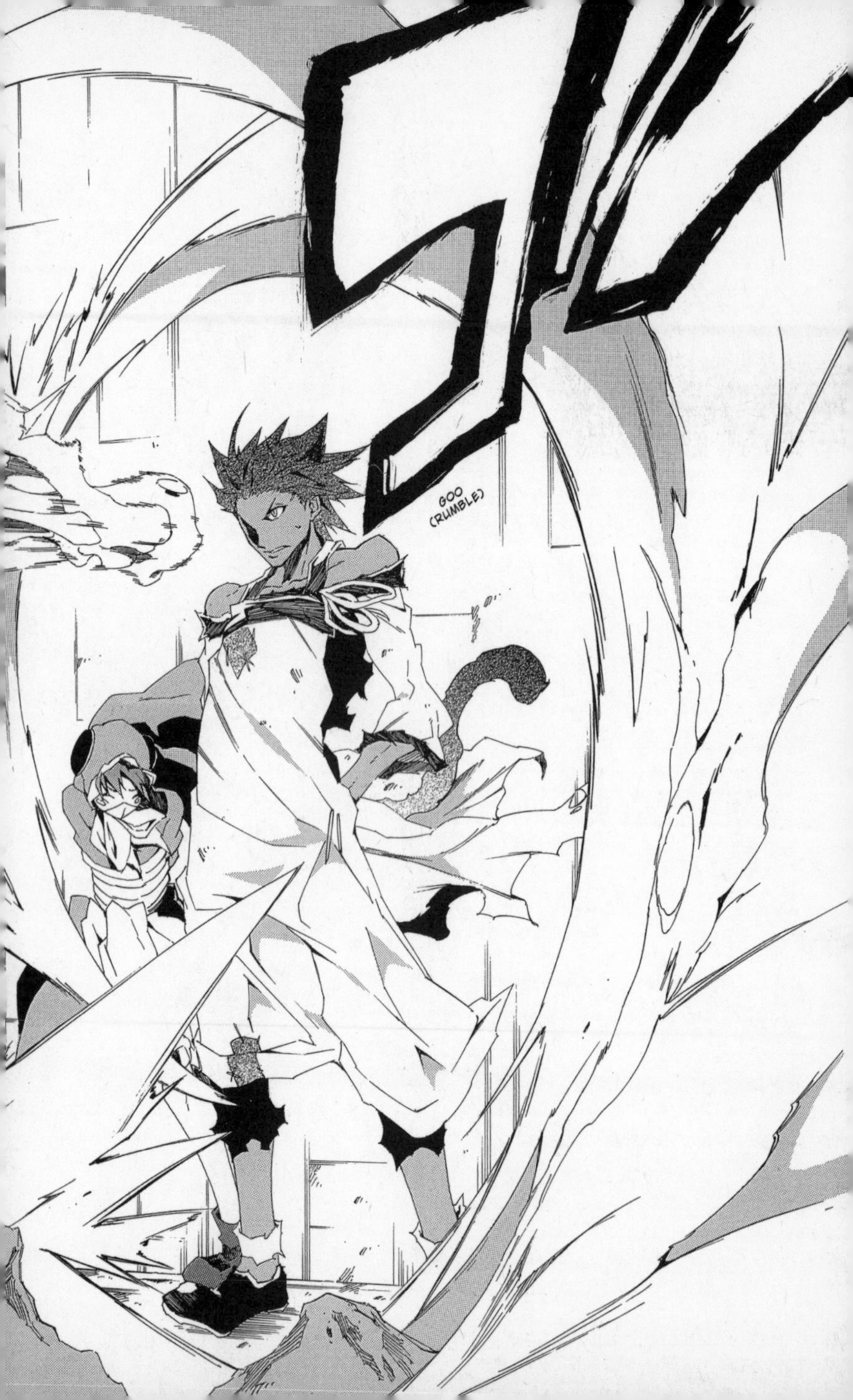
GOO
(RUMBLE)

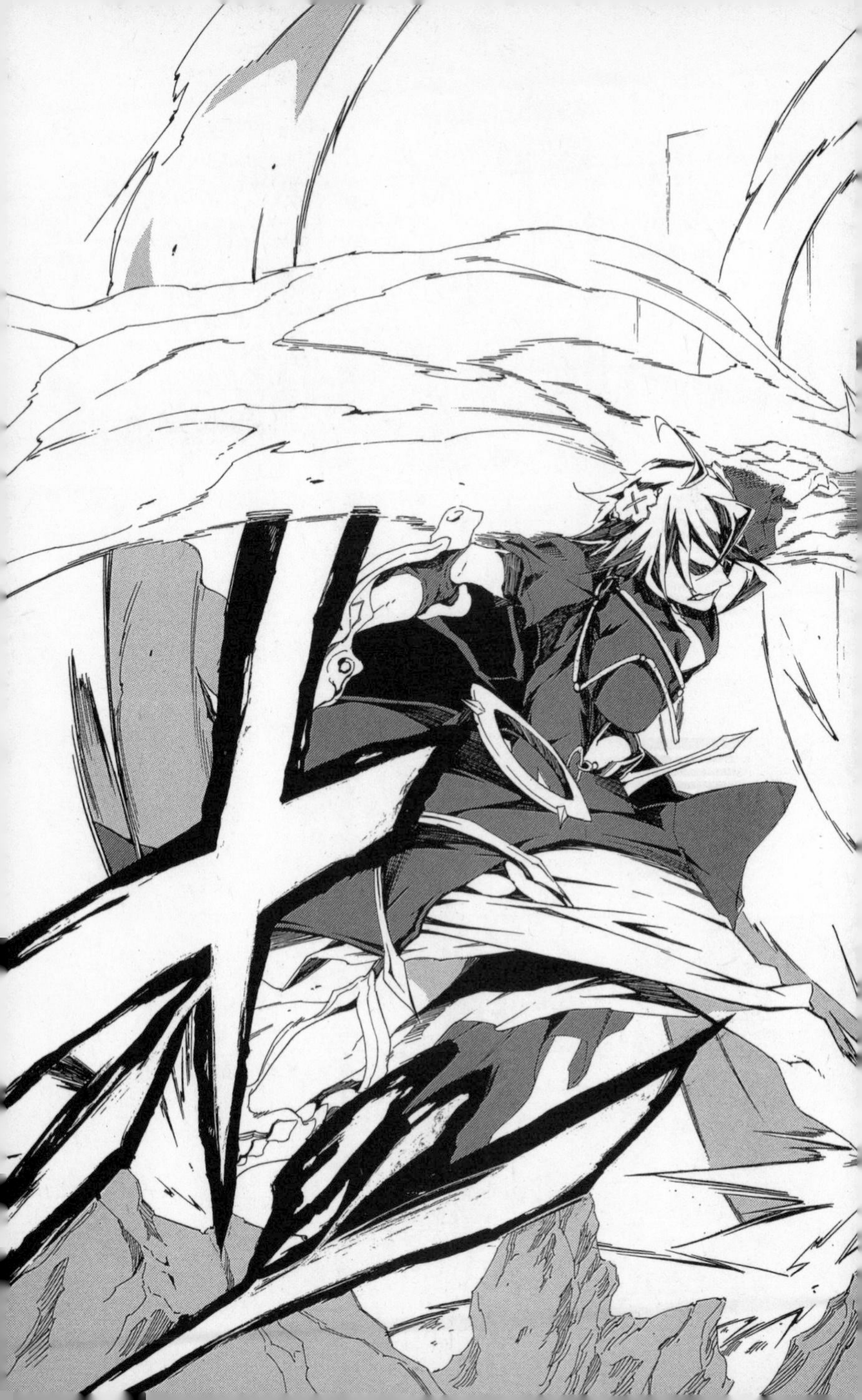

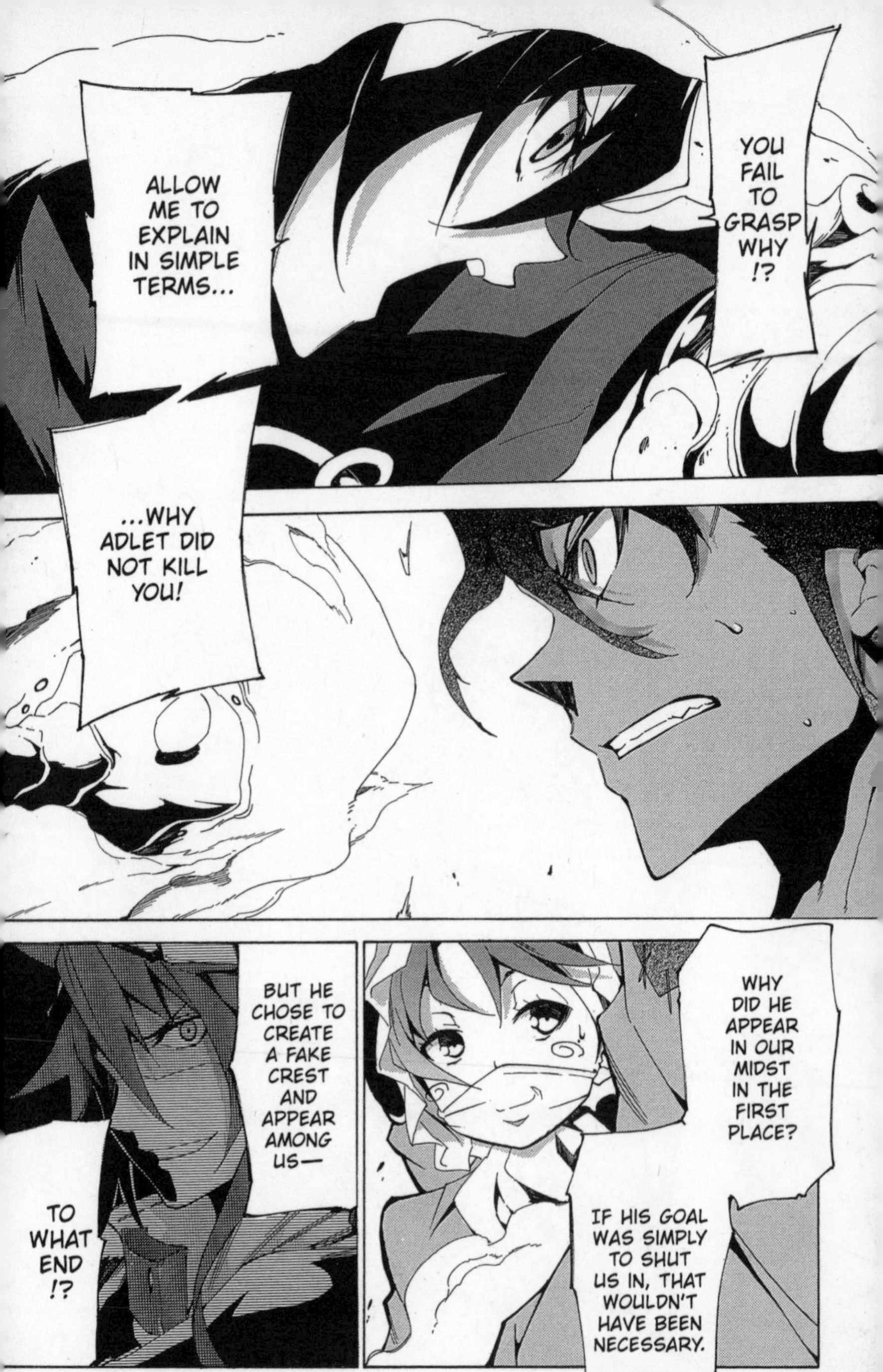
YOU FAIL TO GRASP WHY!?
ALLOW ME TO EXPLAIN IN SIMPLE TERMS...
...WHY ADLET DID NOT KILL YOU!
WHY DID HE APPEAR IN OUR MIDST IN THE FIRST PLACE?
IF HIS GOAL WAS SIMPLY TO SHUT US IN, THAT WOULDN'T HAVE BEEN NECESSARY.
BUT HE CHOSE TO CREATE A FAKE CREST AND APPEAR AMONG US—
TO WHAT END!?

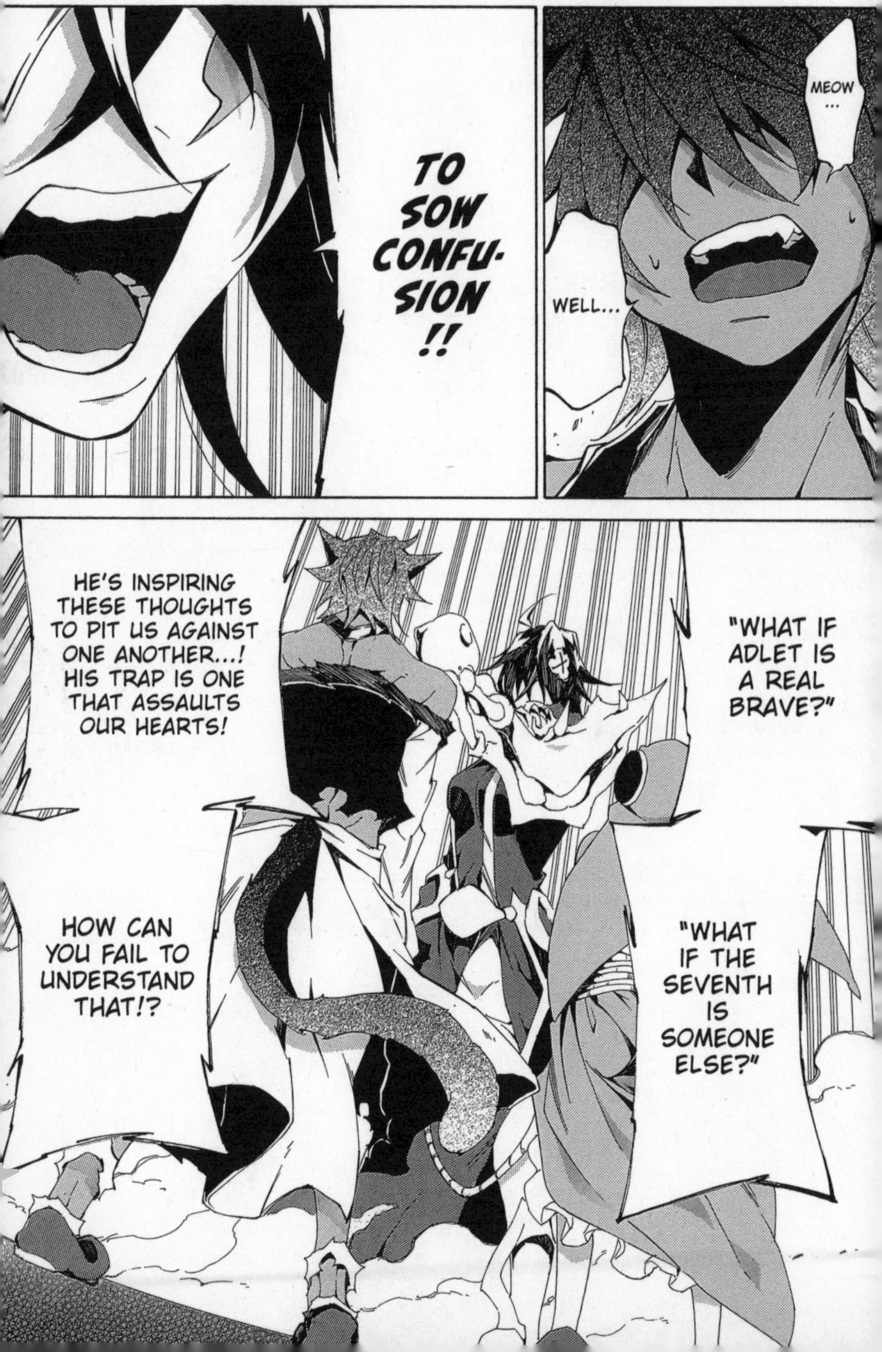
MEOW ...
WELL...
TO SOW CONFU-SION !!
"WHAT IF ADLET IS A REAL BRAVE?"
"WHAT IF THE SEVENTH IS SOMEONE ELSE?"
HE'S INSPIRING THESE THOUGHTS TO PIT US AGAINST ONE ANOTHER...! HIS TRAP IS ONE THAT ASSAULTS OUR HEARTS!
HOW CAN YOU FAIL TO UNDERSTAND THAT!?

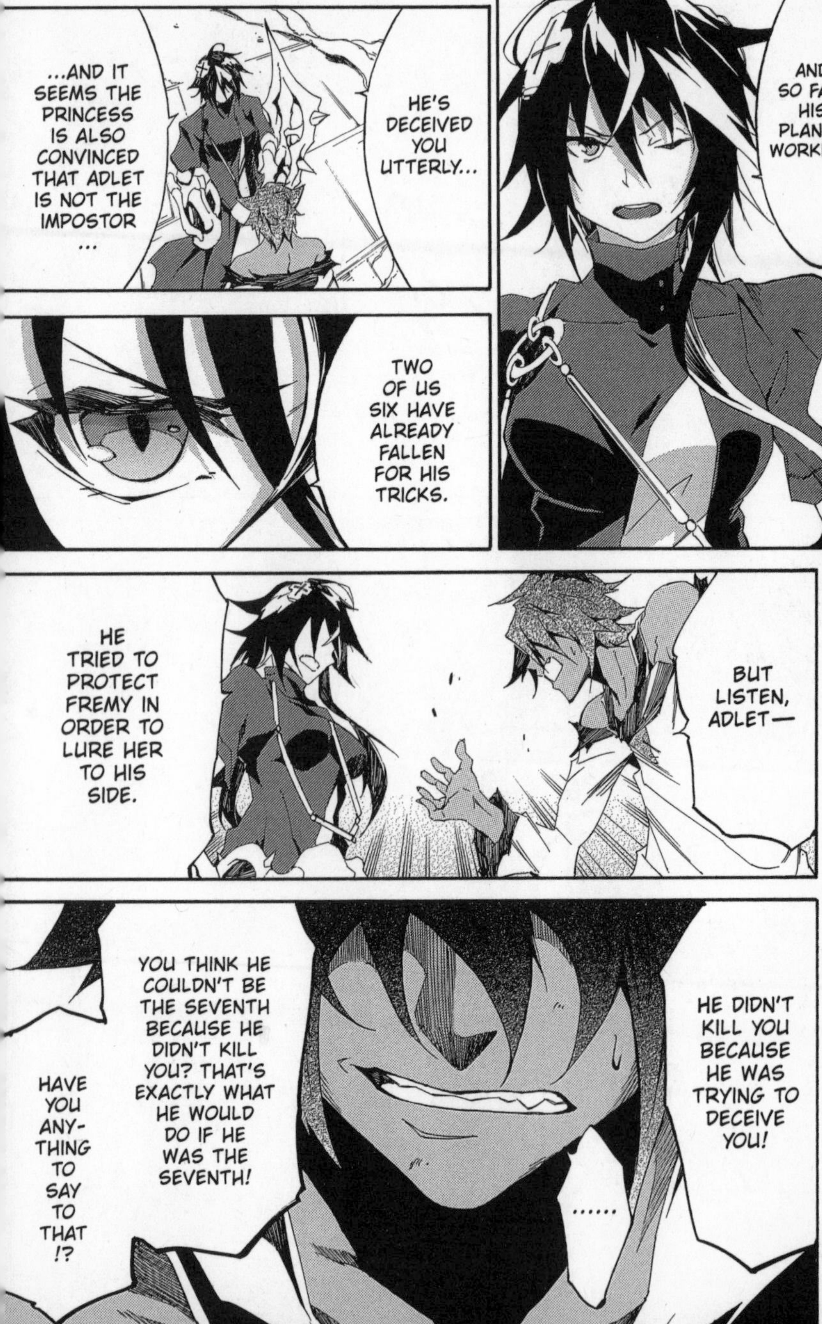
AND SO FAR, HIS PLAN IS WORKING.
HE'S DECEIVED YOU UTTERLY...
...AND IT SEEMS THE PRINCESS IS ALSO CONVINCED THAT ADLET IS NOT THE IMPOSTOR...
TWO OF US SIX HAVE ALREADY FALLEN FOR HIS TRICKS.
BUT LISTEN, ADLET—
HE TRIED TO PROTECT FREMY IN ORDER TO LURE HER TO HIS SIDE.
HE DIDN'T KILL YOU BECAUSE HE WAS TRYING TO DECEIVE YOU!
......
YOU THINK HE COULDN'T BE THE SEVENTH BECAUSE HE DIDN'T KILL YOU? THAT'S EXACTLY WHAT HE WOULD DO IF HE WAS THE SEVENTH!
HAVE YOU ANY-THING TO SAY TO THAT!?

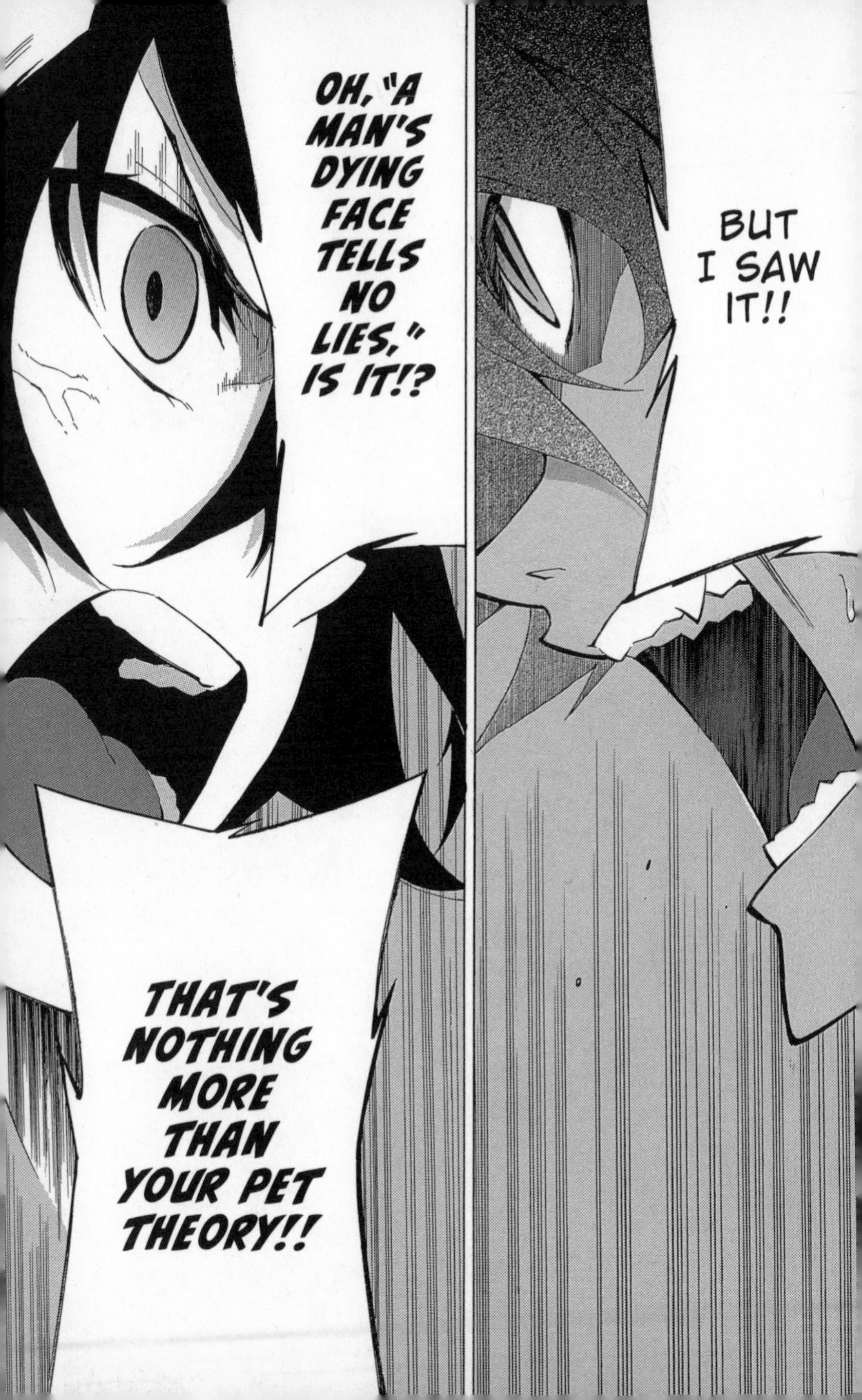
BUT I SAW IT!!
OH, "A MAN'S DYING FACE TELLS NO LIES," IS IT!?
THAT'S NOTHING MORE THAN YOUR PET THEORY!!

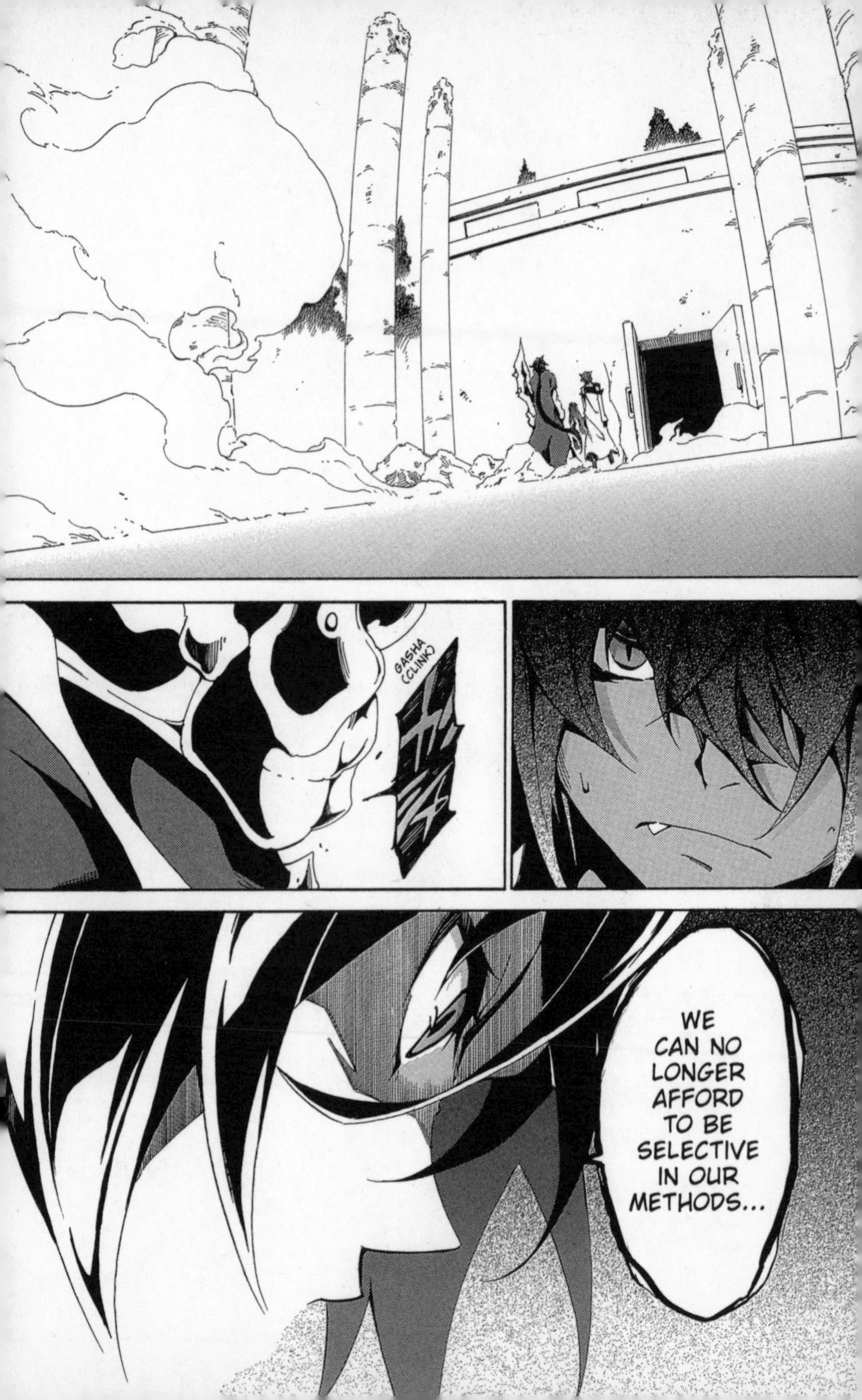
GASHA (CLINK)
WE CAN NO LONGER AFFORD TO BE SELECTIVE IN OUR METHODS...

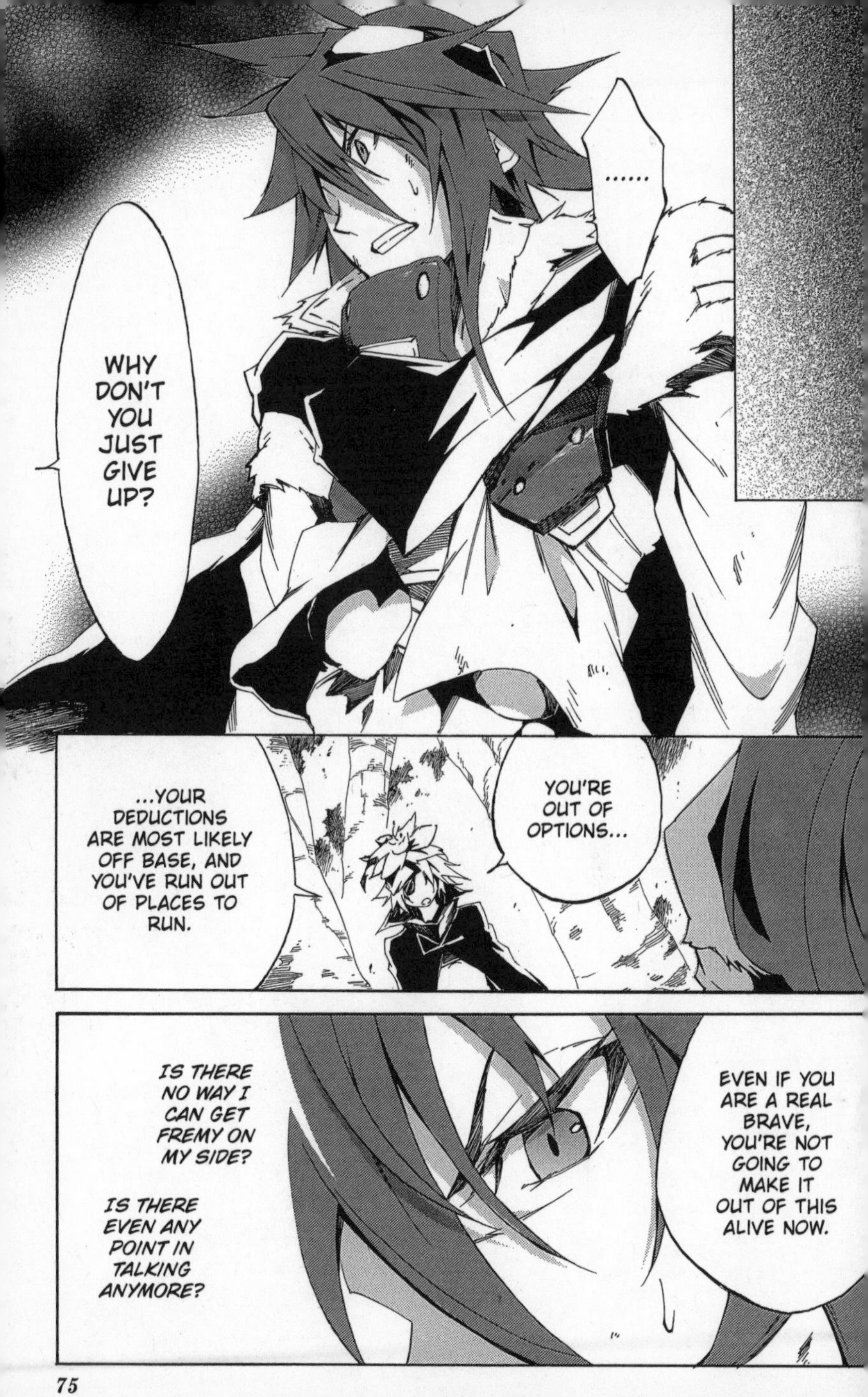
......
WHY DON'T YOU JUST GIVE UP?
YOU'RE OUT OF OPTIONS...
...YOUR DEDUCTIONS ARE MOST LIKELY OFF BASE, AND YOU'VE RUN OUT OF PLACES TO RUN.
EVEN IF YOU ARE A REAL BRAVE, YOU'RE NOT GOING TO MAKE IT OUT OF THIS ALIVE NOW.
IS THERE NO WAY I CAN GET FREMY ON MY SIDE?
IS THERE EVEN ANY POINT IN TALKING ANYMORE?

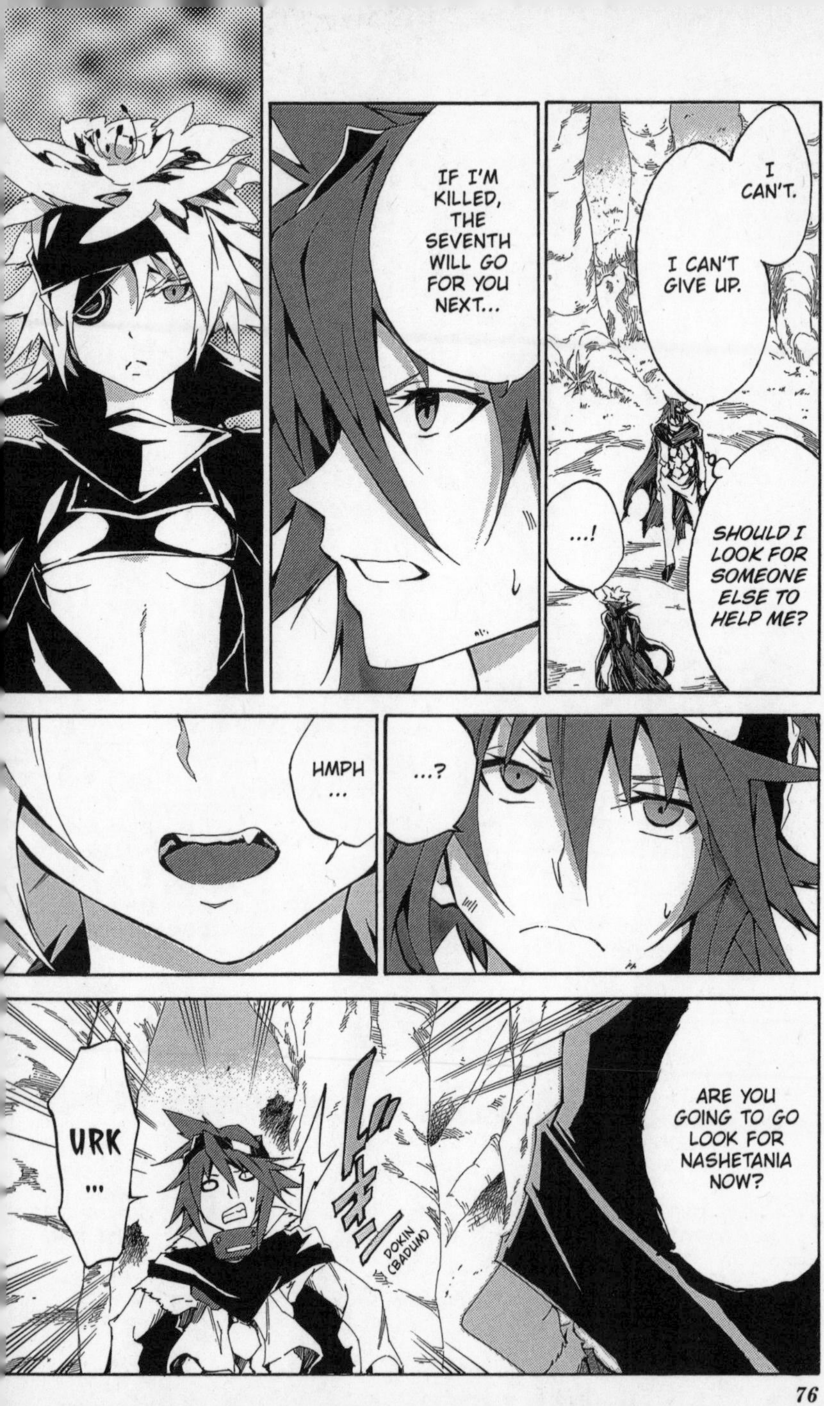
I CAN'T.
I CAN'T GIVE UP.
SHOULD I LOOK FOR SOMEONE ELSE TO HELP ME?
...!
IF I'M KILLED, THE SEVENTH WILL GO FOR YOU NEXT...
...?
HMPH ...
ARE YOU GOING TO GO LOOK FOR NASHETANIA NOW?
DOKIN (BADUM)
URK ...

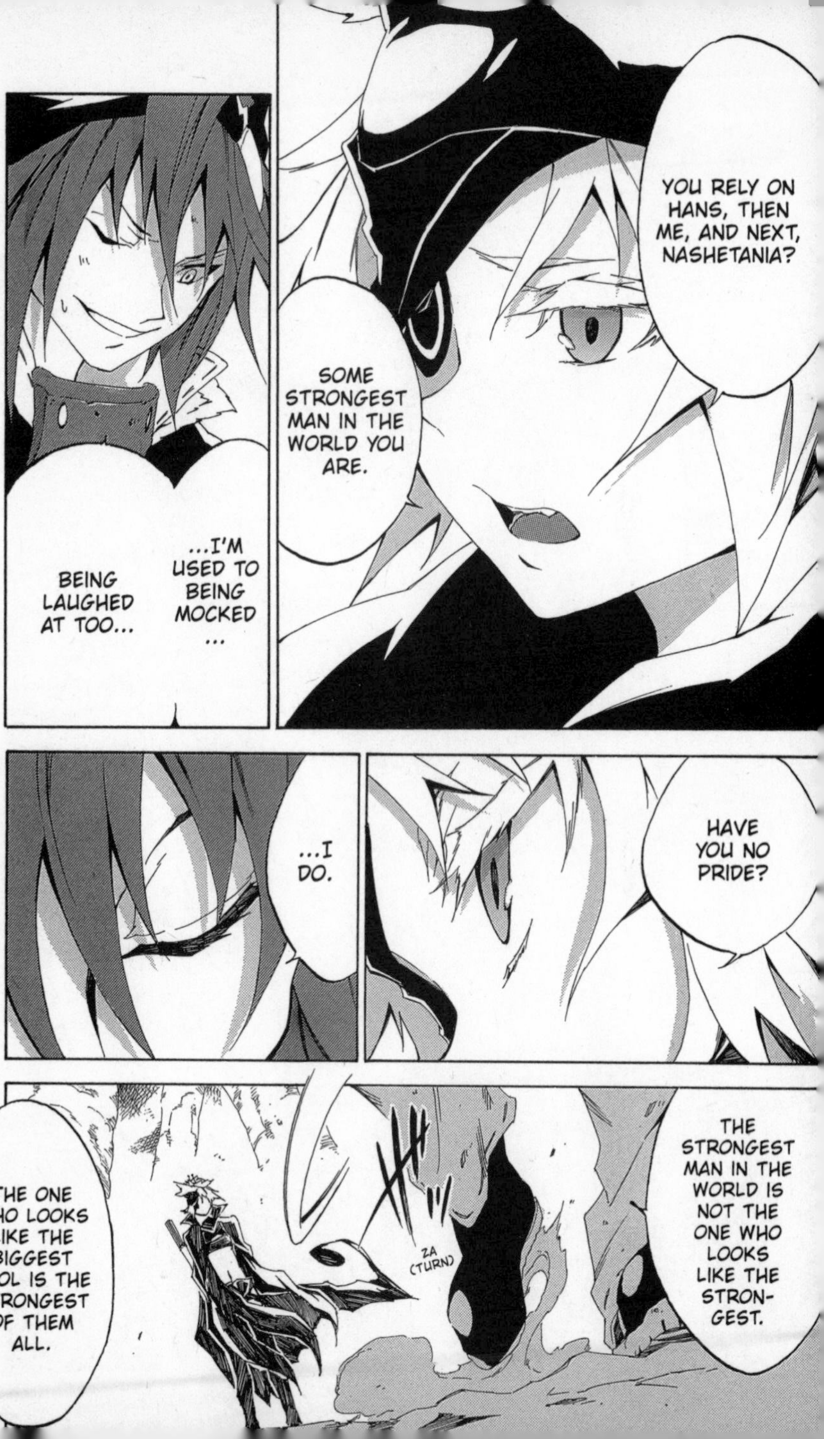
YOU RELY ON HANS, THEN ME, AND NEXT, NASHETANIA?
SOME STRONGEST MAN IN THE WORLD YOU ARE.
...I'M USED TO BEING MOCKED ...
BEING LAUGHED AT TOO...
HAVE YOU NO PRIDE?
...I DO.
THE STRONGEST MAN IN THE WORLD IS NOT THE ONE WHO LOOKS LIKE THE STRON-GEST.
ZA (TURN)
THE ONE WHO LOOKS LIKE THE BIGGEST FOOL IS THE STRONGEST OF THEM ALL.

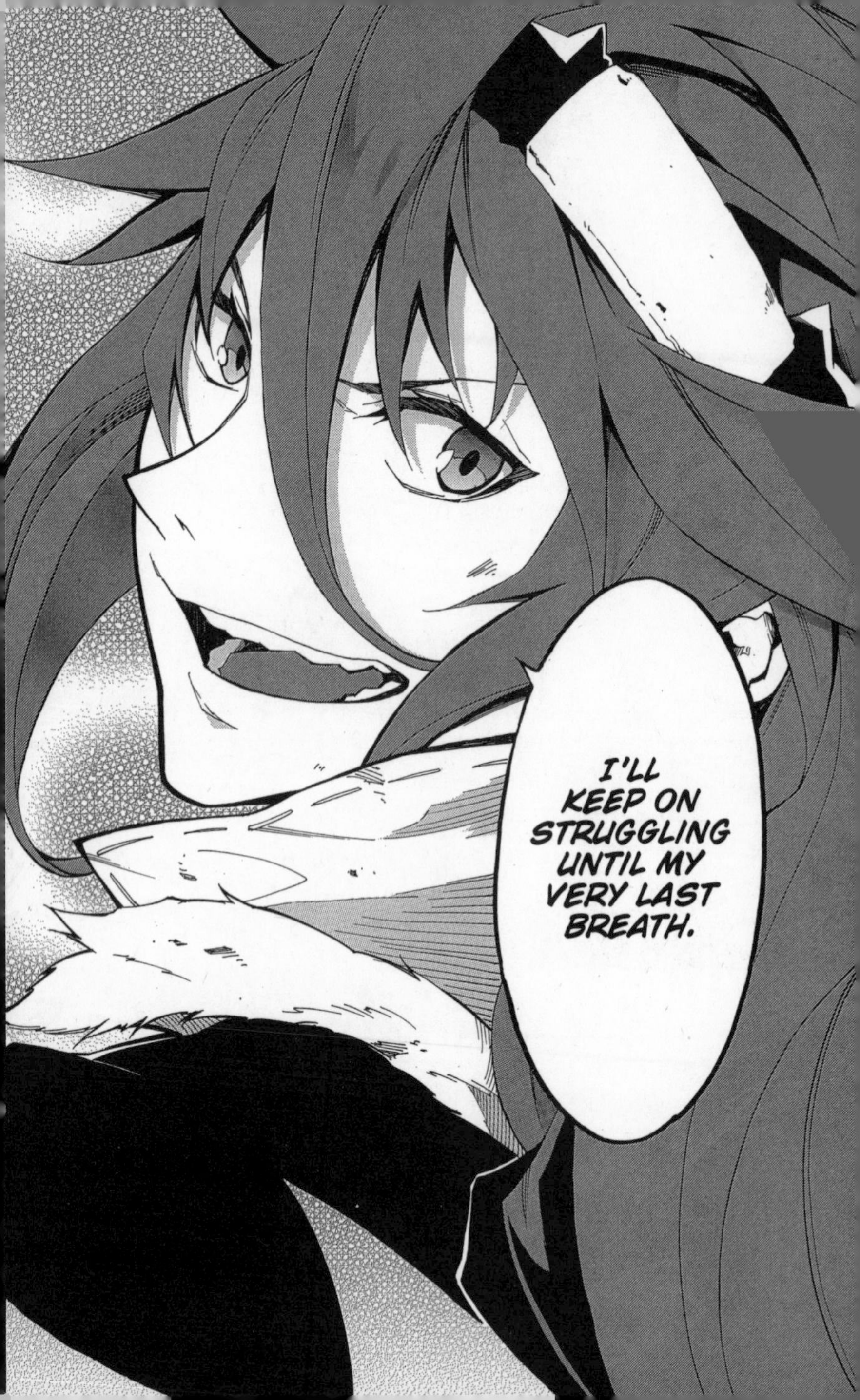
I'LL KEEP ON STRUGGLING UNTIL MY VERY LAST BREATH.

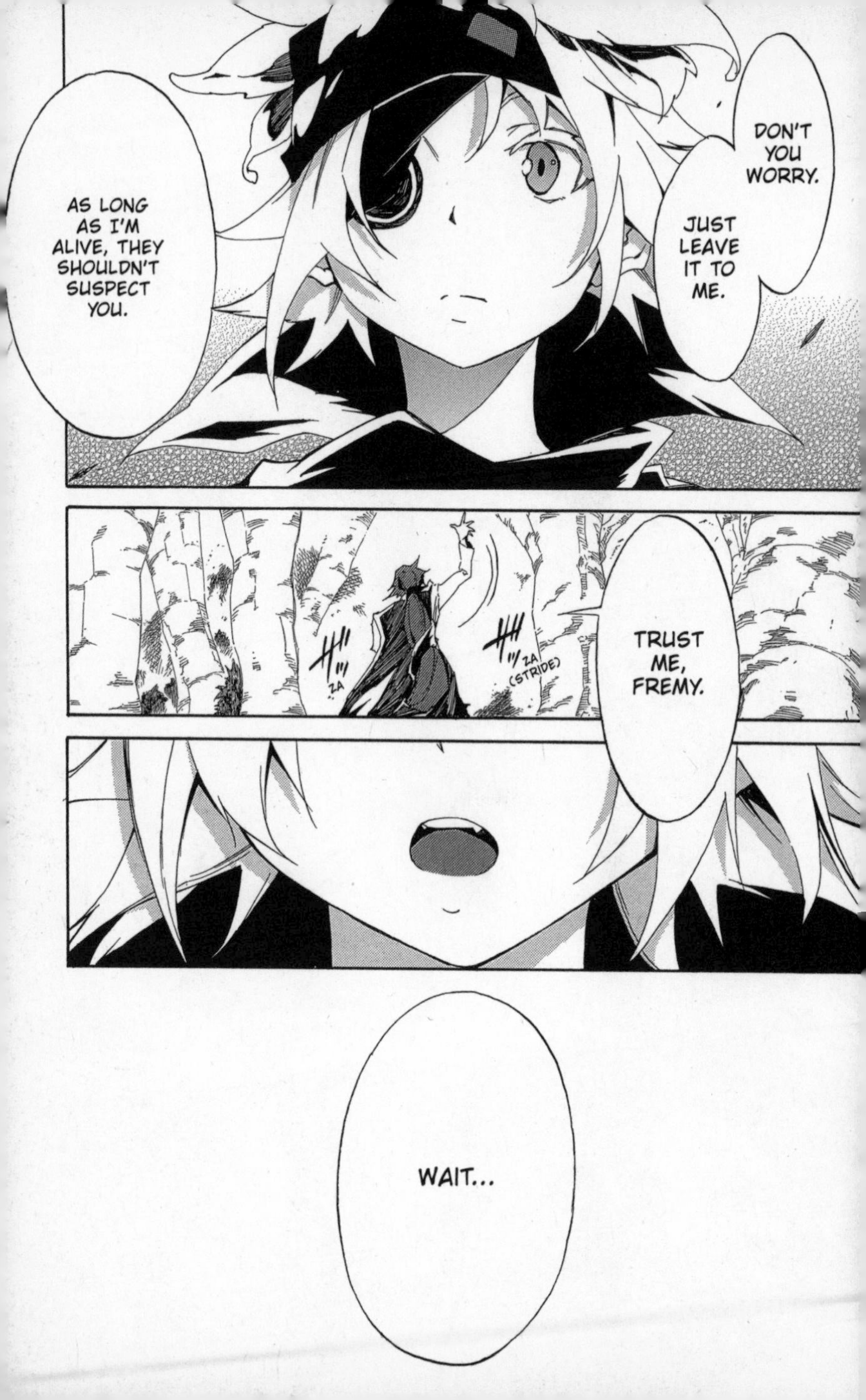
DON'T YOU WORRY.
JUST LEAVE IT TO ME.
AS LONG AS I'M ALIVE, THEY SHOULDN'T SUSPECT YOU.
TRUST ME, FREMY.
ZA (STRIDE)
ZA
WAIT...

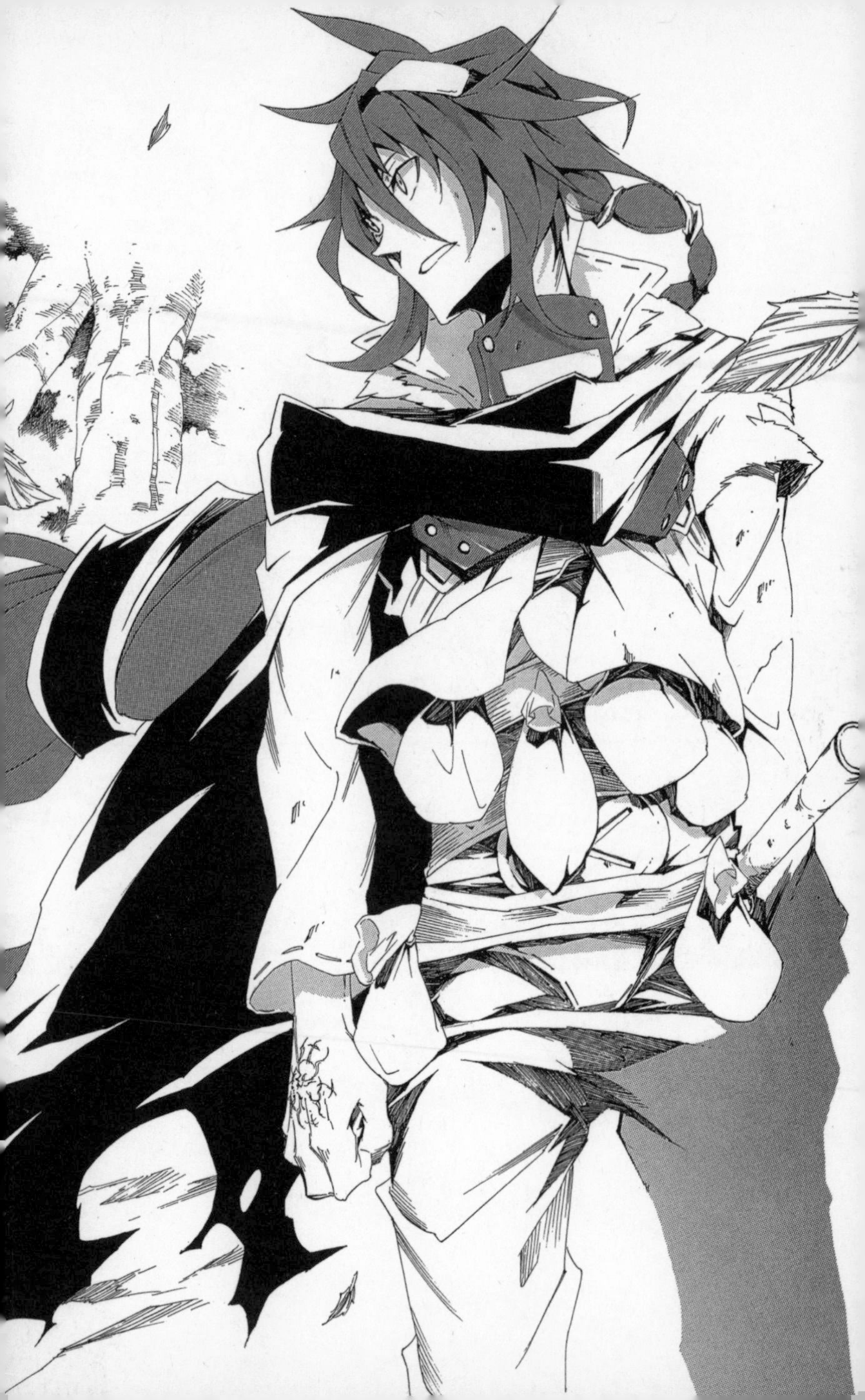

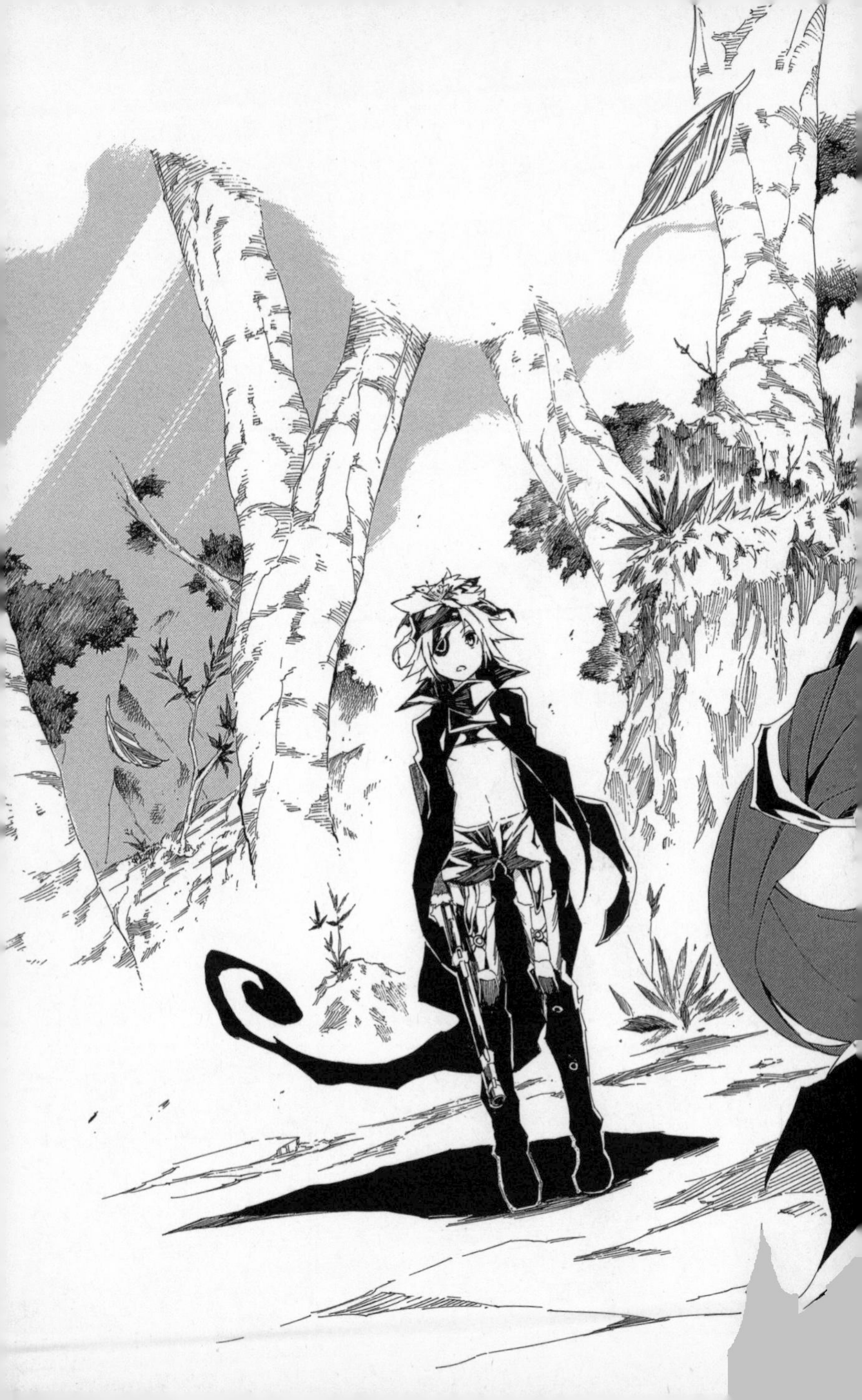

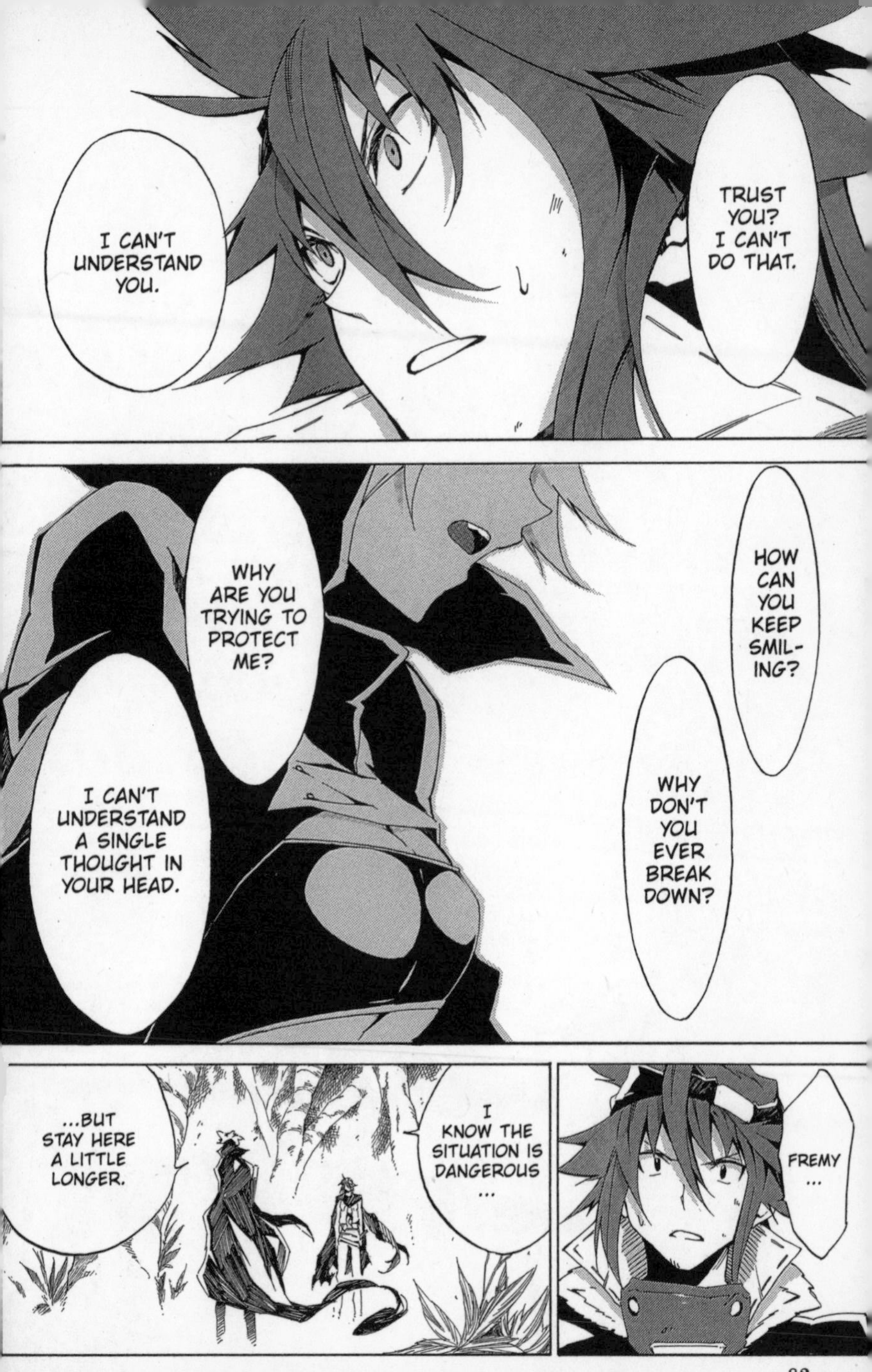
TRUST YOU? I CAN'T DO THAT.
I CAN'T UNDERSTAND YOU.
HOW CAN YOU KEEP SMIL-ING?
WHY DON'T YOU EVER BREAK DOWN?
WHY ARE YOU TRYING TO PROTECT ME?
I CAN'T UNDERSTAND A SINGLE THOUGHT IN YOUR HEAD.
FREMY ...
I KNOW THE SITUATION IS DANGEROUS ...
...BUT STAY HERE A LITTLE LONGER.

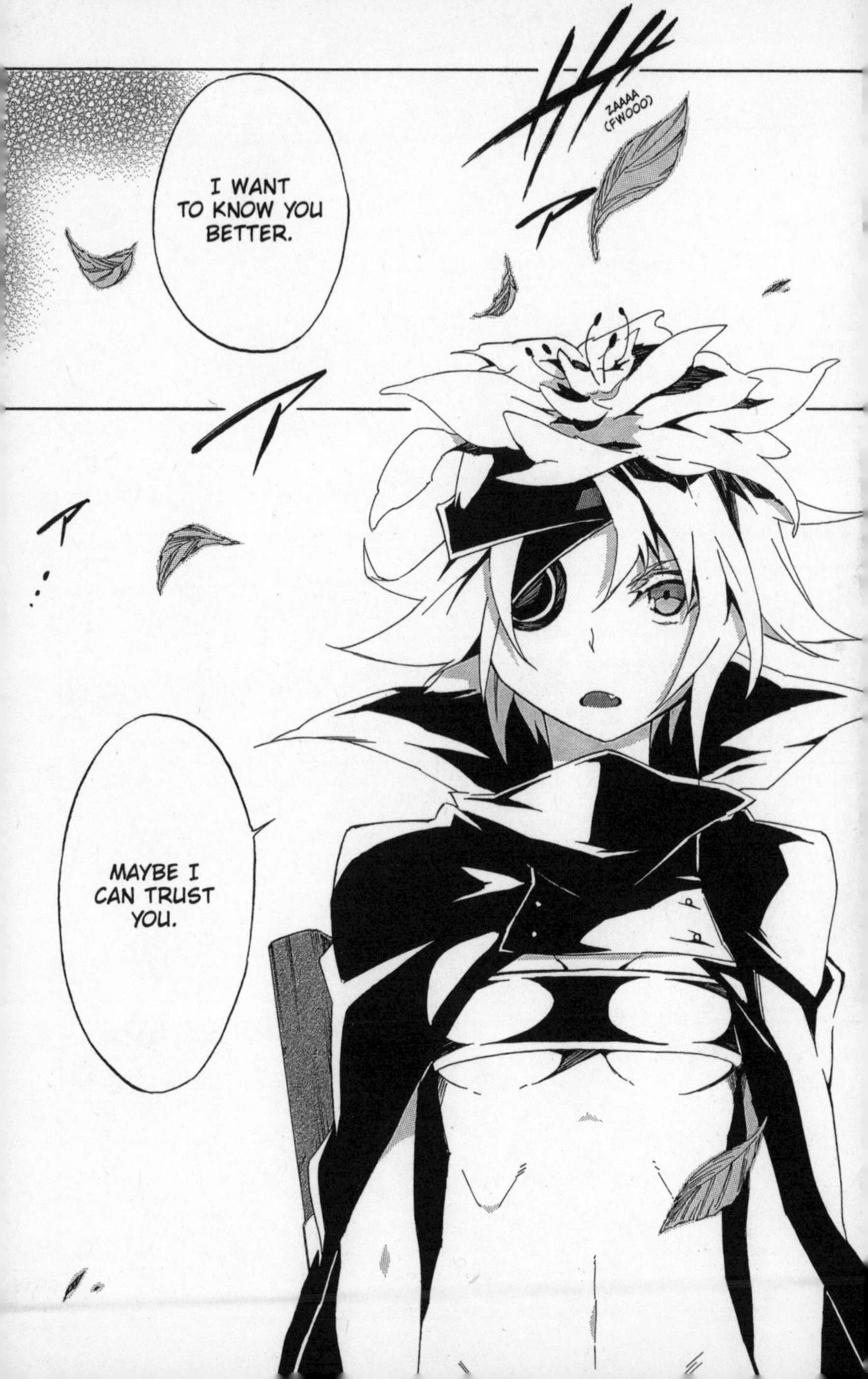
ZAAAA (FWOOO)
I WANT TO KNOW YOU BETTER.
MAYBE I CAN TRUST YOU.

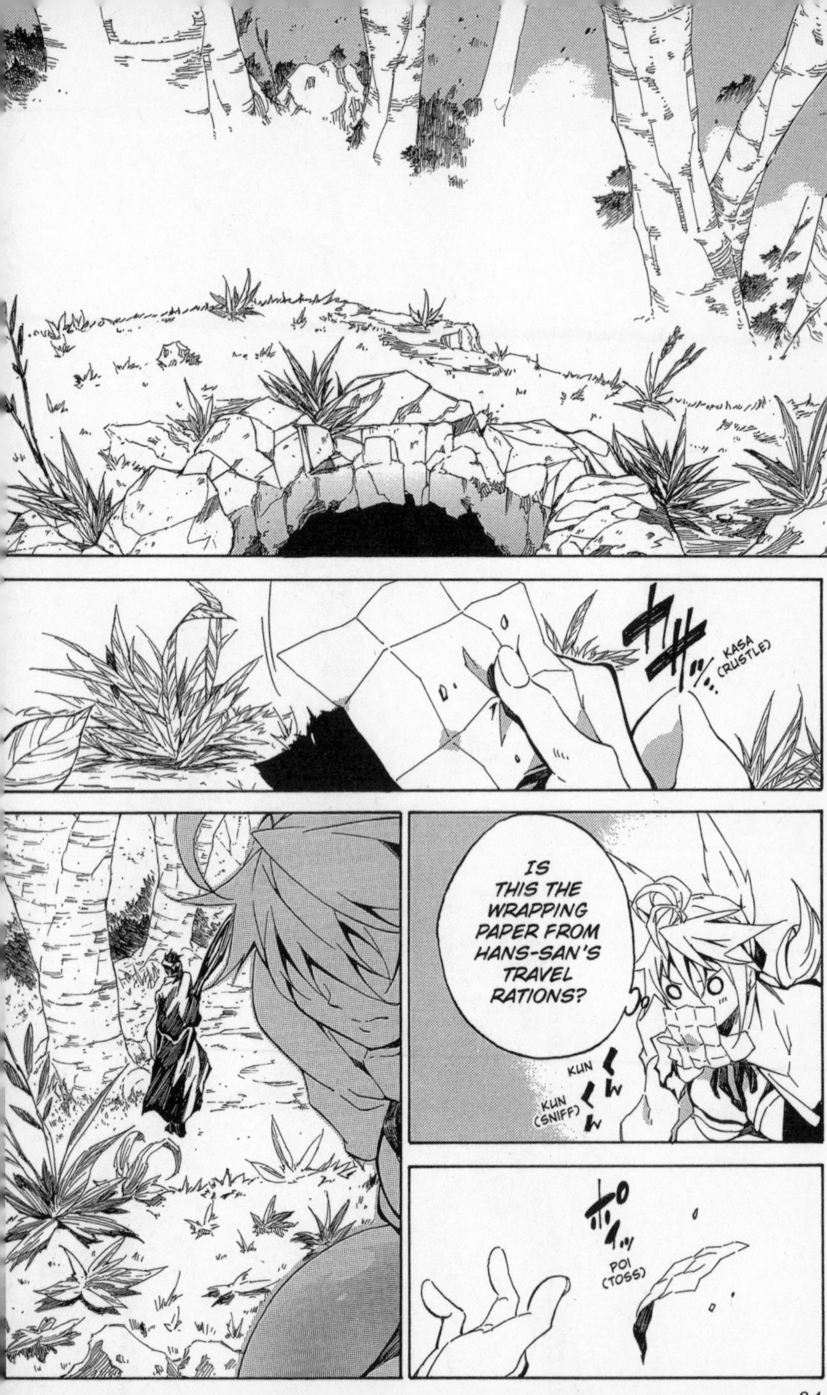
KASA (RUSTLE)
IS THIS THE WRAPPING PAPER FROM HANS-SAN'S TRAVEL RATIONS?
KUN KUN (SNIFF)
POI (TOSS)

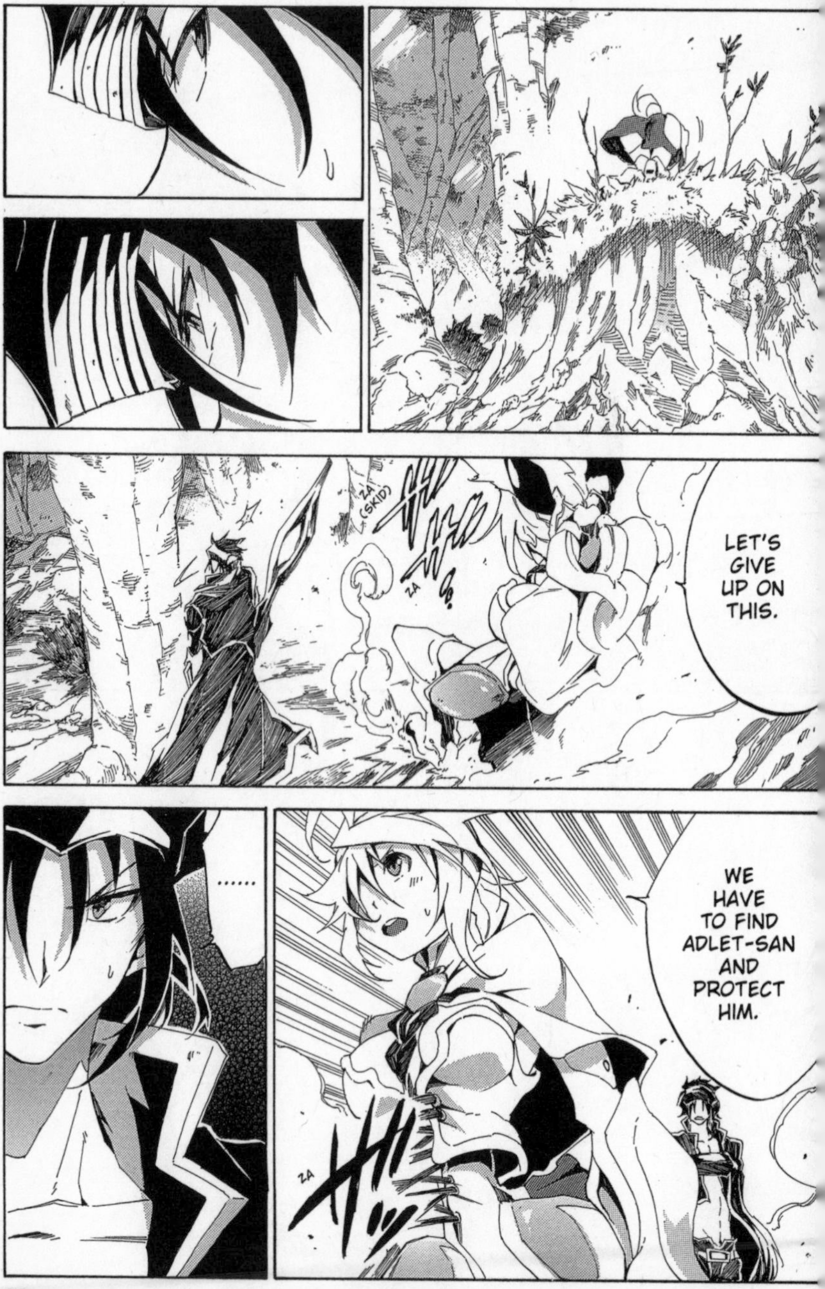
ZA (SKID)
ZA
LET'S GIVE UP ON THIS.
WE HAVE TO FIND ADLET-SAN AND PROTECT HIM.
ZA
......

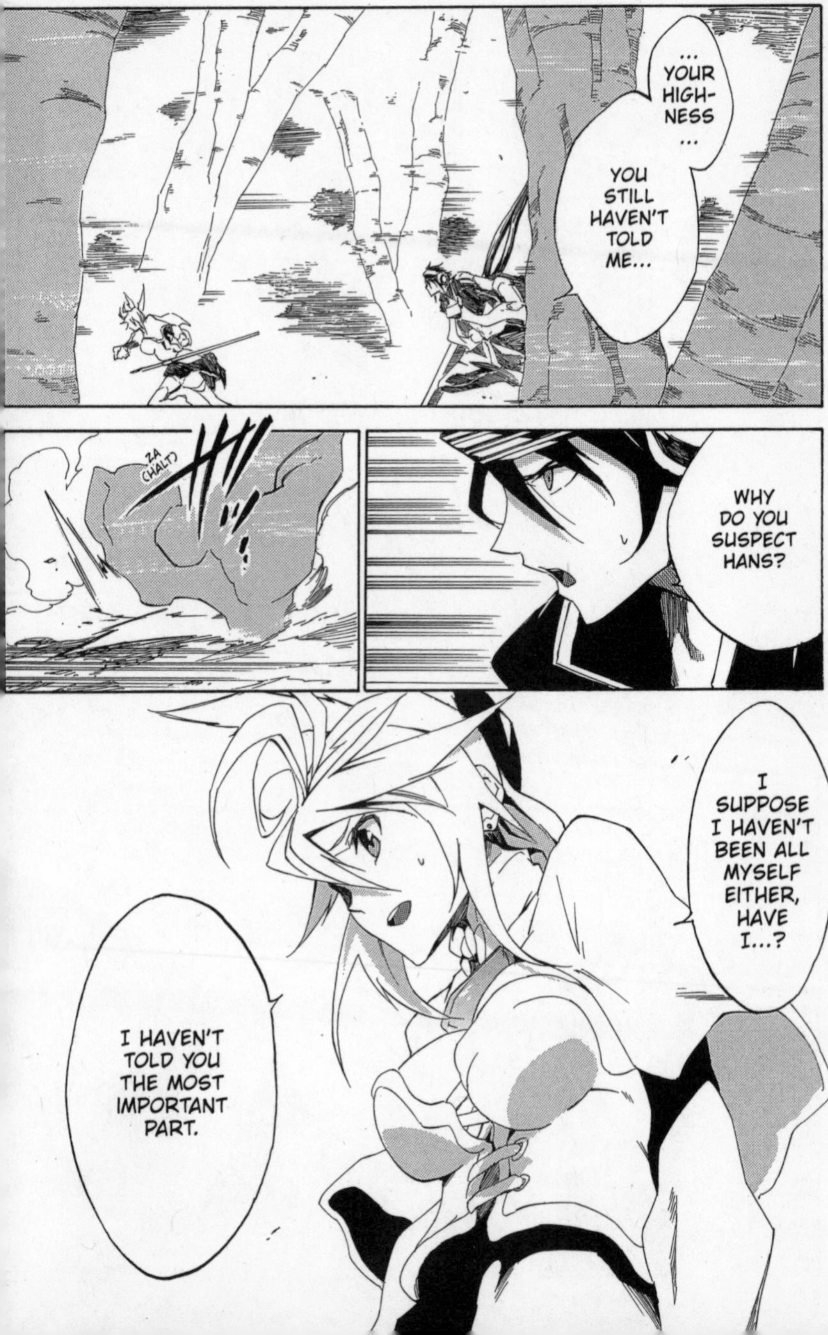
...YOUR HIGH-NESS...
YOU STILL HAVEN'T TOLD ME...
WHY DO YOU SUSPECT HANS?
ZA (HALT)
I SUPPOSE I HAVEN'T BEEN ALL MYSELF EITHER, HAVE I...?
I HAVEN'T TOLD YOU THE MOST IMPORTANT PART.

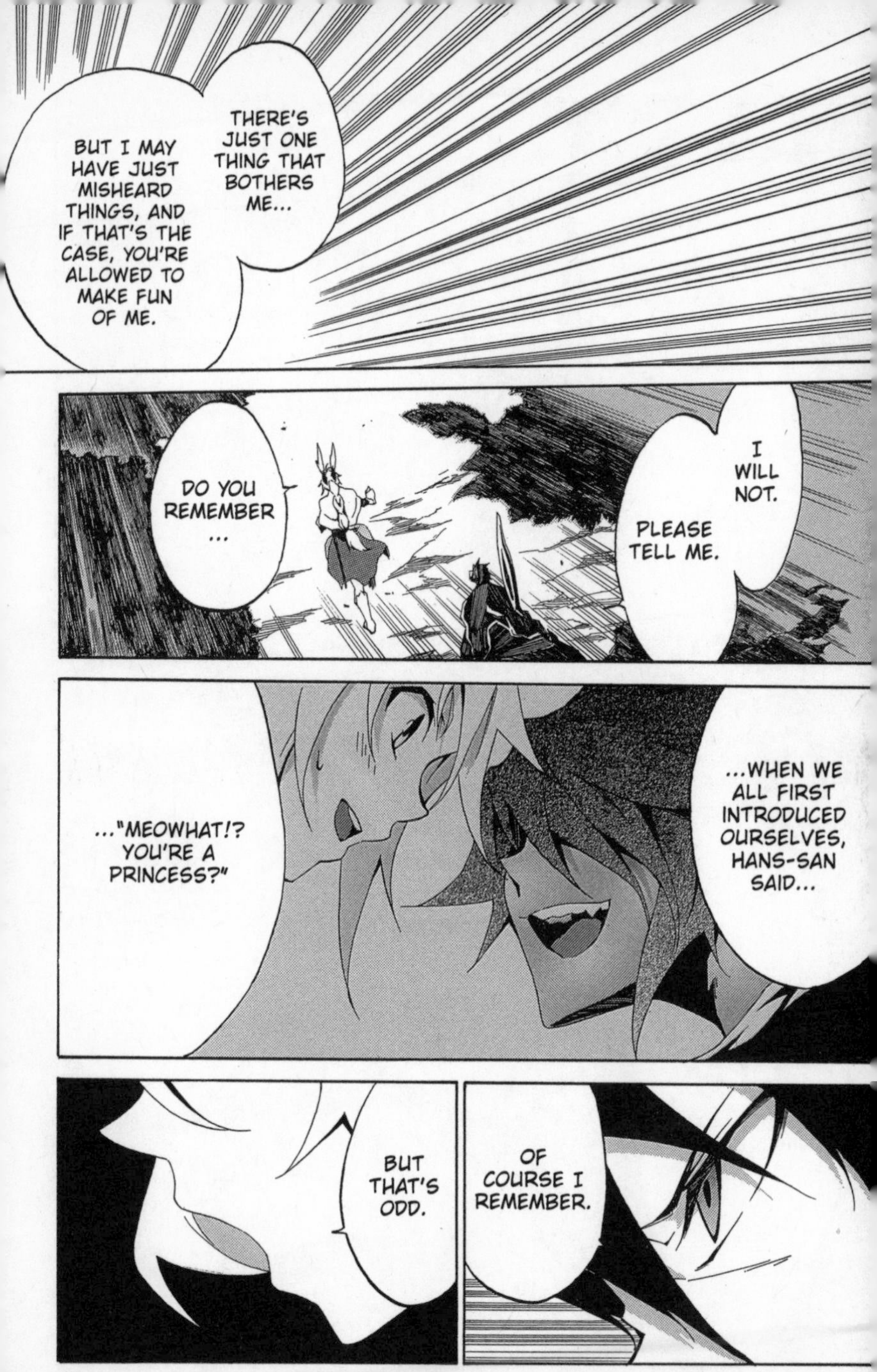
THERE'S JUST ONE THING THAT BOTHERS ME...
BUT I MAY HAVE JUST MISHEARD THINGS, AND IF THAT'S THE CASE, YOU'RE ALLOWED TO MAKE FUN OF ME.
I WILL NOT.
PLEASE TELL ME.
DO YOU REMEMBER...
...WHEN WE ALL FIRST INTRODUCED OURSELVES, HANS-SAN SAID...
..."MEOWHAT!? YOU'RE A PRINCESS?"
OF COURSE I REMEMBER.
BUT THAT'S ODD.

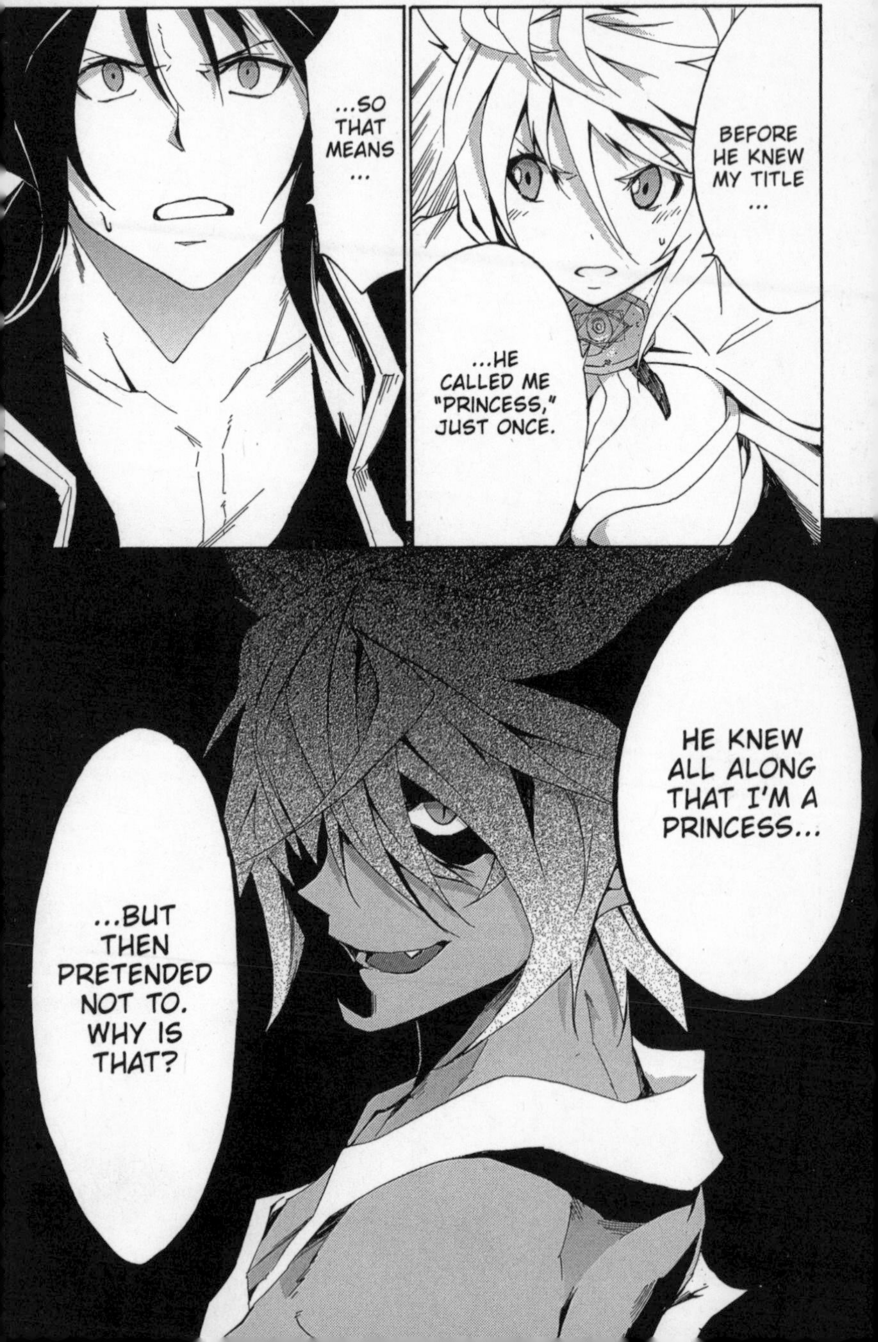
BEFORE HE KNEW MY TITLE ...
...HE CALLED ME "PRINCESS," JUST ONCE.
...SO THAT MEANS ...
HE KNEW ALL ALONG THAT I'M A PRINCESS...
...BUT THEN PRETENDED NOT TO. WHY IS THAT?

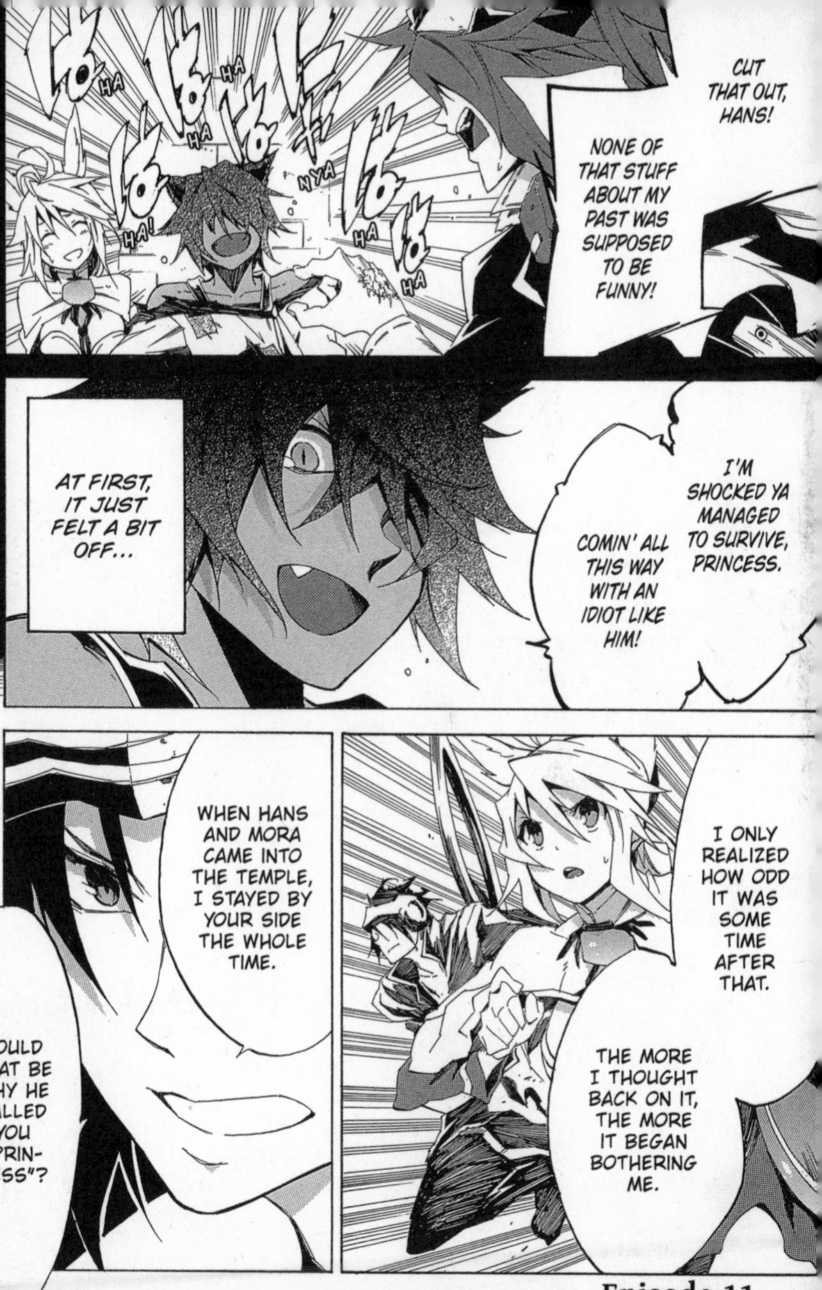
CUT THAT OUT, HANS!
NONE OF THAT STUFF ABOUT MY PAST WAS SUPPOSED TO BE FUNNY!
HA
HA
HA
HA!
NYA
HA
HA
HA
I'M SHOCKED YA MANAGED TO SURVIVE, PRINCESS.
COMIN' ALL THIS WAY WITH AN IDIOT LIKE HIM!
AT FIRST, IT JUST FELT A BIT OFF...
I ONLY REALIZED HOW ODD IT WAS SOME TIME AFTER THAT.
THE MORE I THOUGHT BACK ON IT, THE MORE IT BEGAN BOTHERING ME.
WHEN HANS AND MORA CAME INTO THE TEMPLE, I STAYED BY YOUR SIDE THE WHOLE TIME.
COULD THAT BE WHY HE CALLED YOU "PRIN-CESS"?

Episode.11

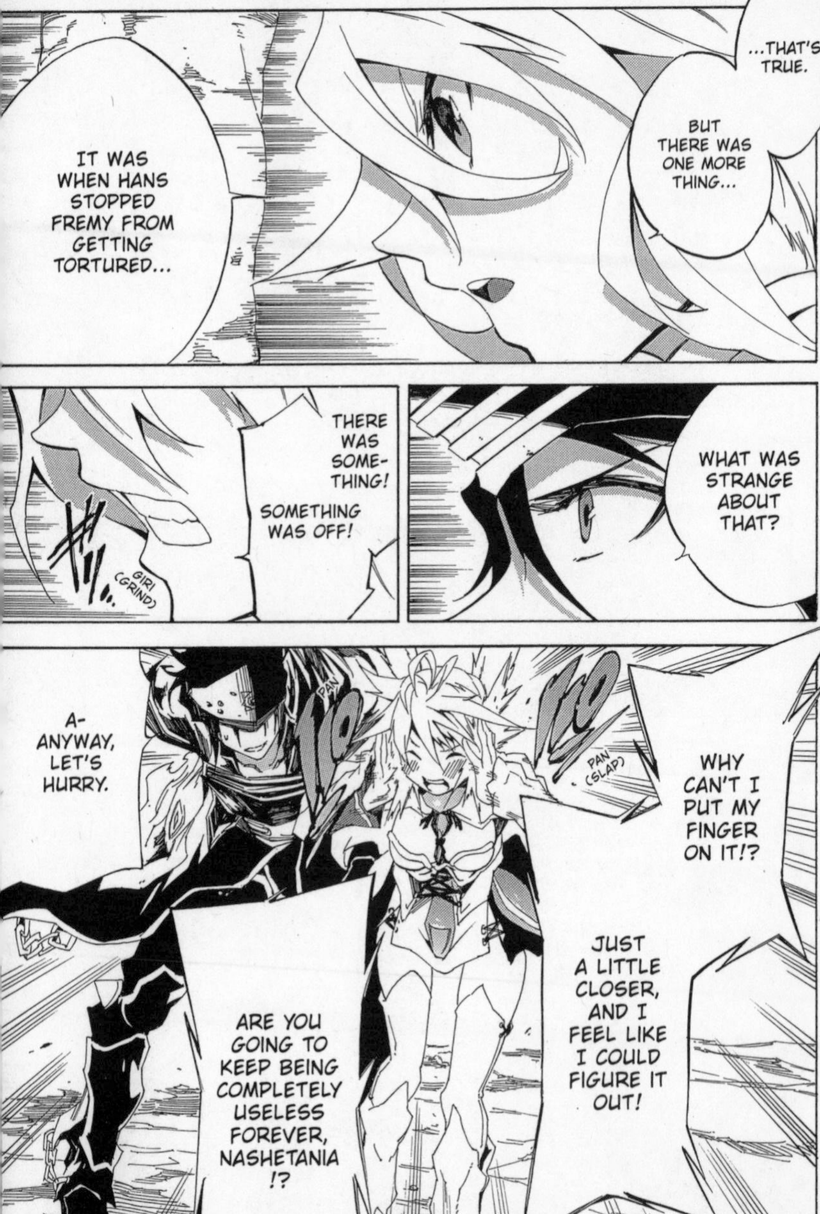
...THAT'S TRUE.
BUT THERE WAS ONE MORE THING...
IT WAS WHEN HANS STOPPED FREMY FROM GETTING TORTURED...
WHAT WAS STRANGE ABOUT THAT?
THERE WAS SOME-THING!
SOMETHING WAS OFF!
GIRI (GRIND)
WHY CAN'T I PUT MY FINGER ON IT!?
PAN (SLAP)
JUST A LITTLE CLOSER, AND I FEEL LIKE I COULD FIGURE IT OUT!
PAN
ARE YOU GOING TO KEEP BEING COMPLETELY USELESS FOREVER, NASHETANIA!?
A-ANYWAY, LET'S HURRY.

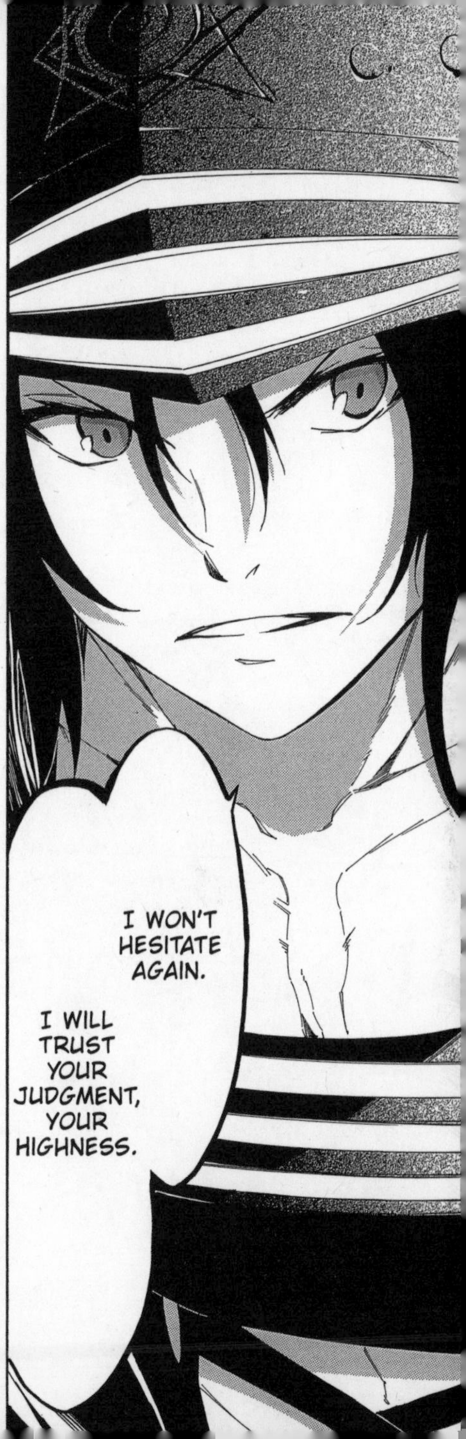
I WON'T HESITATE AGAIN.
I WILL TRUST YOUR JUDGMENT, YOUR HIGHNESS.

Episode.11

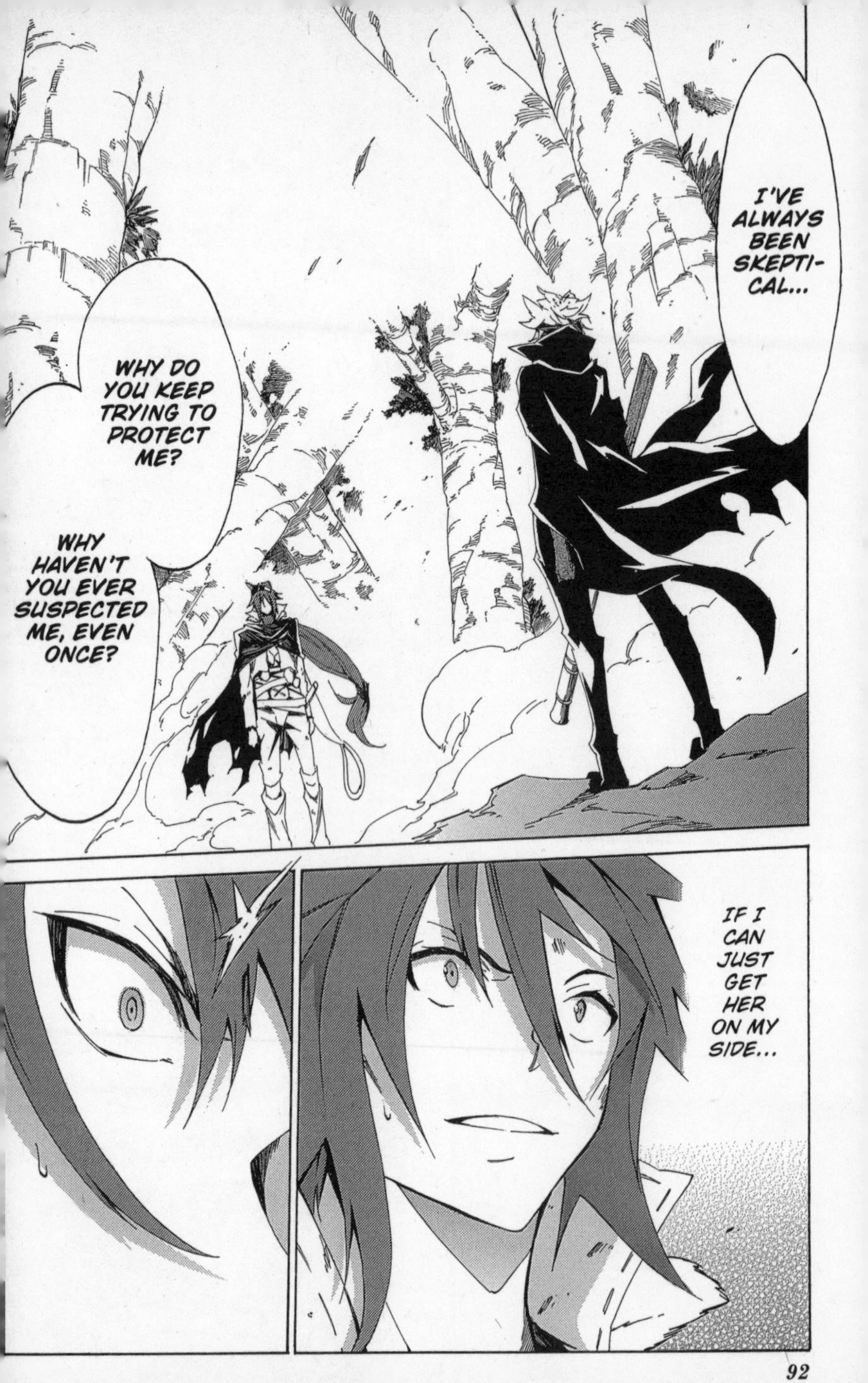
I'VE ALWAYS BEEN SKEPTI-CAL...
WHY DO YOU KEEP TRYING TO PROTECT ME?
WHY HAVEN'T YOU EVER SUSPECTED ME, EVEN ONCE?
IF I CAN JUST GET HER ON MY SIDE...

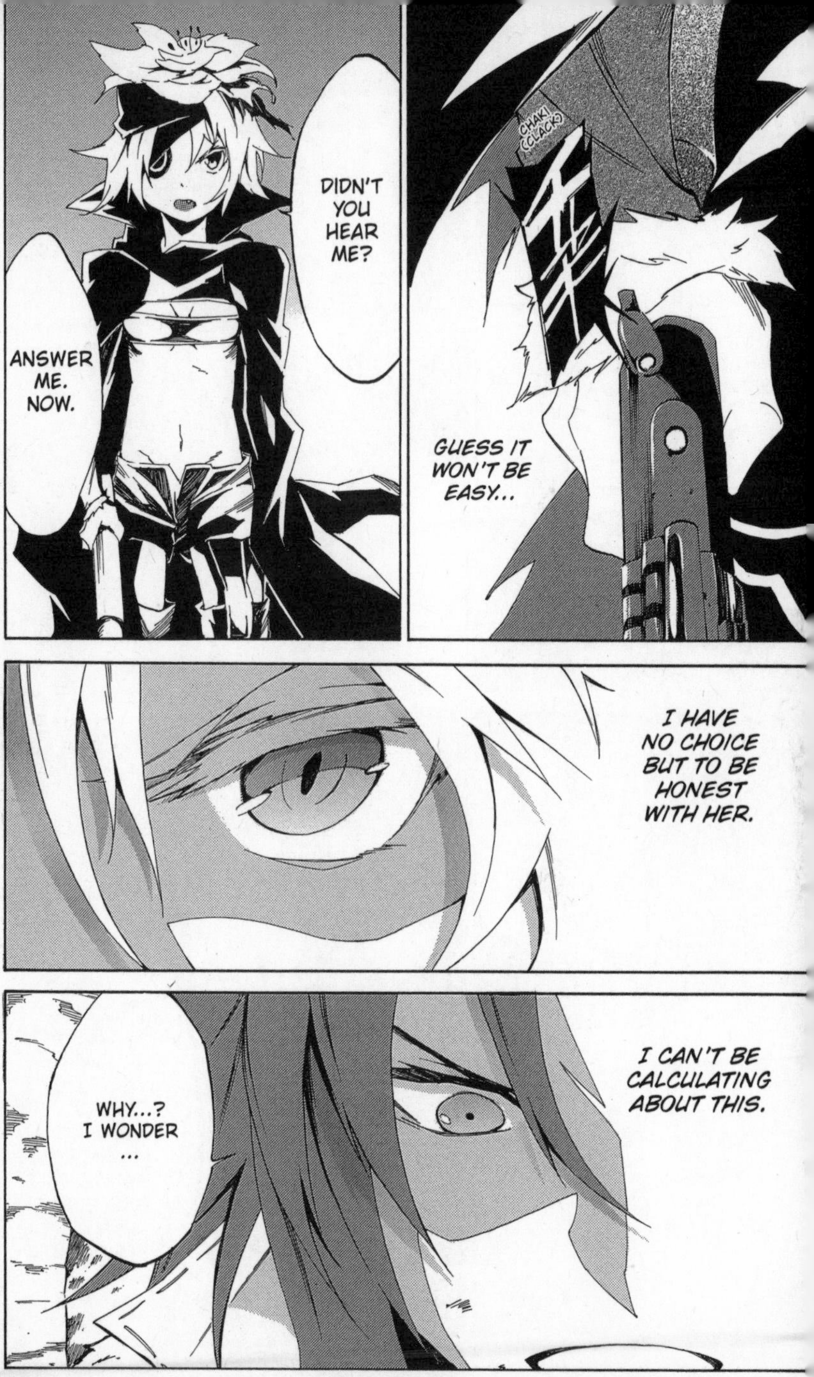
CHAKI (CLACK)
GUESS IT WON'T BE EASY...
DIDN'T YOU HEAR ME?
ANSWER ME. NOW.
I HAVE NO CHOICE BUT TO BE HONEST WITH HER.
I CAN'T BE CALCULATING ABOUT THIS.
WHY...? I WONDER ...

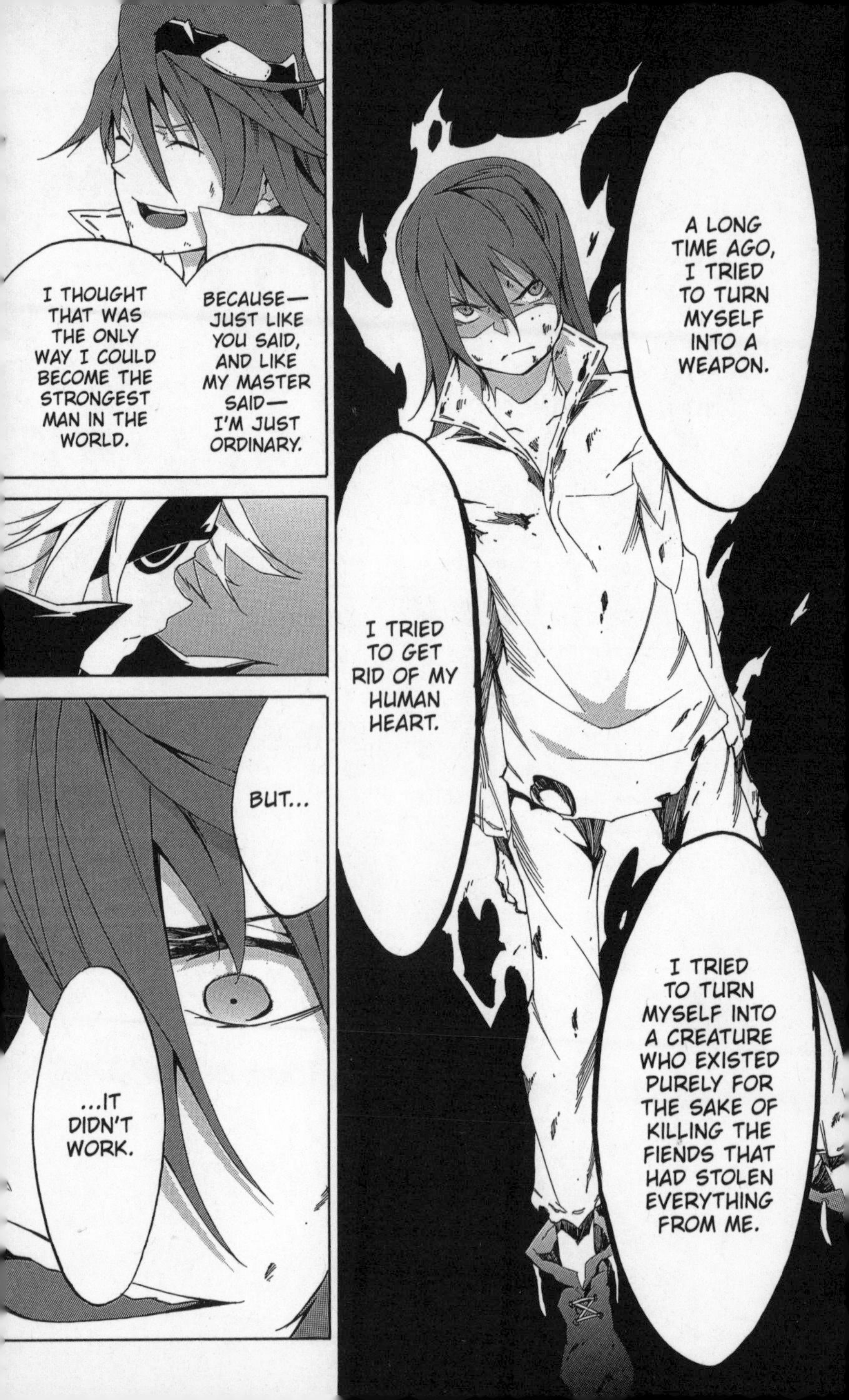
A LONG TIME AGO, I TRIED TO TURN MYSELF INTO A WEAPON.
I TRIED TO GET RID OF MY HUMAN HEART.
I TRIED TO TURN MYSELF INTO A CREATURE WHO EXISTED PURELY FOR THE SAKE OF KILLING THE FIENDS THAT HAD STOLEN EVERYTHING FROM ME.
BECAUSE— JUST LIKE YOU SAID, AND LIKE MY MASTER SAID— I'M JUST ORDINARY.
I THOUGHT THAT WAS THE ONLY WAY I COULD BECOME THE STRONGEST MAN IN THE WORLD.
BUT...
...IT DIDN'T WORK.

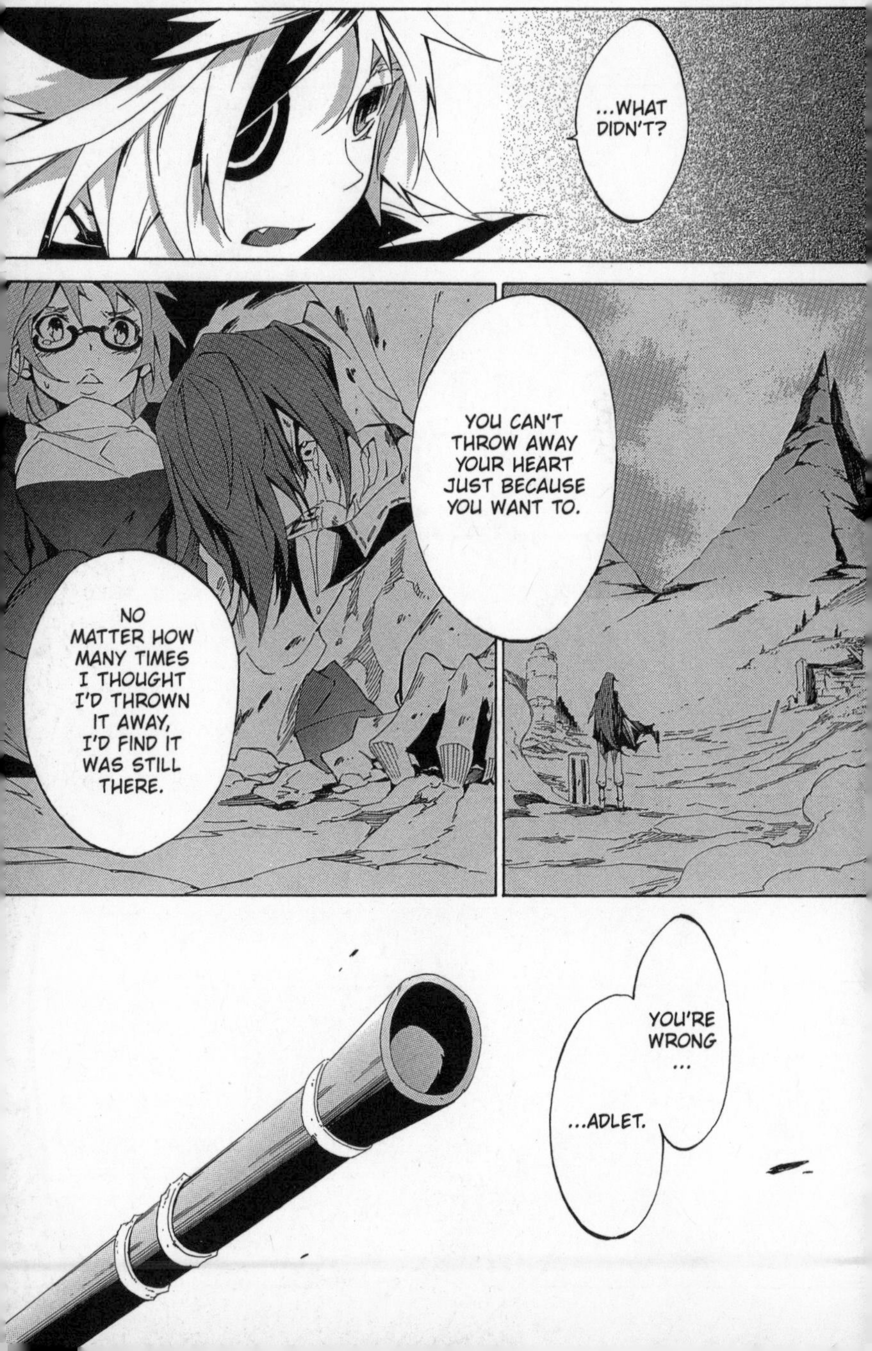
...WHAT DIDN'T?
YOU CAN'T THROW AWAY YOUR HEART JUST BECAUSE YOU WANT TO.
NO MATTER HOW MANY TIMES I THOUGHT I'D THROWN IT AWAY, I'D FIND IT WAS STILL THERE.
YOU'RE WRONG ...
...ADLET.

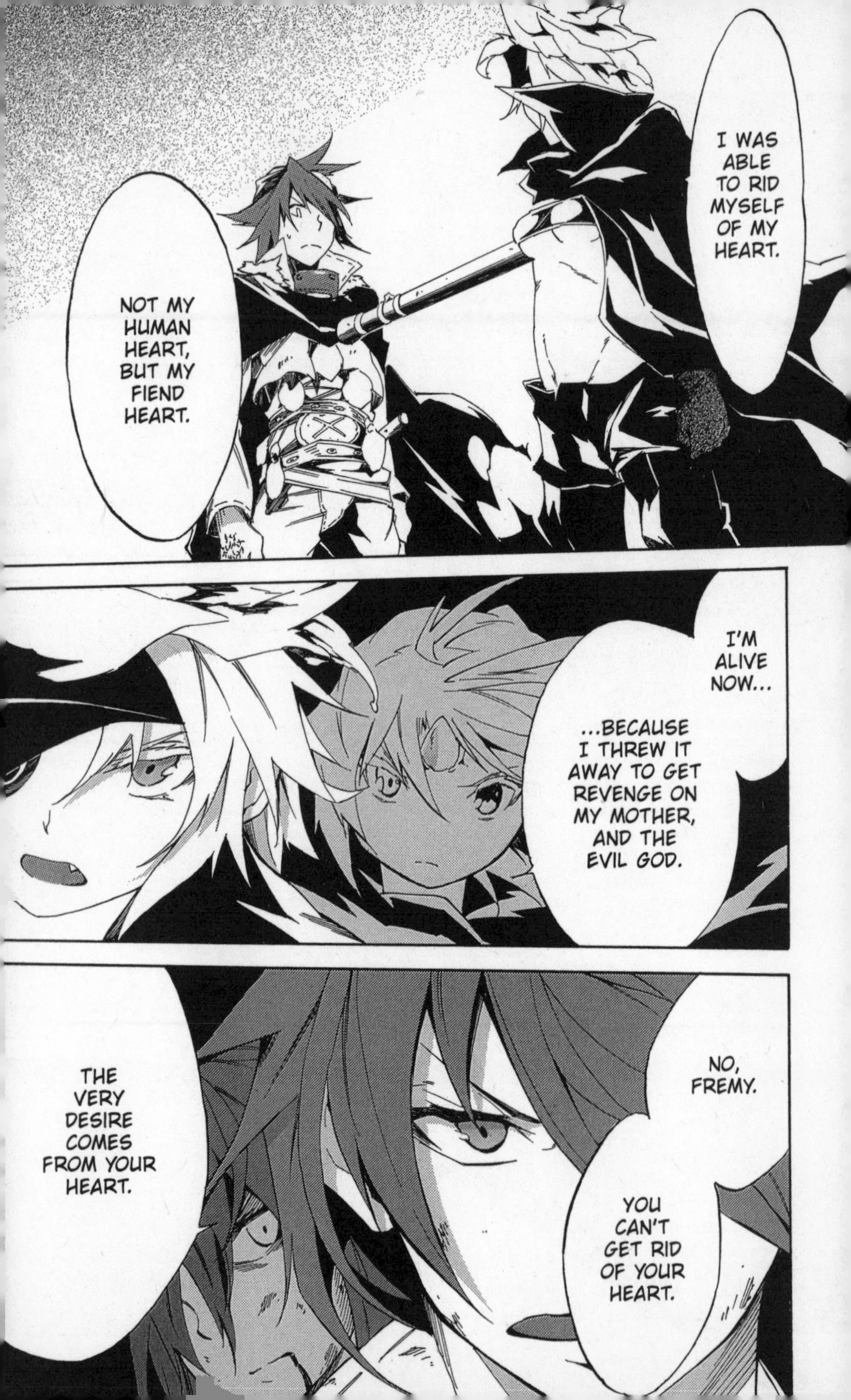
I WAS ABLE TO RID MYSELF OF MY HEART.
NOT MY HUMAN HEART, BUT MY FIEND HEART.
I'M ALIVE NOW...
...BECAUSE I THREW IT AWAY TO GET REVENGE ON MY MOTHER, AND THE EVIL GOD.
NO, FREMY.
YOU CAN'T GET RID OF YOUR HEART.
THE VERY DESIRE COMES FROM YOUR HEART.

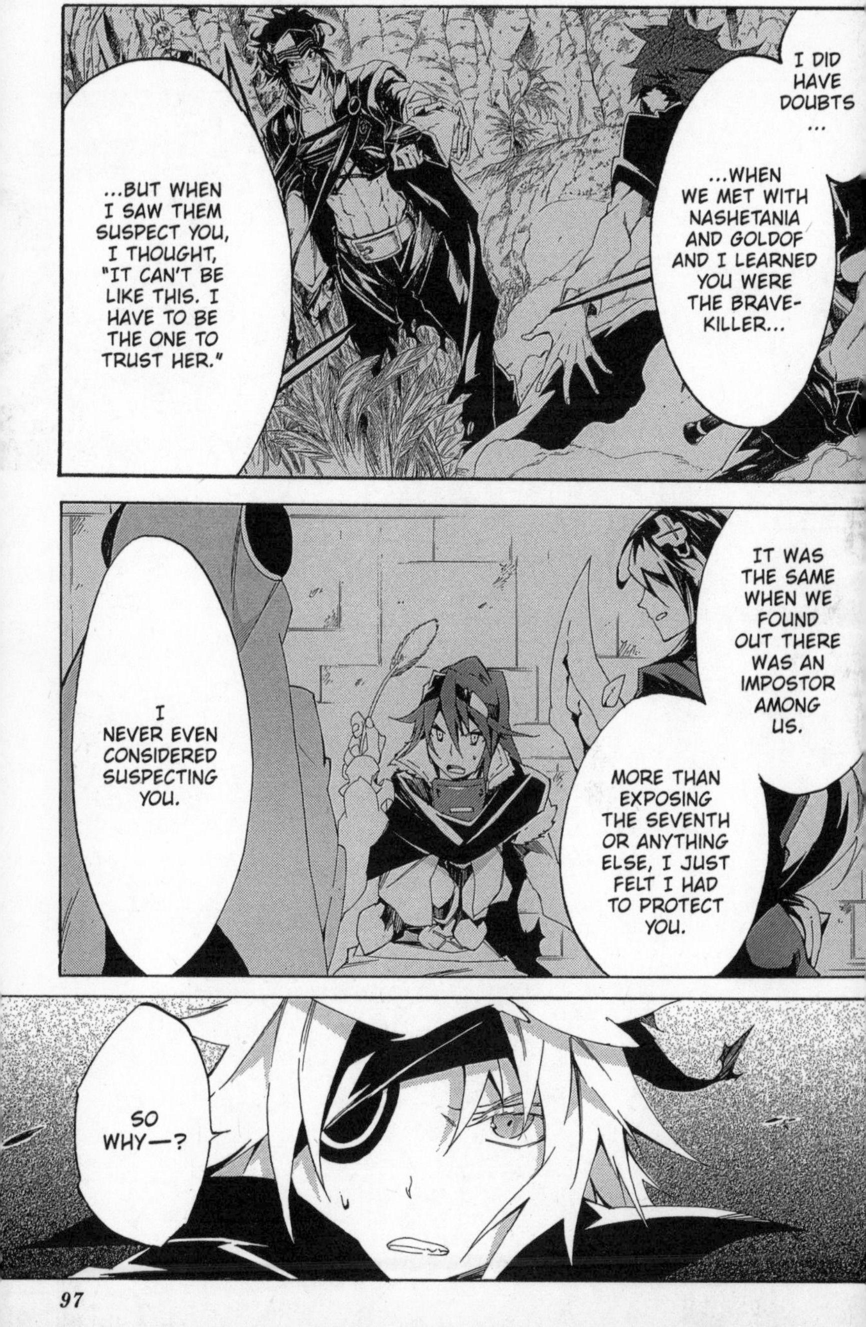
I DID HAVE DOUBTS...
...WHEN WE MET WITH NASHETANIA AND GOLDOF AND I LEARNED YOU WERE THE BRAVE-KILLER...
...BUT WHEN I SAW THEM SUSPECT YOU, I THOUGHT, "IT CAN'T BE LIKE THIS. I HAVE TO BE THE ONE TO TRUST HER."
IT WAS THE SAME WHEN WE FOUND OUT THERE WAS AN IMPOSTOR AMONG US.
MORE THAN EXPOSING THE SEVENTH OR ANYTHING ELSE, I JUST FELT I HAD TO PROTECT YOU.
I NEVER EVEN CONSIDERED SUSPECTING YOU.
SO WHY—?

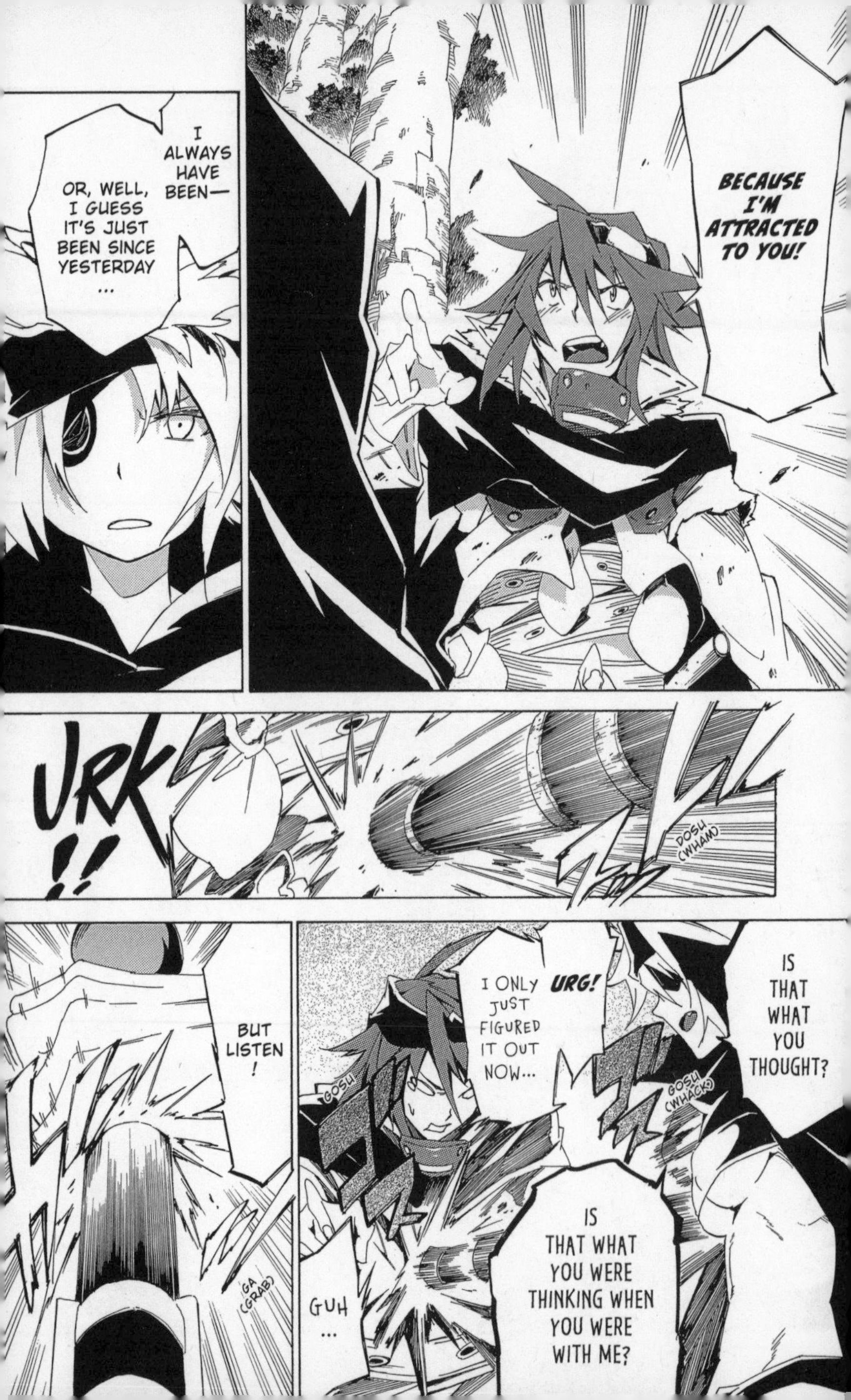
BECAUSE I'M ATTRACTED TO YOU!
I ALWAYS HAVE BEEN—
OR, WELL, I GUESS IT'S JUST BEEN SINCE YESTERDAY ...
DOSU (WHAM)
URK !!
IS THAT WHAT YOU THOUGHT?
GOSU (WHACK)
URG!
I ONLY JUST FIGURED IT OUT NOW...
GOSU
IS THAT WHAT YOU WERE THINKING WHEN YOU WERE WITH ME?
GUH ...
BUT LISTEN!
GA (GRAB)

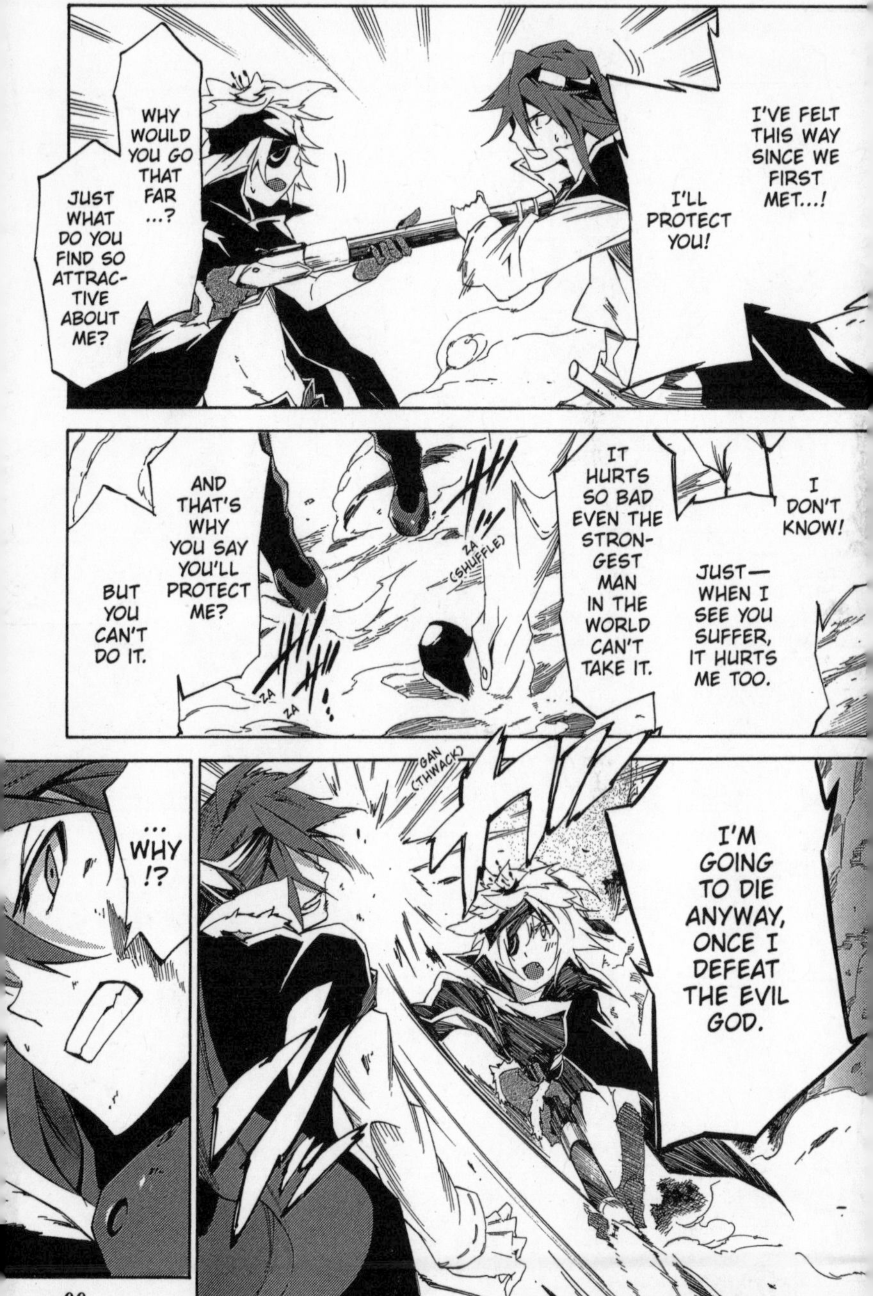
I'VE FELT THIS WAY SINCE WE FIRST MET...!
I'LL PROTECT YOU!
WHY WOULD YOU GO THAT FAR ...?
JUST WHAT DO YOU FIND SO ATTRACTIVE ABOUT ME?
I DON'T KNOW!
JUST— WHEN I SEE YOU SUFFER, IT HURTS ME TOO.
IT HURTS SO BAD EVEN THE STRONGEST MAN IN THE WORLD CAN'T TAKE IT.
ZA (SHUFFLE)
AND THAT'S WHY YOU SAY YOU'LL PROTECT ME?
ZA
ZA
BUT YOU CAN'T DO IT.
I'M GOING TO DIE ANYWAY, ONCE I DEFEAT THE EVIL GOD.
GAN (THWACK)
... WHY !?

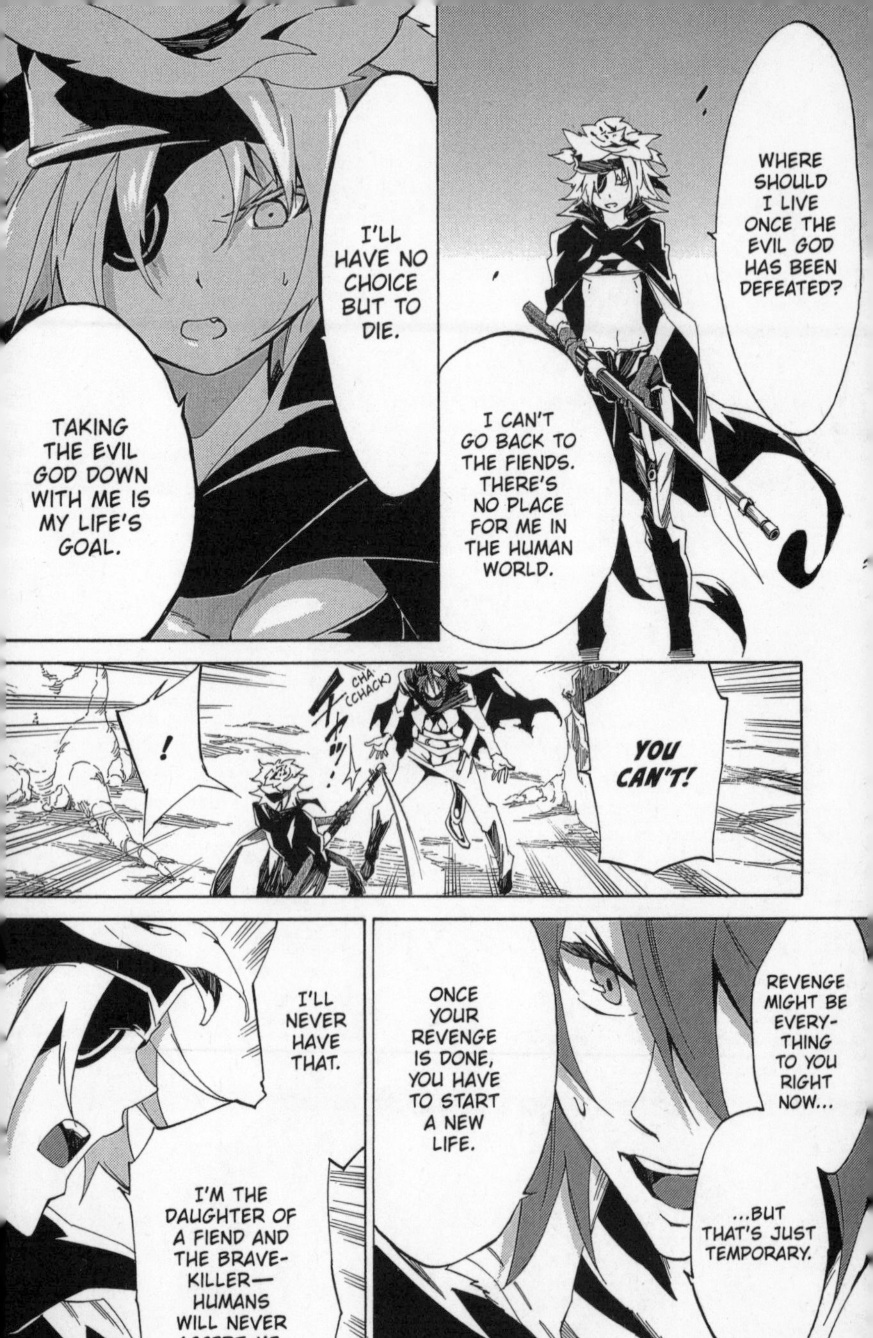
WHERE SHOULD I LIVE ONCE THE EVIL GOD HAS BEEN DEFEATED?
I CAN'T GO BACK TO THE FIENDS. THERE'S NO PLACE FOR ME IN THE HUMAN WORLD.
I'LL HAVE NO CHOICE BUT TO DIE.
TAKING THE EVIL GOD DOWN WITH ME IS MY LIFE'S GOAL.
YOU CAN'T!
CHA CHACK
!
REVENGE MIGHT BE EVERY-THING TO YOU RIGHT NOW...
...BUT THAT'S JUST TEMPORARY.
ONCE YOUR REVENGE IS DONE, YOU HAVE TO START A NEW LIFE.
I'LL NEVER HAVE THAT.
I'M THE DAUGHTER OF A FIEND AND THE BRAVE-KILLER—HUMANS WILL NEVER ACCEPT ME.

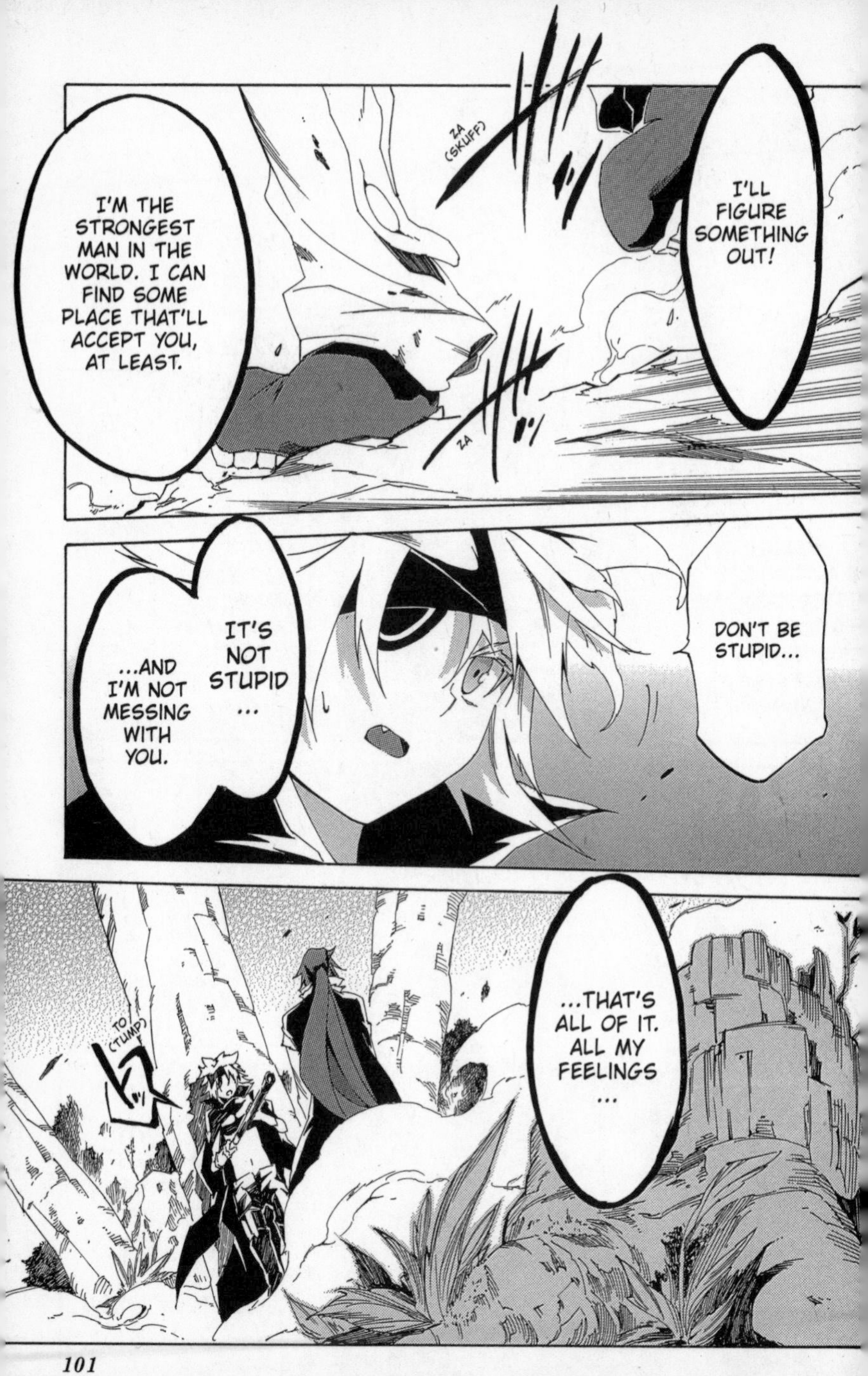
I'LL FIGURE SOMETHING OUT!
ZA (SKUFF)
ZA
I'M THE STRONGEST MAN IN THE WORLD. I CAN FIND SOME PLACE THAT'LL ACCEPT YOU, AT LEAST.
DON'T BE STUPID...
IT'S NOT STUPID ...
...AND I'M NOT MESSING WITH YOU.
...THAT'S ALL OF IT. ALL MY FEELINGS ...
TO (TUMP)

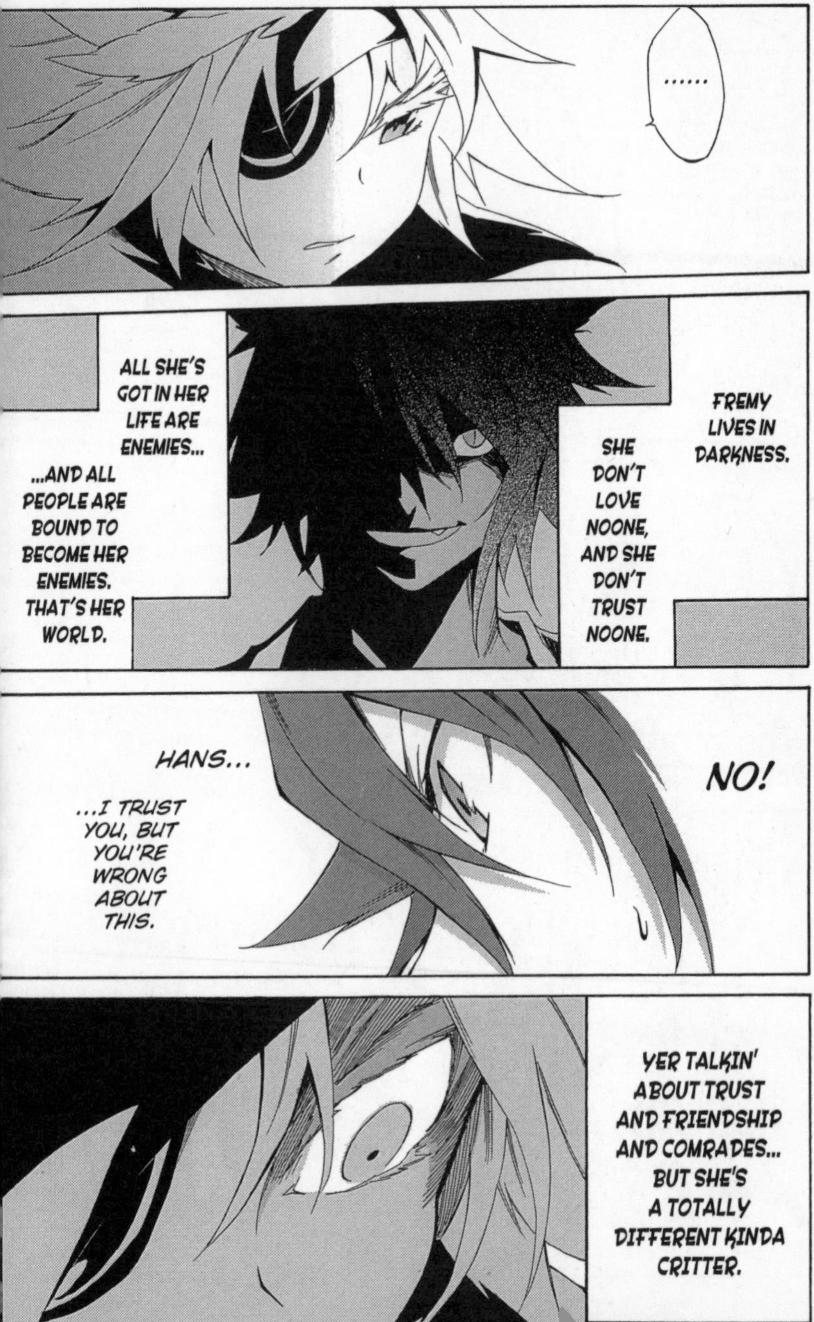
......
FREMY LIVES IN DARKNESS.
SHE DON'T LOVE NOONE, AND SHE DON'T TRUST NOONE.
ALL SHE'S GOT IN HER LIFE ARE ENEMIES...
...AND ALL PEOPLE ARE BOUND TO BECOME HER ENEMIES. THAT'S HER WORLD.
NO!
HANS...
...I TRUST YOU, BUT YOU'RE WRONG ABOUT THIS.
YER TALKIN' ABOUT TRUST AND FRIENDSHIP AND COMRADES... BUT SHE'S A TOTALLY DIFFERENT KINDA CRITTER.

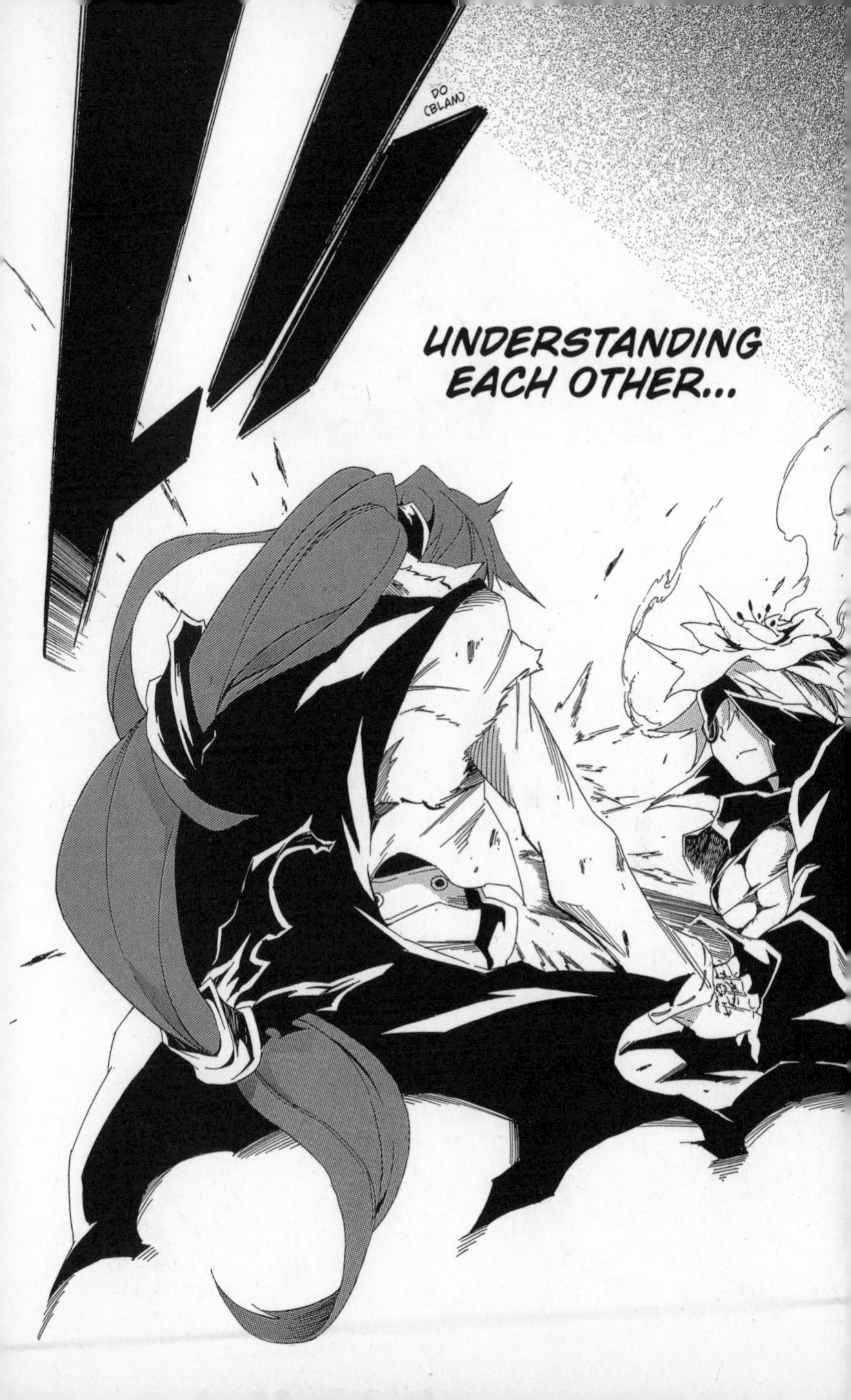
DO
(BLAM)
UNDERSTANDING EACH OTHER...

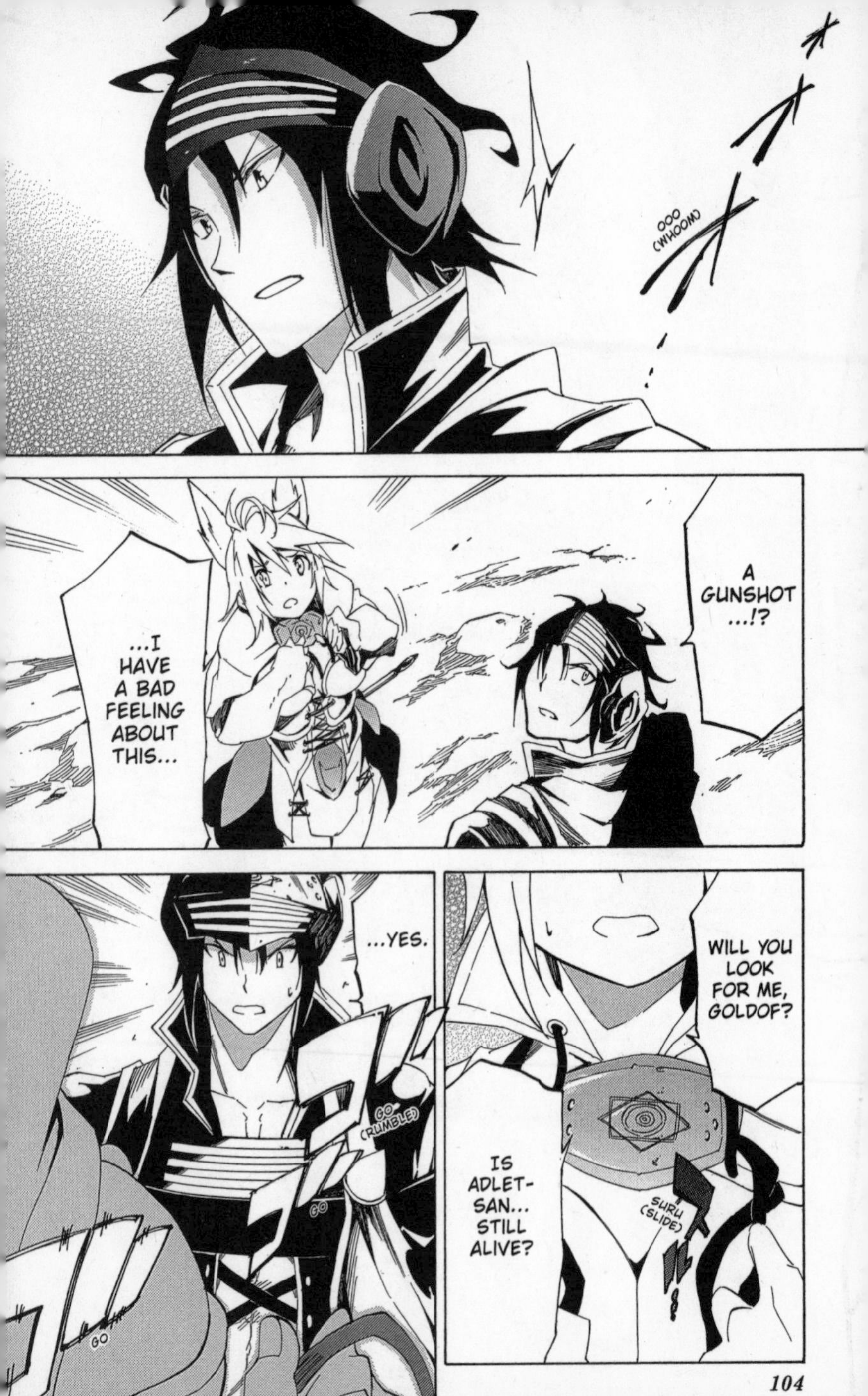
OOO (WHOOM)
A GUNSHOT ...!?
...I HAVE A BAD FEELING ABOUT THIS...
WILL YOU LOOK FOR ME, GOLDOF?
IS ADLET-SAN... STILL ALIVE?
SURU (SLIDE)
...YES.
GO- (RUMBLE)
GO
GO

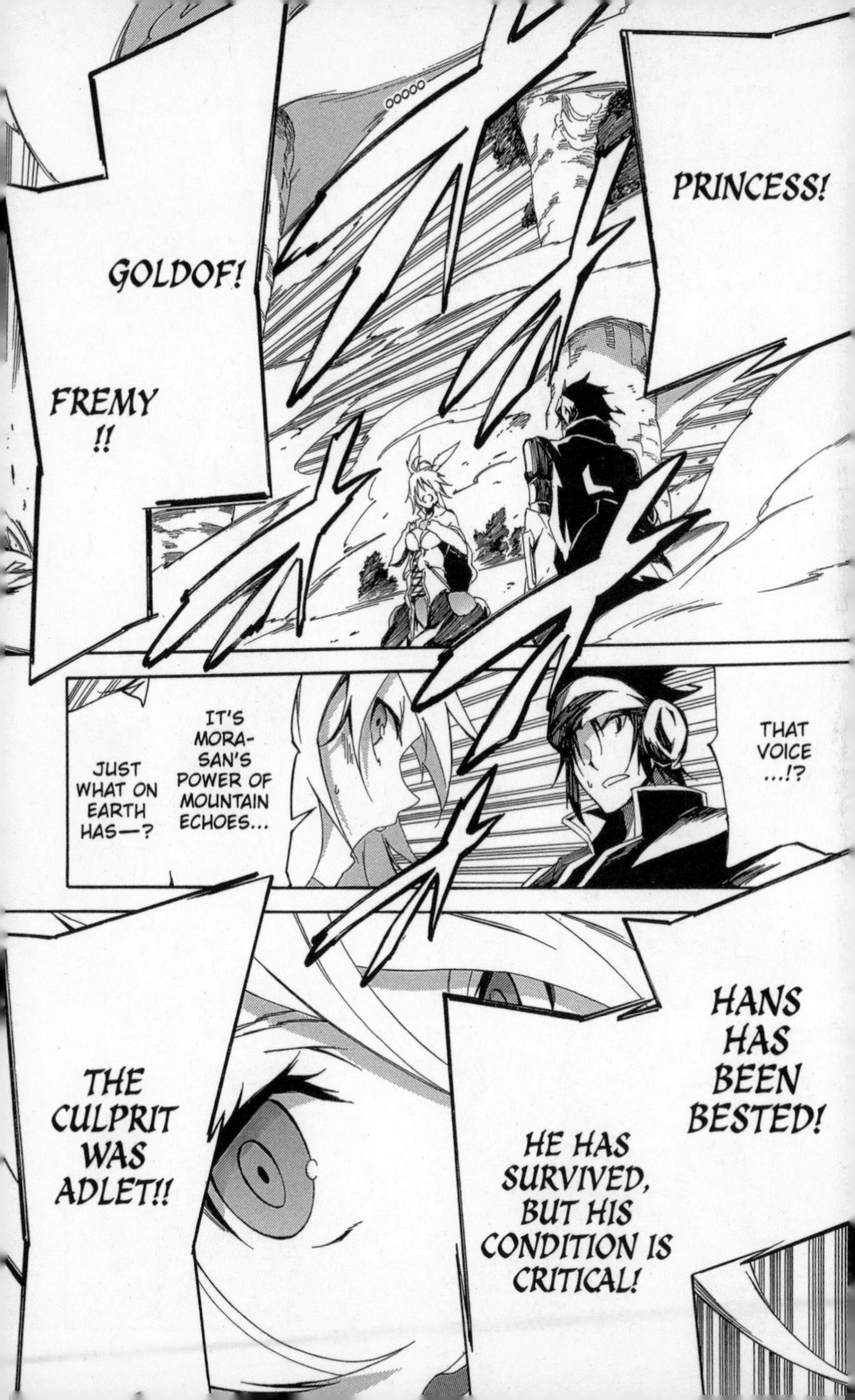
PRINCESS!
GOLDOF!
FREMY !!
THAT VOICE ...!?
IT'S MORA-SAN'S POWER OF MOUNTAIN ECHOES...
JUST WHAT ON EARTH HAS—?
HANS HAS BEEN BESTED!
HE HAS SURVIVED, BUT HIS CONDITION IS CRITICAL!
THE CULPRIT WAS ADLET!!

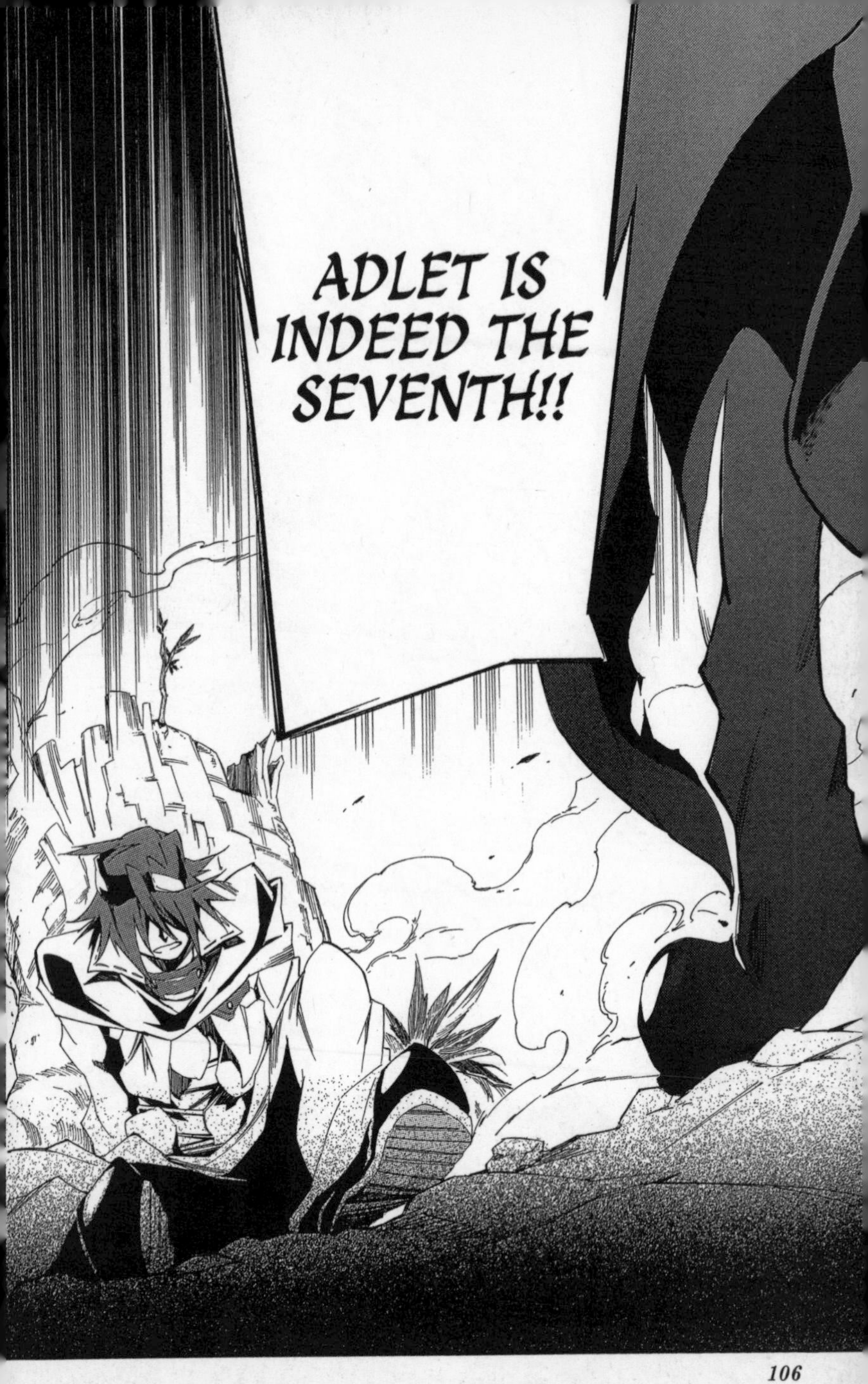
ADLET IS INDEED THE SEVENTH!!

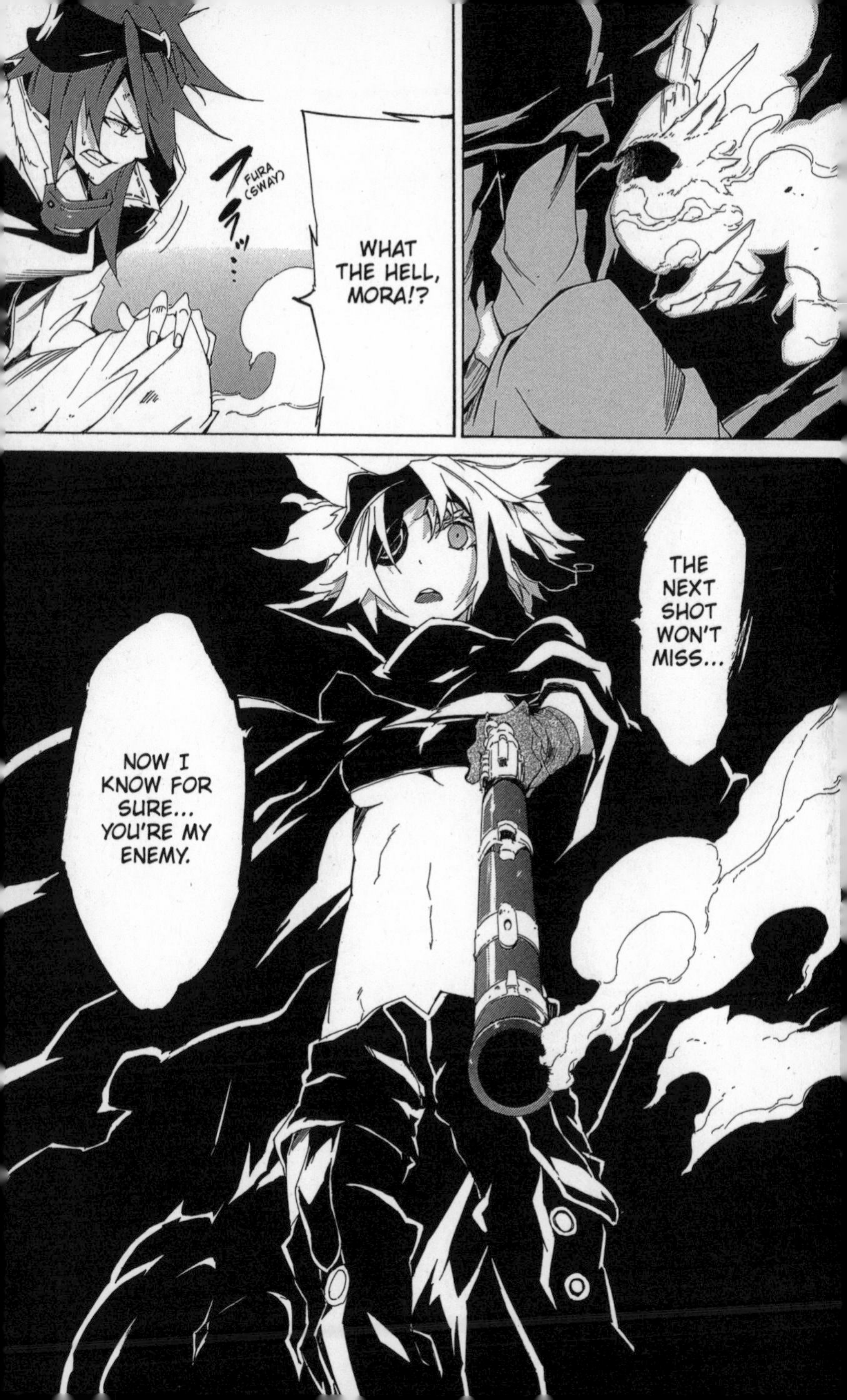
FURA (SWAY)
WHAT THE HELL, MORA!?
THE NEXT SHOT WON'T MISS...
NOW I KNOW FOR SURE... YOU'RE MY ENEMY.

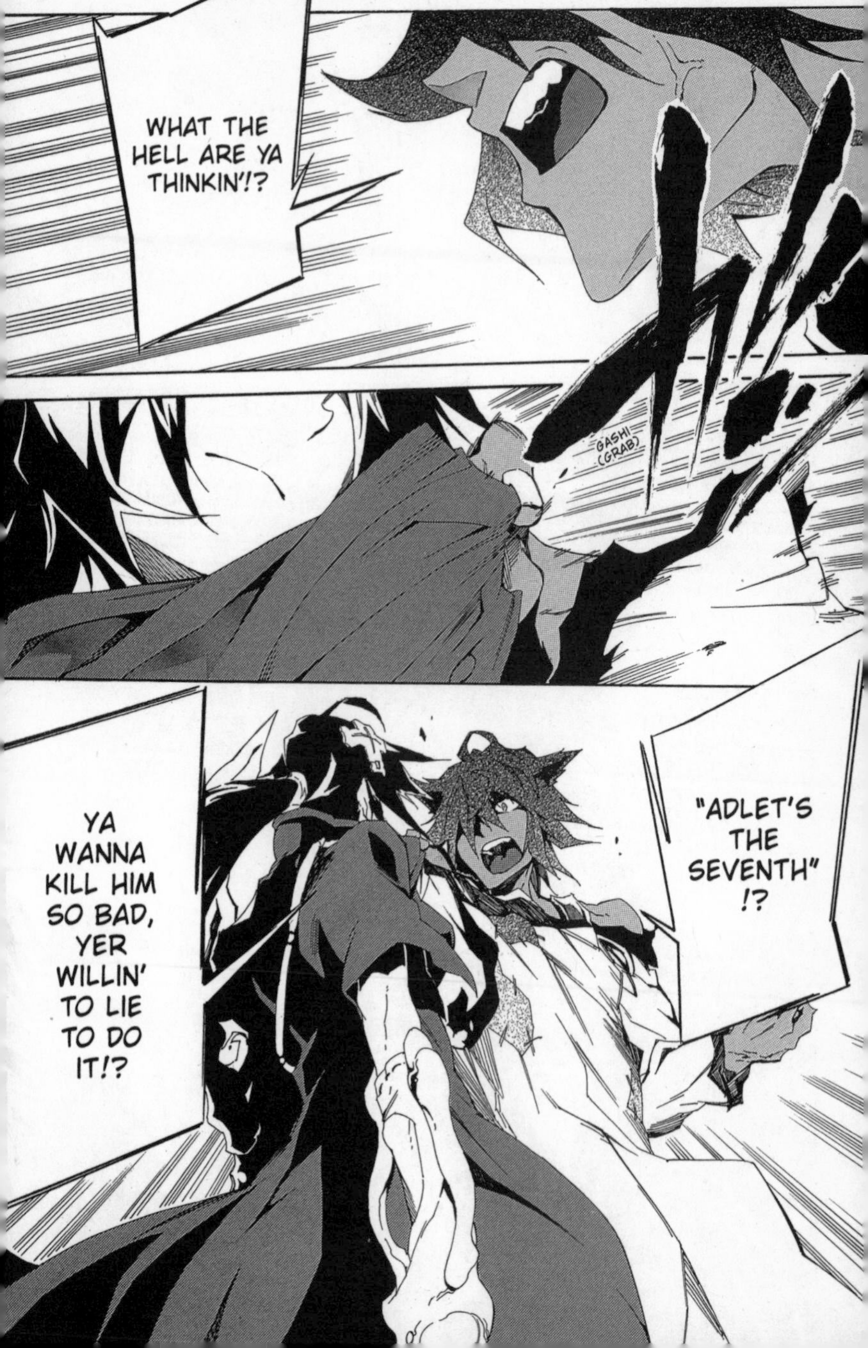
WHAT THE HELL ARE YA THINKIN'!?
GASHI (GRAB)
"ADLET'S THE SEVENTH" !?
YA WANNA KILL HIM SO BAD, YER WILLIN' TO LIE TO DO IT!?

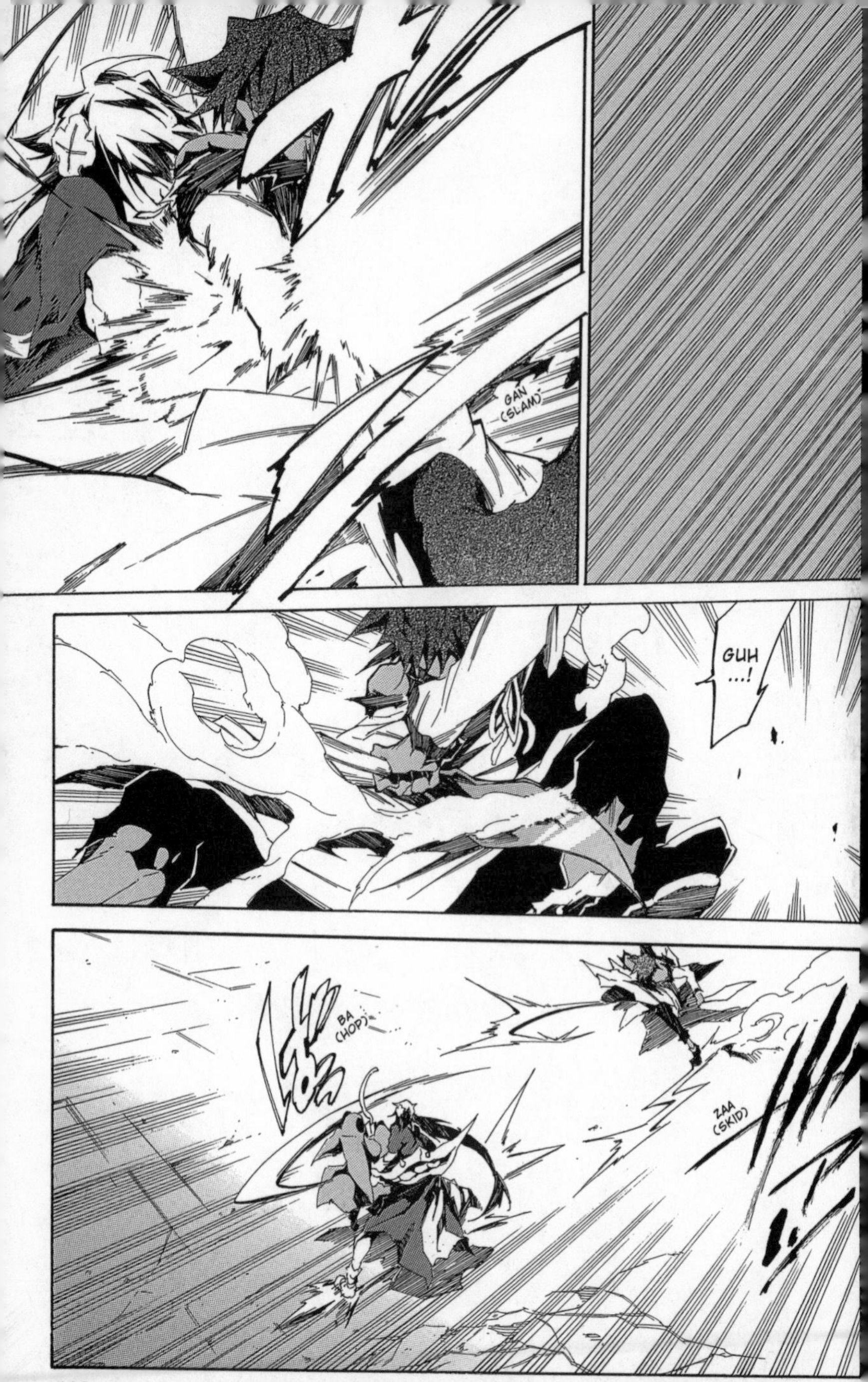
GAN (SLAM)
GUH ...!
ZAA (SKID)
BA (HOP)

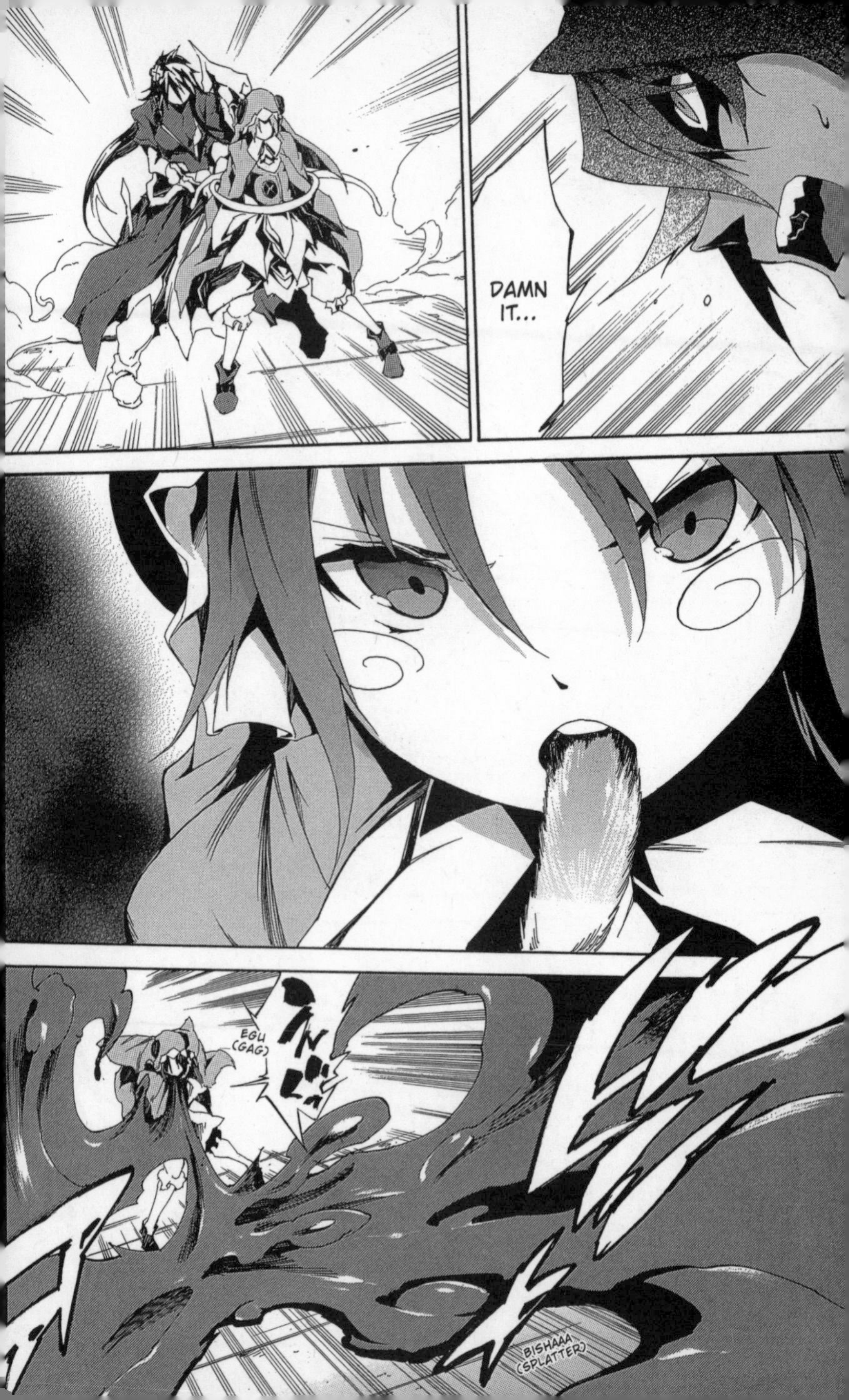
DAMN IT...
EGU (GAG)
BISHAAA (SPLATTER)

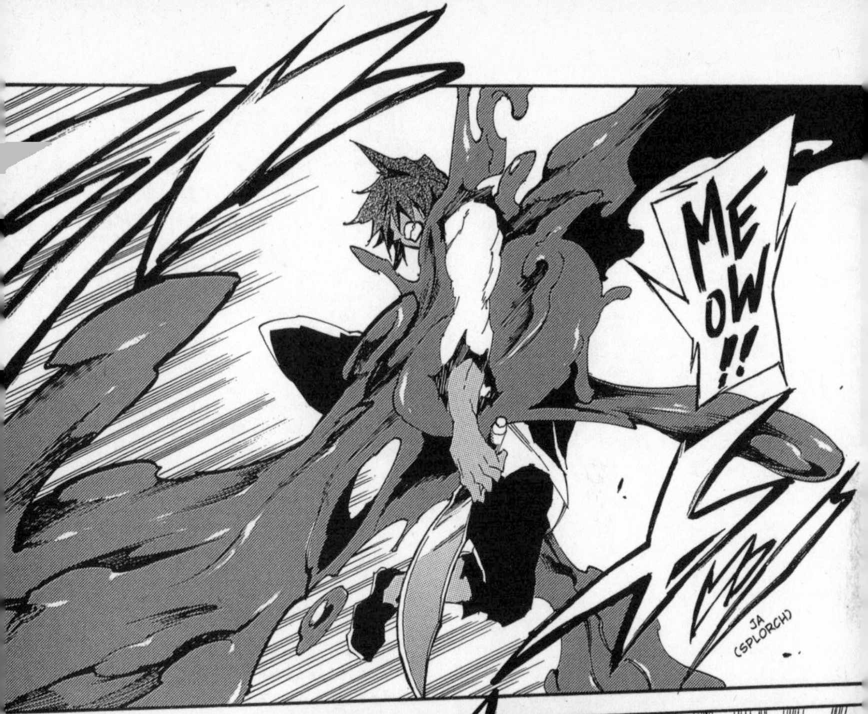
MEOW!!
JA (SPLORCH)

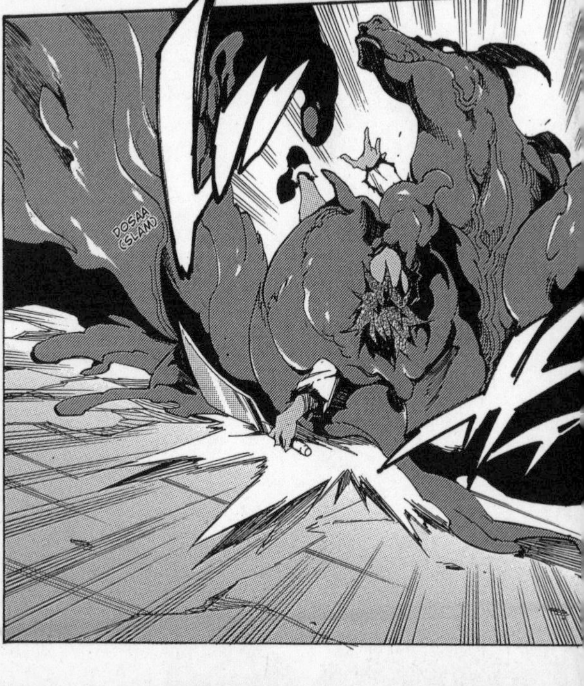
DOSAA (SLAM)

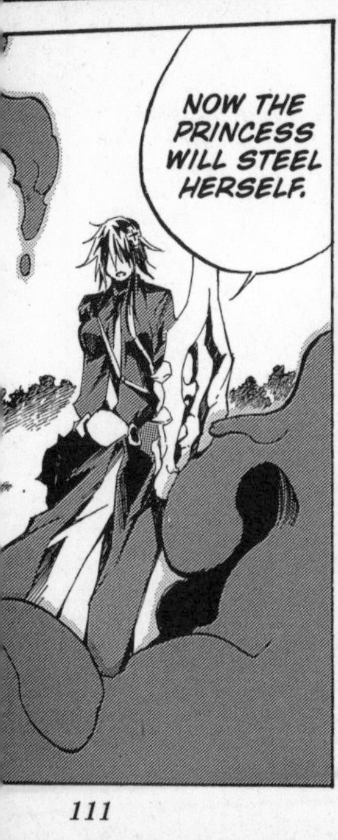
NOW THE PRINCESS WILL STEEL HERSELF.

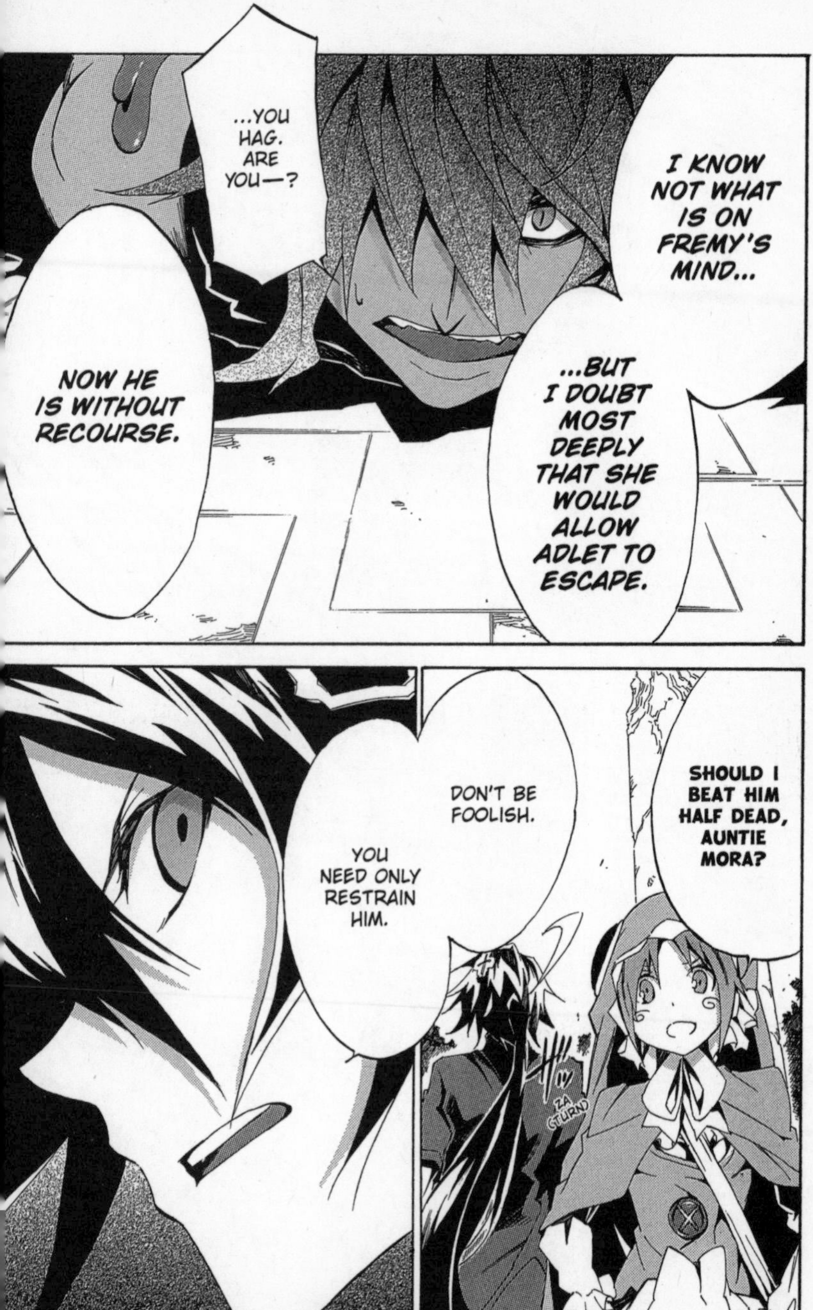
I KNOW NOT WHAT IS ON FREMY'S MIND...
...BUT I DOUBT MOST DEEPLY THAT SHE WOULD ALLOW ADLET TO ESCAPE.
...YOU HAG. ARE YOU—?
NOW HE IS WITHOUT RECOURSE.
SHOULD I BEAT HIM HALF DEAD, AUNTIE MORA?
DON'T BE FOOLISH.
YOU NEED ONLY RESTRAIN HIM.
ZA (TURN)

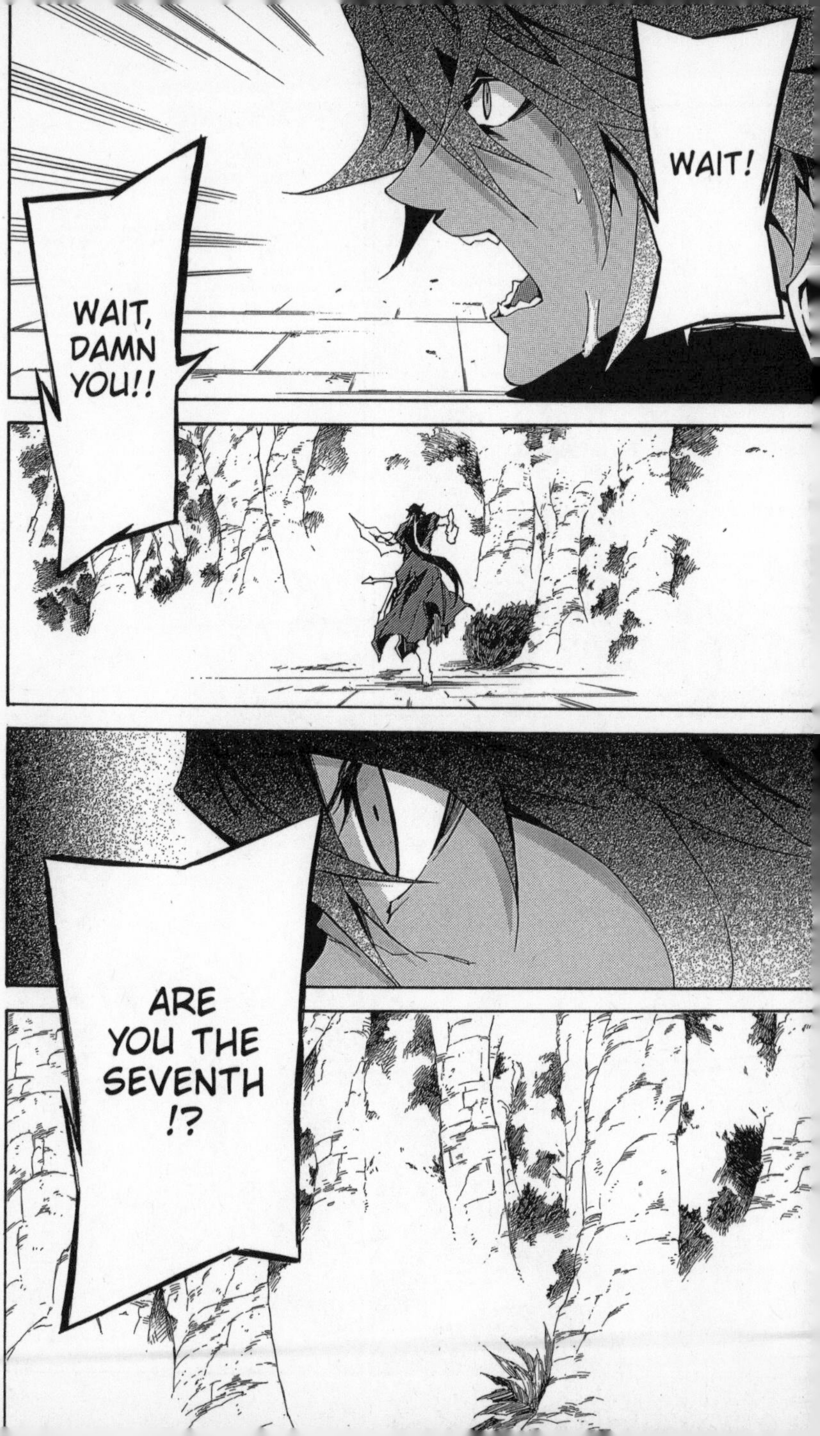
WAIT!
WAIT, DAMN YOU!!
ARE YOU THE SEVENTH !?

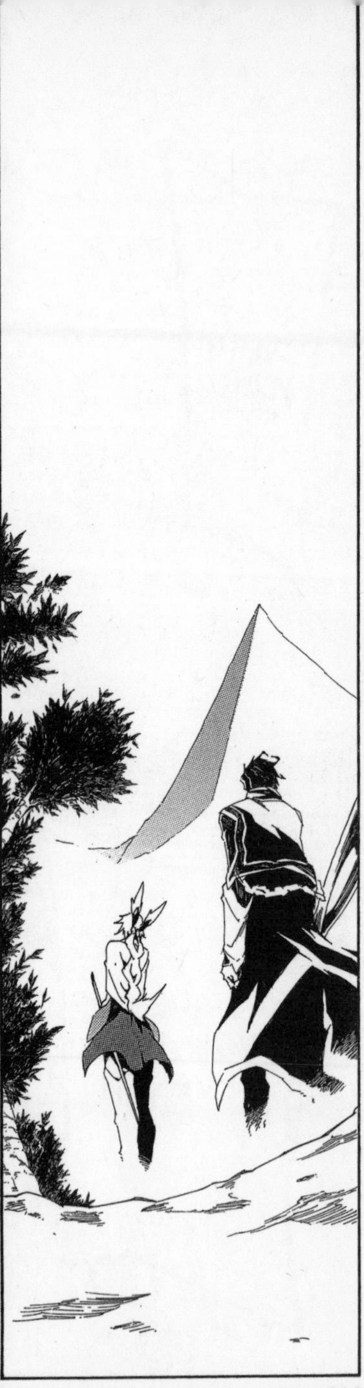

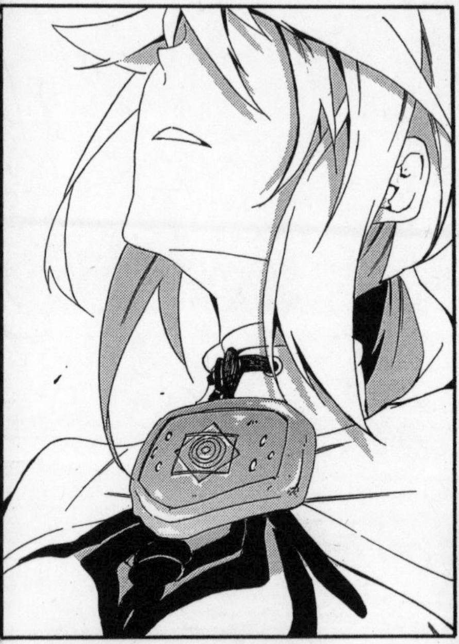

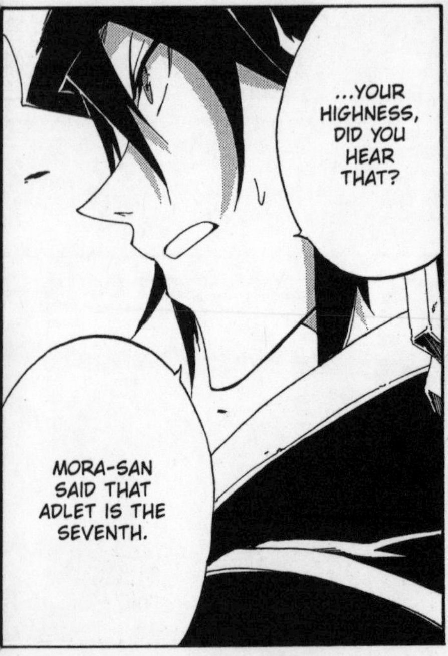
...YOUR HIGHNESS, DID YOU HEAR THAT?
MORA-SAN SAID THAT ADLET IS THE SEVENTH.

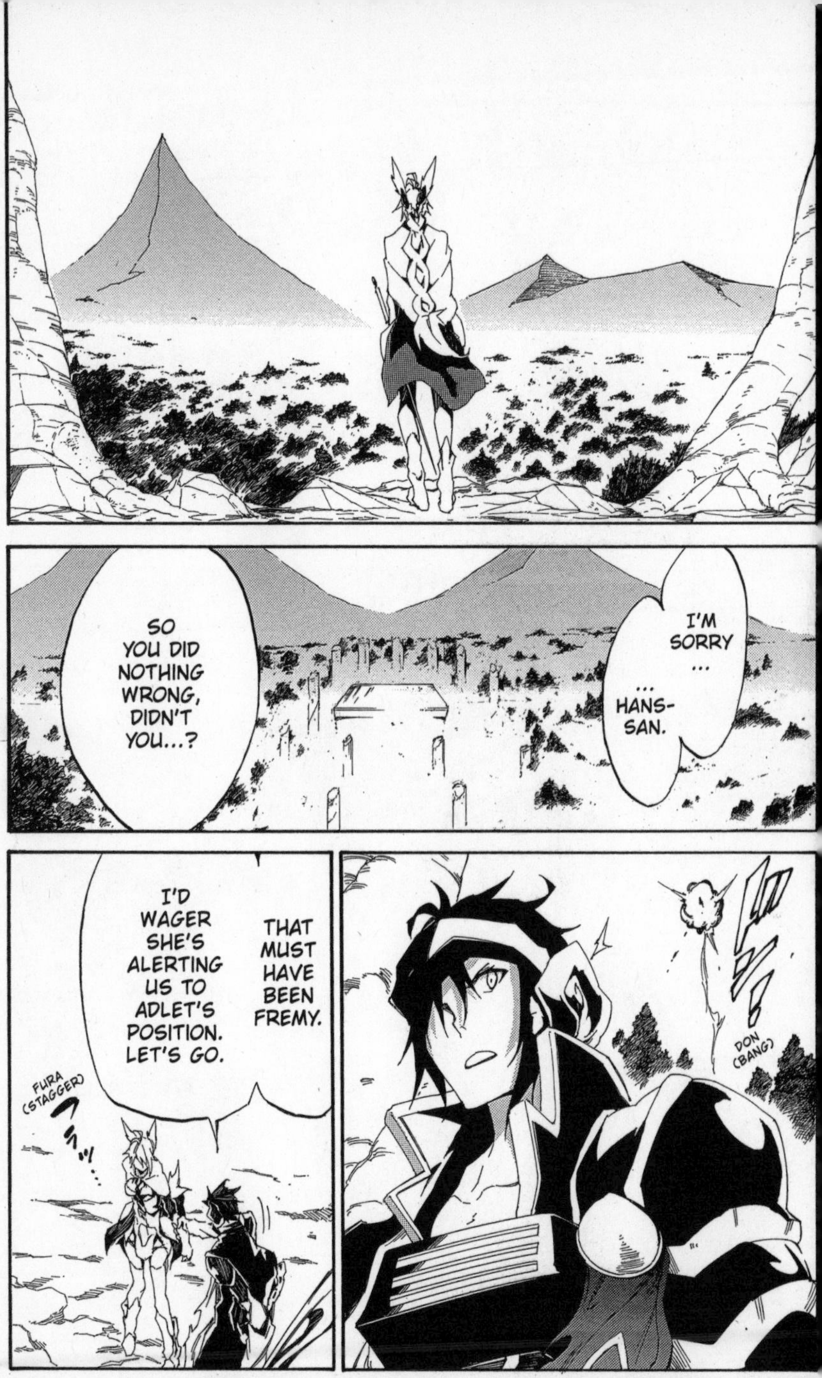
I'M SORRY ... ... HANS-SAN.
SO YOU DID NOTHING WRONG, DIDN'T YOU...?
DON (BANG)
THAT MUST HAVE BEEN FREMY.
I'D WAGER SHE'S ALERTING US TO ADLET'S POSITION. LET'S GO.
FURA (STAGGER)

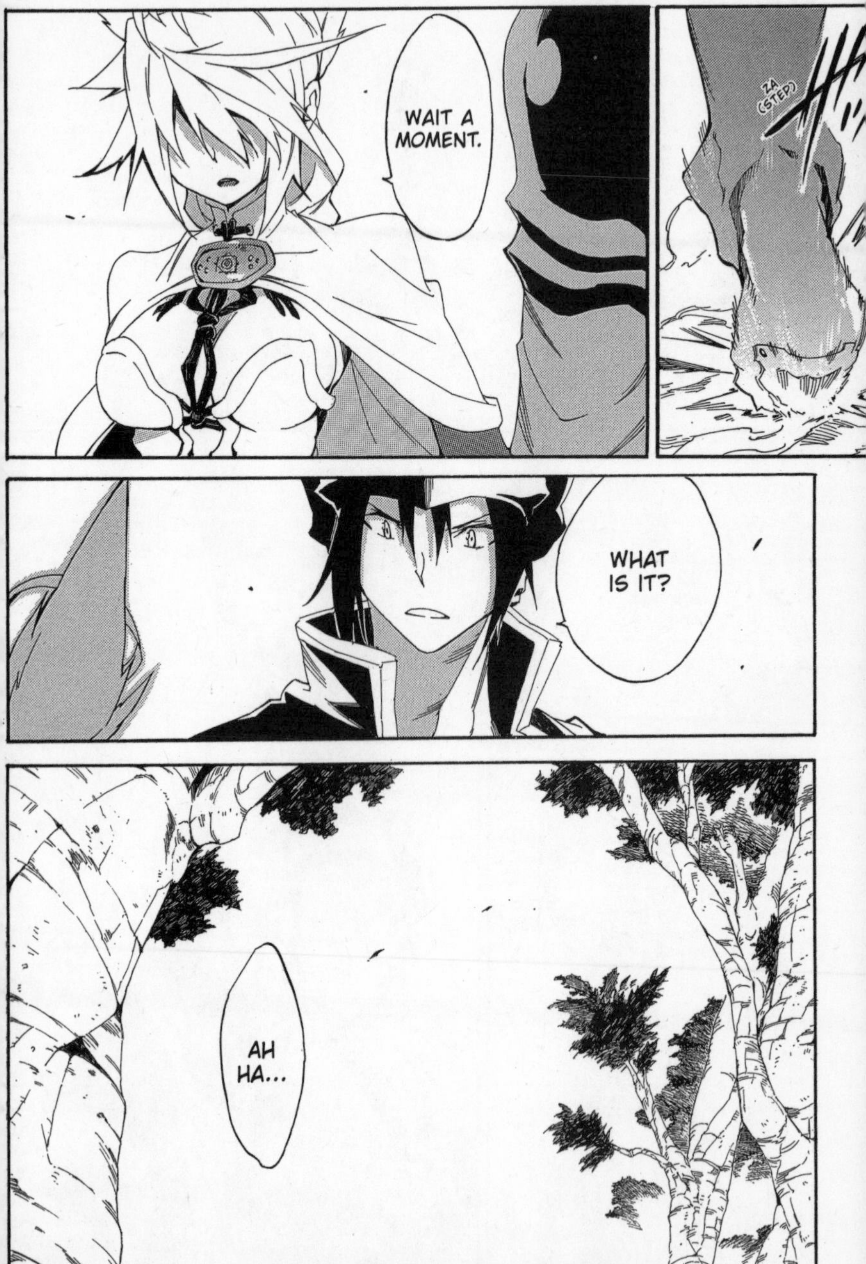
ZA (STEP)
WAIT A MOMENT.
WHAT IS IT?
AH HA...

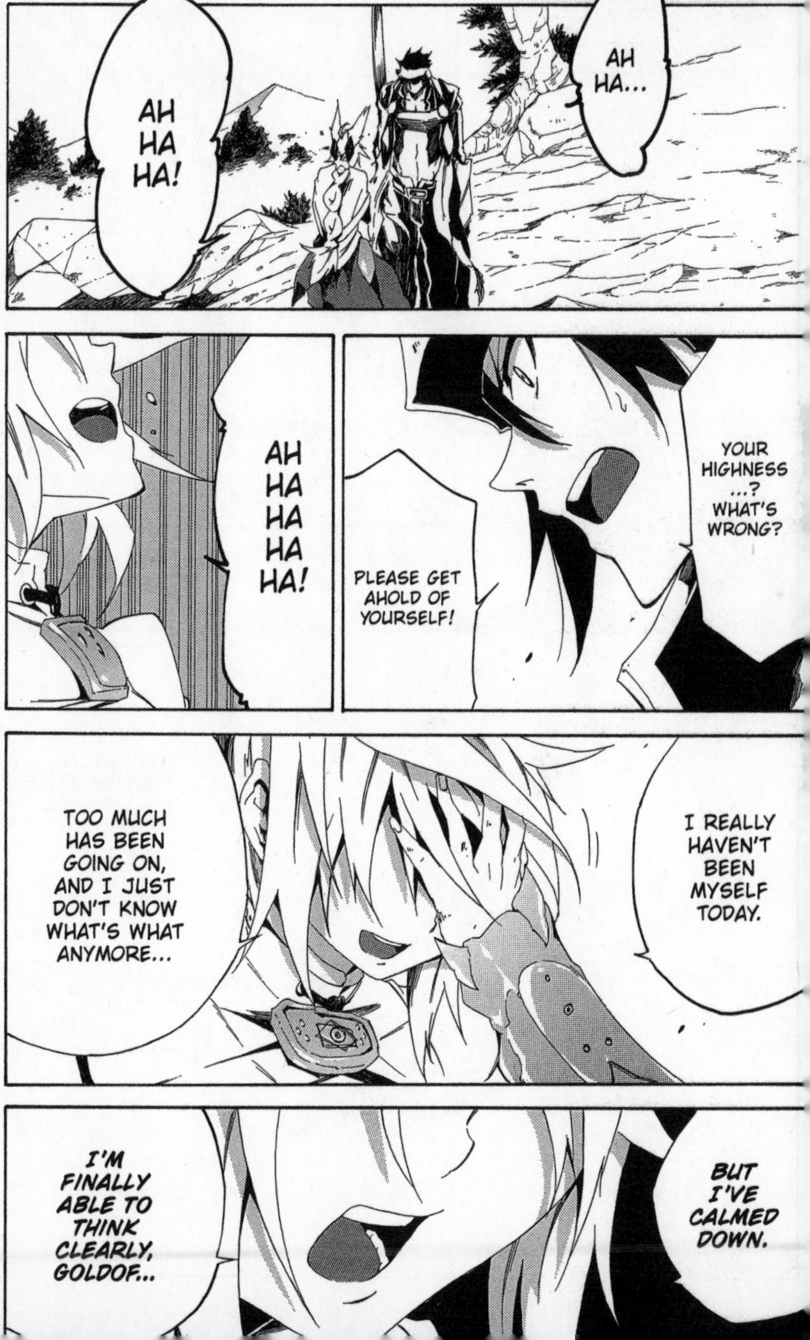
AH HA...
AH HA HA!
YOUR HIGHNESS ...? WHAT'S WRONG?
PLEASE GET AHOLD OF YOURSELF!
AH HA HA HA HA!
I REALLY HAVEN'T BEEN MYSELF TODAY.
TOO MUCH HAS BEEN GOING ON, AND I JUST DON'T KNOW WHAT'S WHAT ANYMORE...
BUT I'VE CALMED DOWN.
I'M FINALLY ABLE TO THINK CLEARLY, GOLDOF...

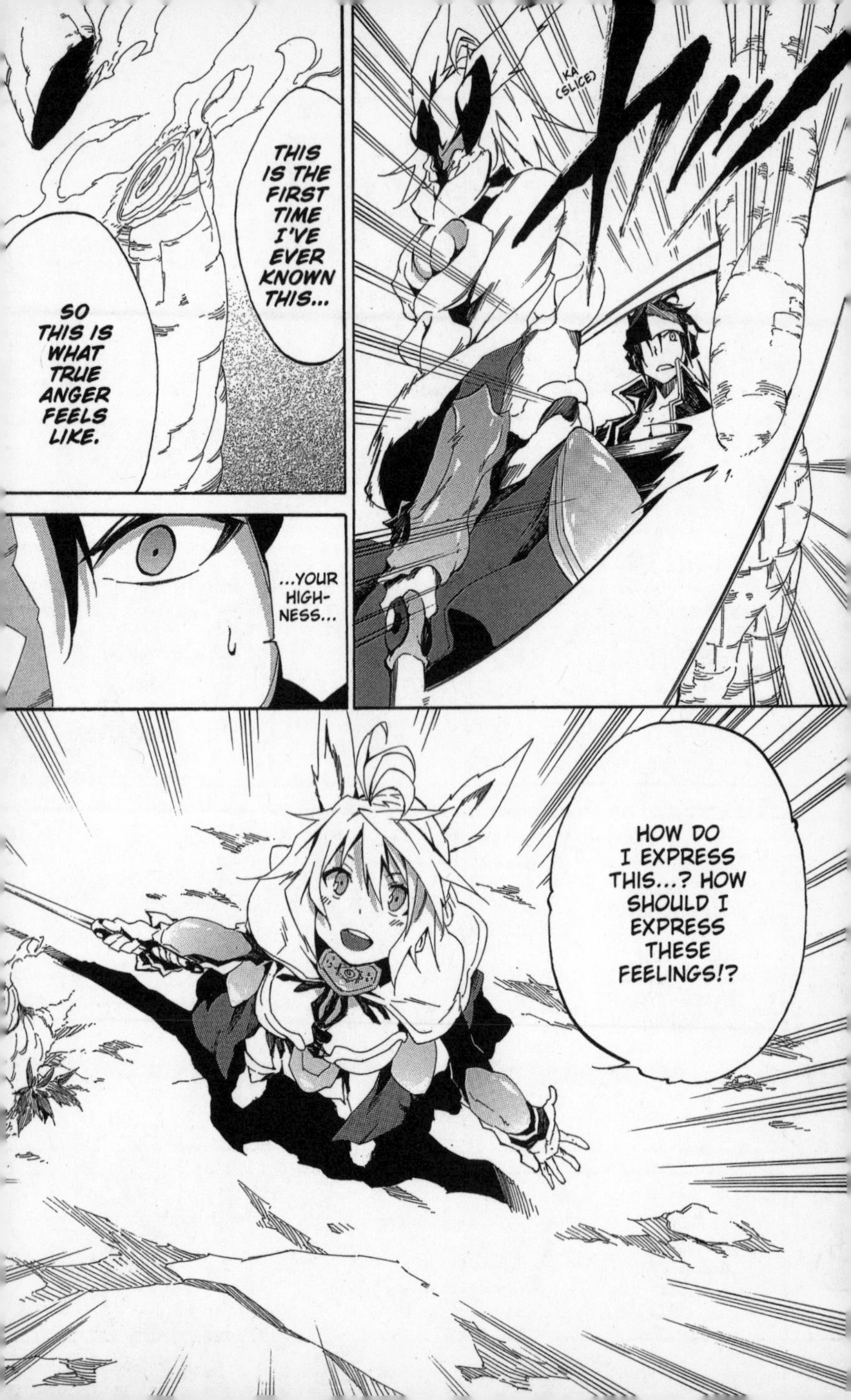
KA (SLICE)
THIS IS THE FIRST TIME I'VE EVER KNOWN THIS...
SO THIS IS WHAT TRUE ANGER FEELS LIKE.
...YOUR HIGH-NESS...
HOW DO I EXPRESS THIS...? HOW SHOULD I EXPRESS THESE FEELINGS!?

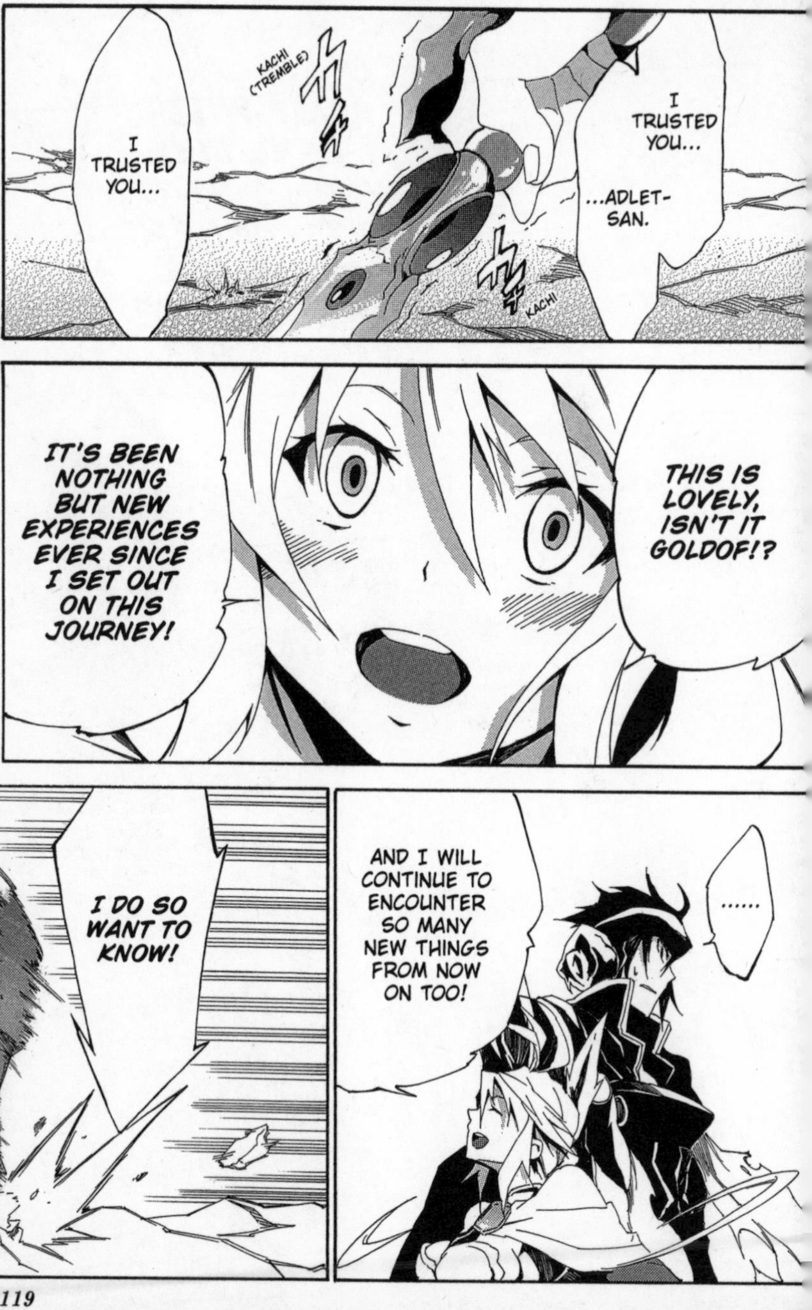
I TRUSTED YOU... ...ADLET-SAN.
KACHI (TREMBLE)
I TRUSTED YOU...
KACHI
THIS IS LOVELY, ISN'T IT GOLDOF!?
IT'S BEEN NOTHING BUT NEW EXPERIENCES EVER SINCE I SET OUT ON THIS JOURNEY!
......
AND I WILL CONTINUE TO ENCOUNTER SO MANY NEW THINGS FROM NOW ON TOO!
I DO SO WANT TO KNOW!

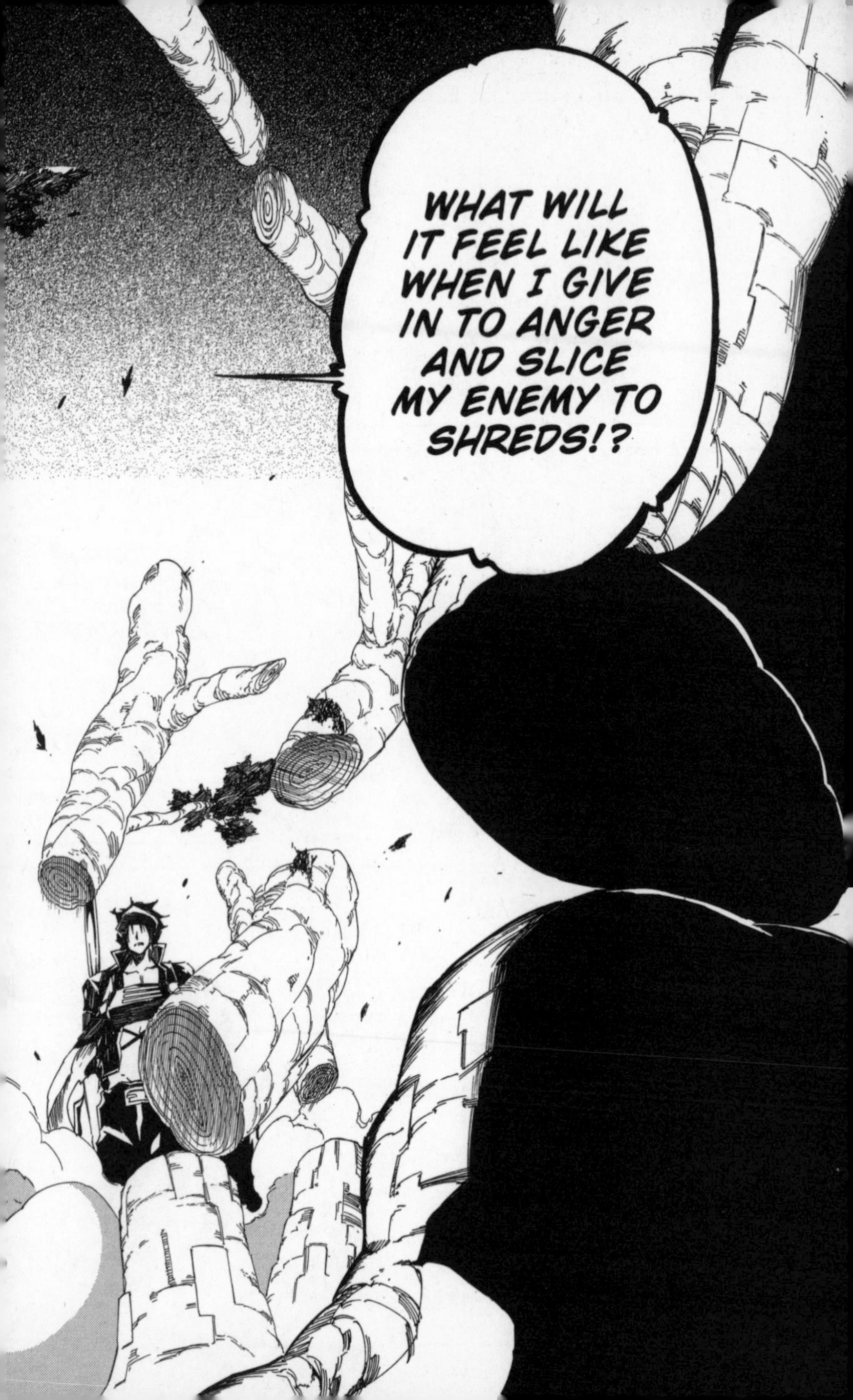
WHAT WILL IT FEEL LIKE WHEN I GIVE IN TO ANGER AND SLICE MY ENEMY TO SHREDS!?

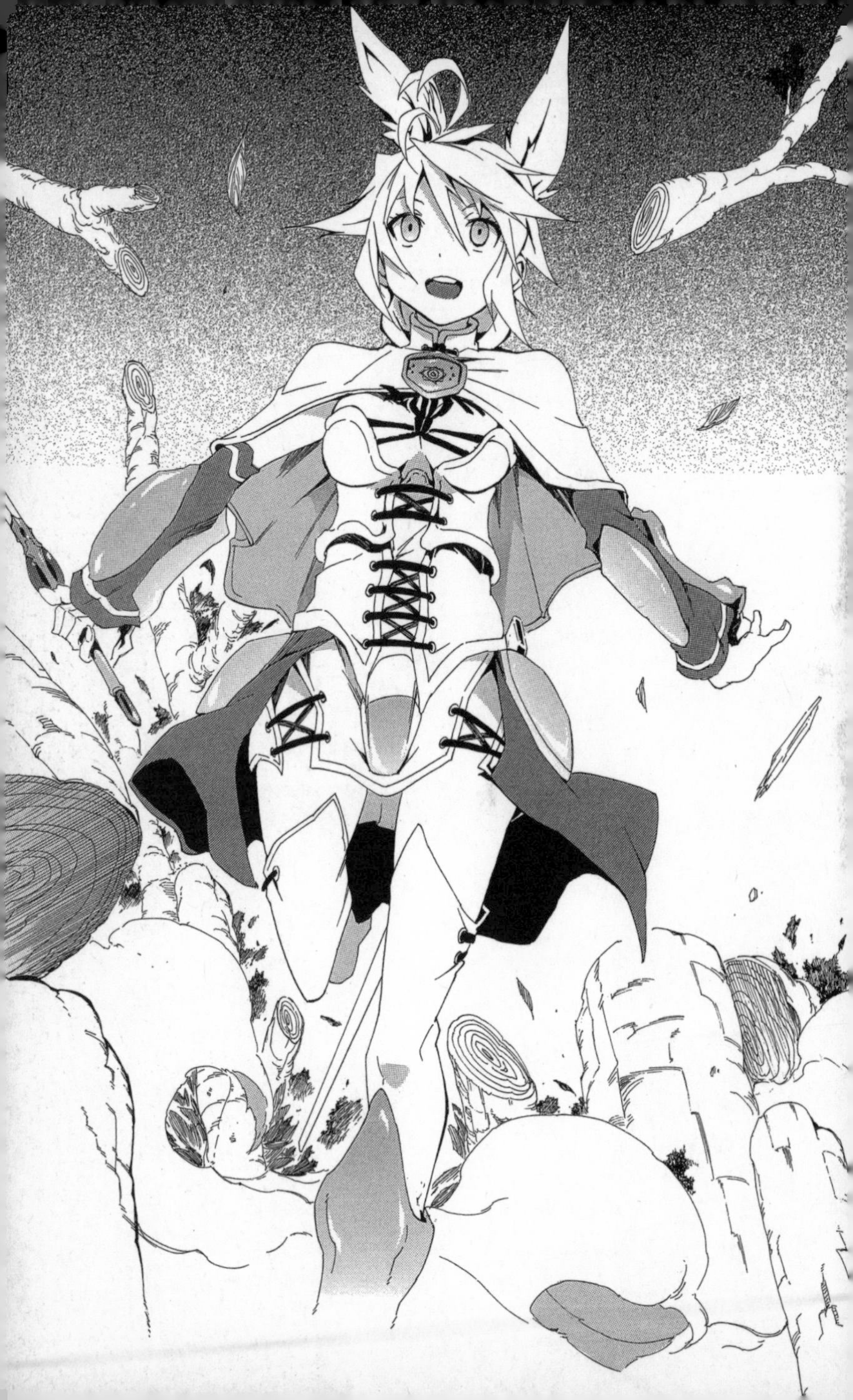

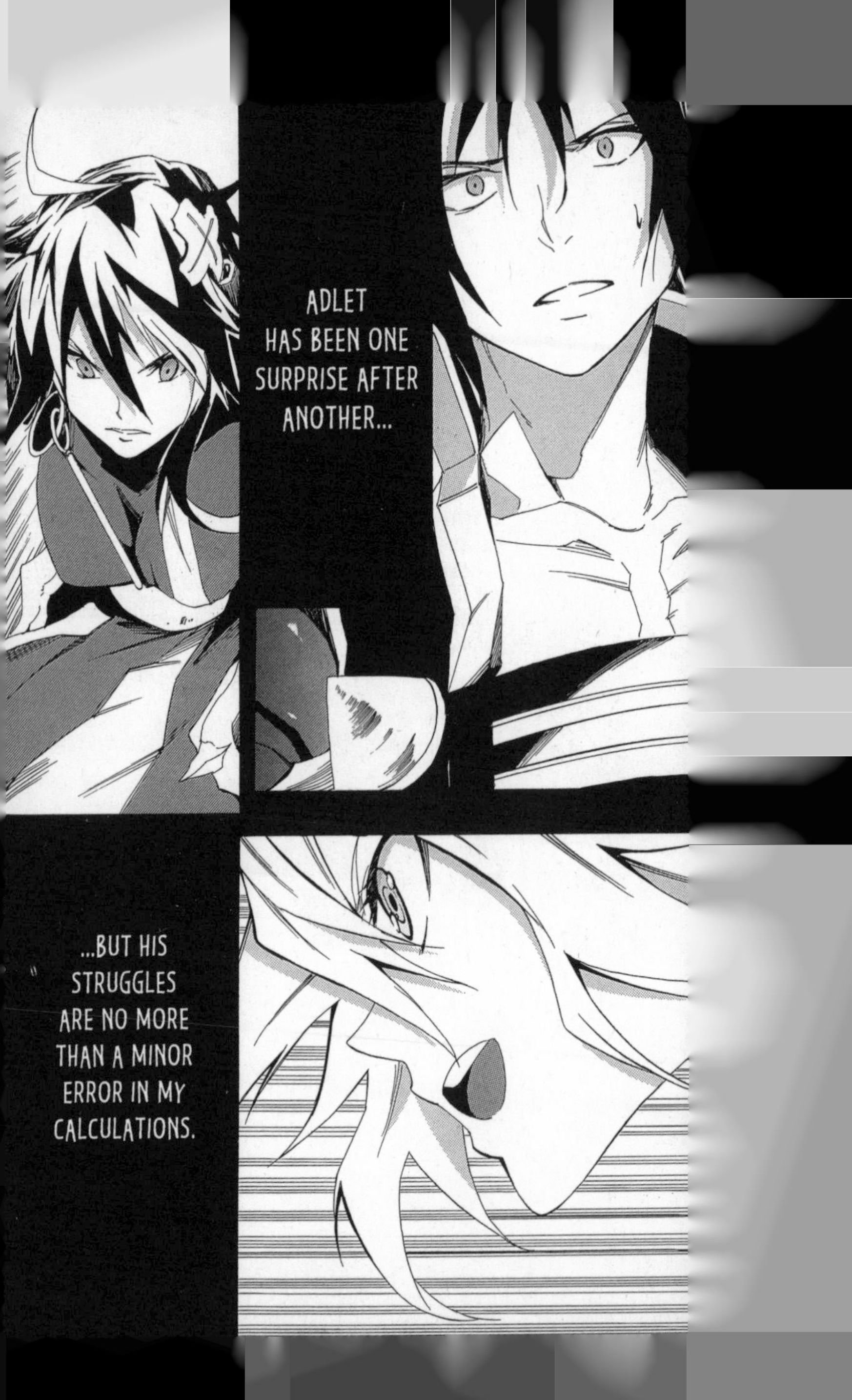
ADLET HAS BEEN ONE SURPRISE AFTER ANOTHER...
...BUT HIS STRUGGLES ARE NO MORE THAN A MINOR ERROR IN MY CALCULATIONS.

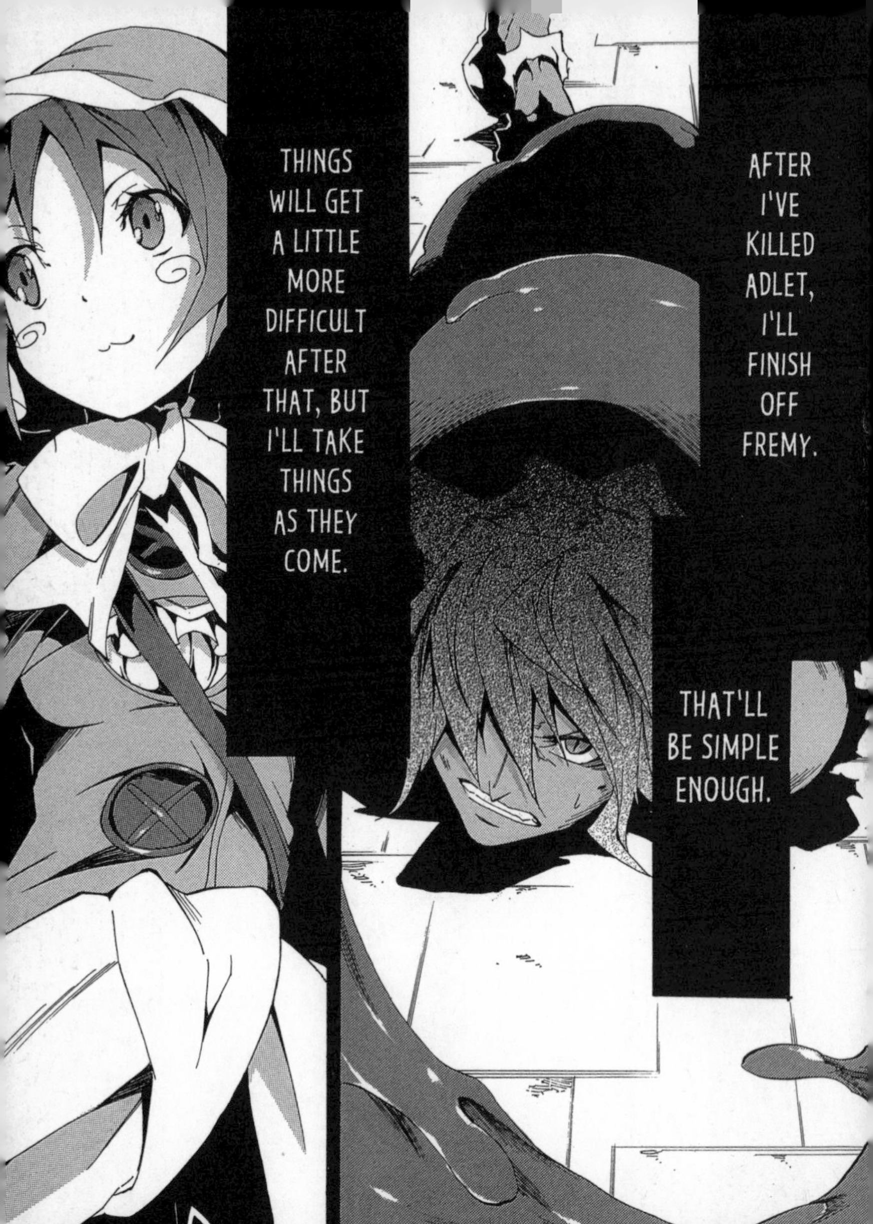
AFTER I'VE KILLED ADLET, I'LL FINISH OFF FREMY.
THAT'LL BE SIMPLE ENOUGH.
THINGS WILL GET A LITTLE MORE DIFFICULT AFTER THAT, BUT I'LL TAKE THINGS AS THEY COME.

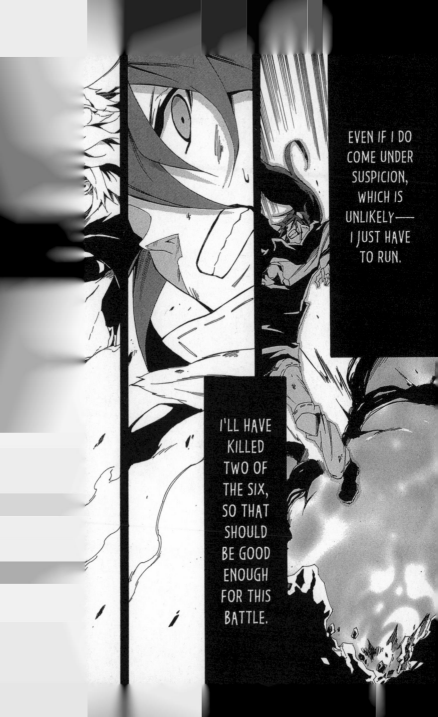

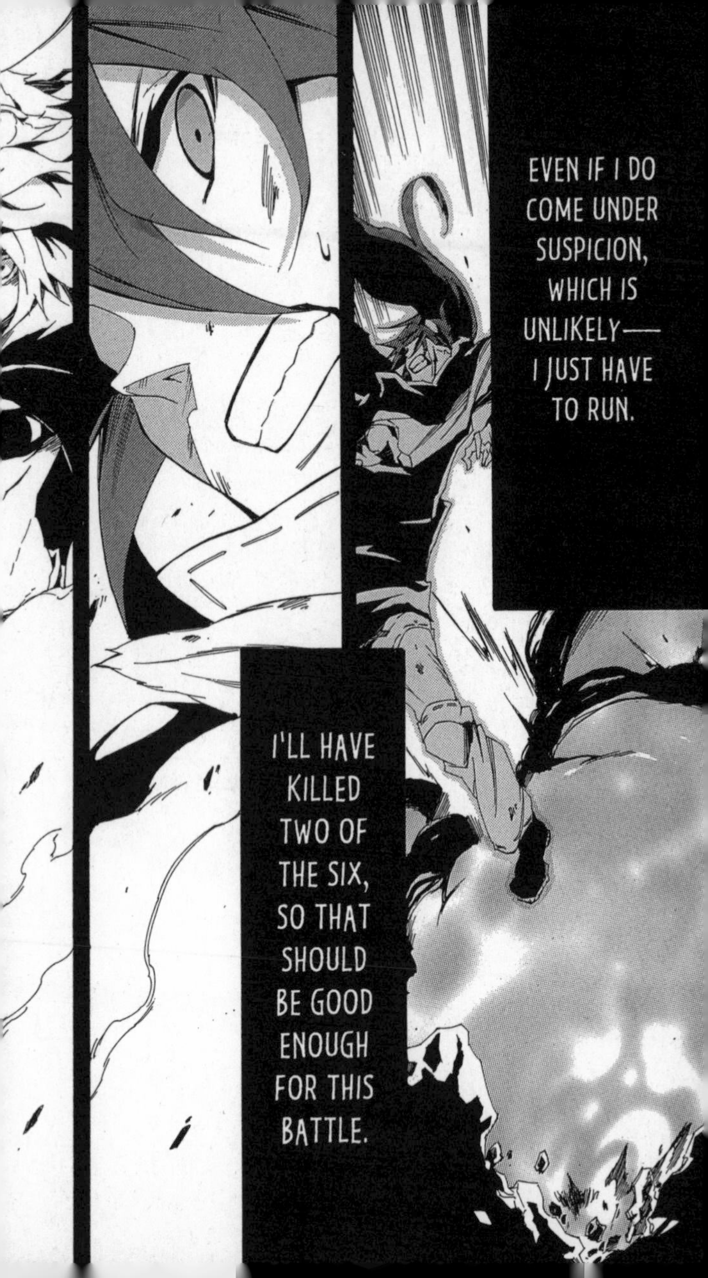
EVEN IF I DO COME UNDER SUSPICION, WHICH IS UNLIKELY—— I JUST HAVE TO RUN.
I'LL HAVE KILLED TWO OF THE SIX, SO THAT SHOULD BE GOOD ENOUGH FOR THIS BATTLE.

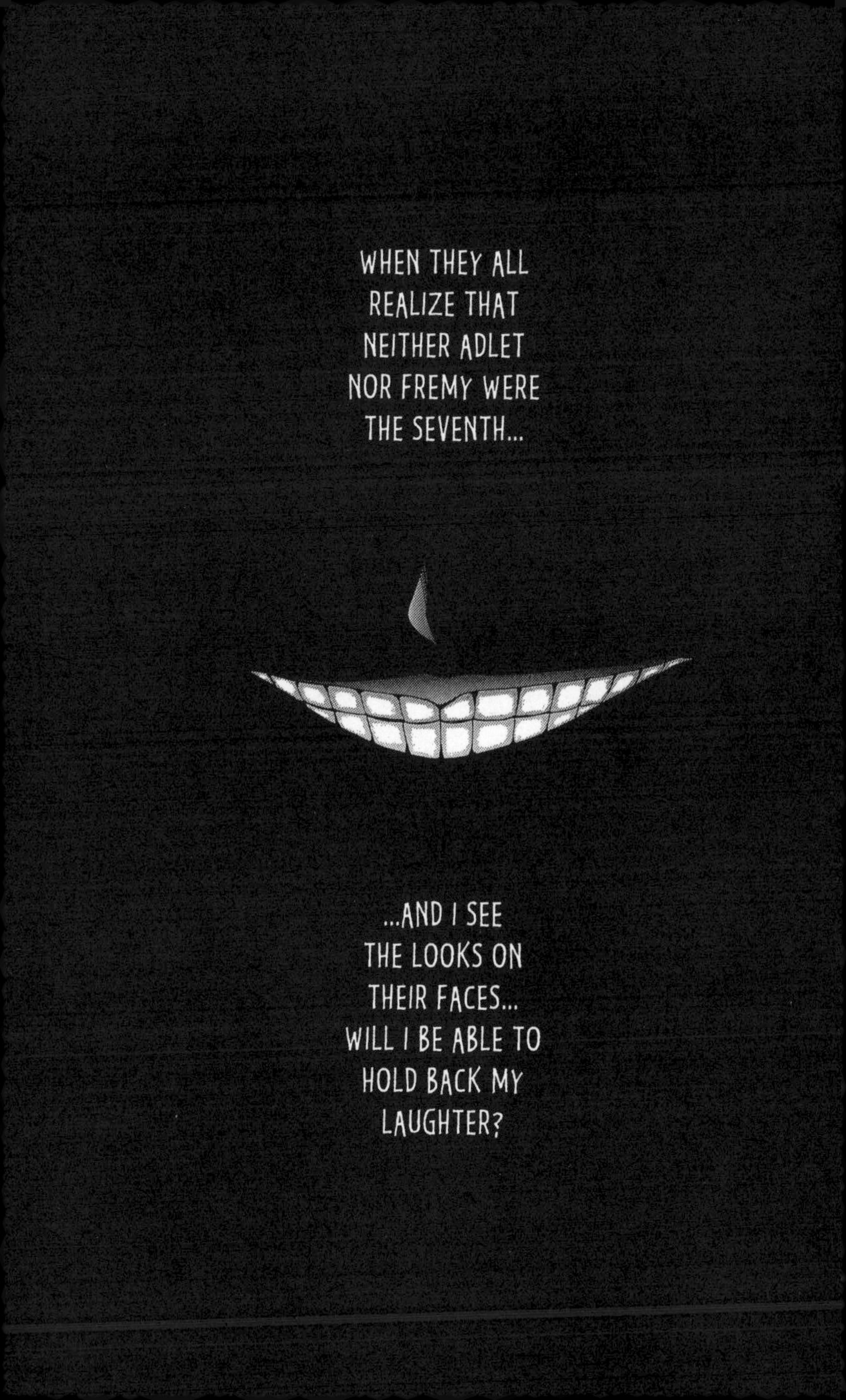
WHEN THEY ALL REALIZE THAT NEITHER ADLET NOR FREMY WERE THE SEVENTH...
...AND I SEE THE LOOKS ON THEIR FACES... WILL I BE ABLE TO HOLD BACK MY LAUGHTER?

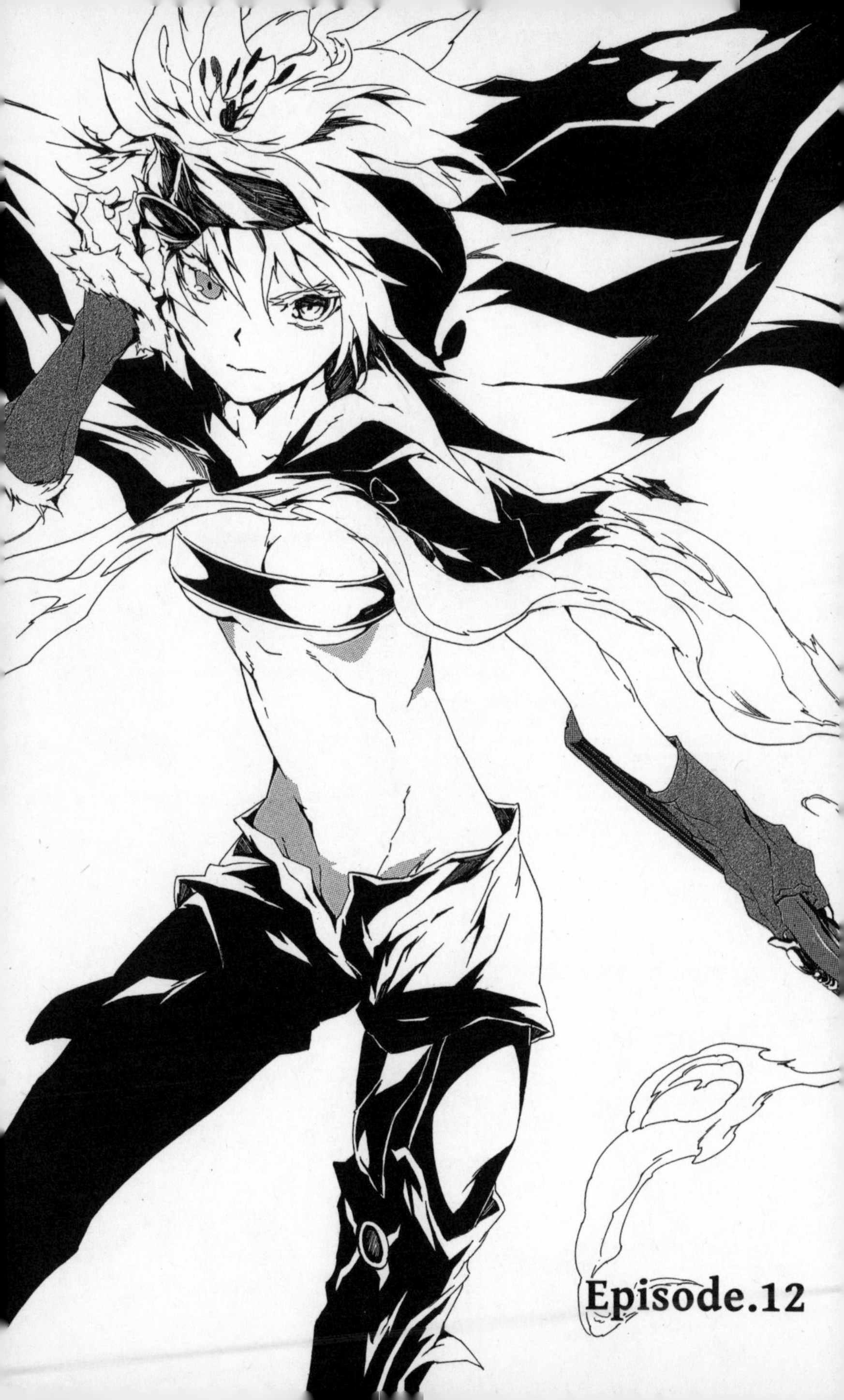

Episode.12

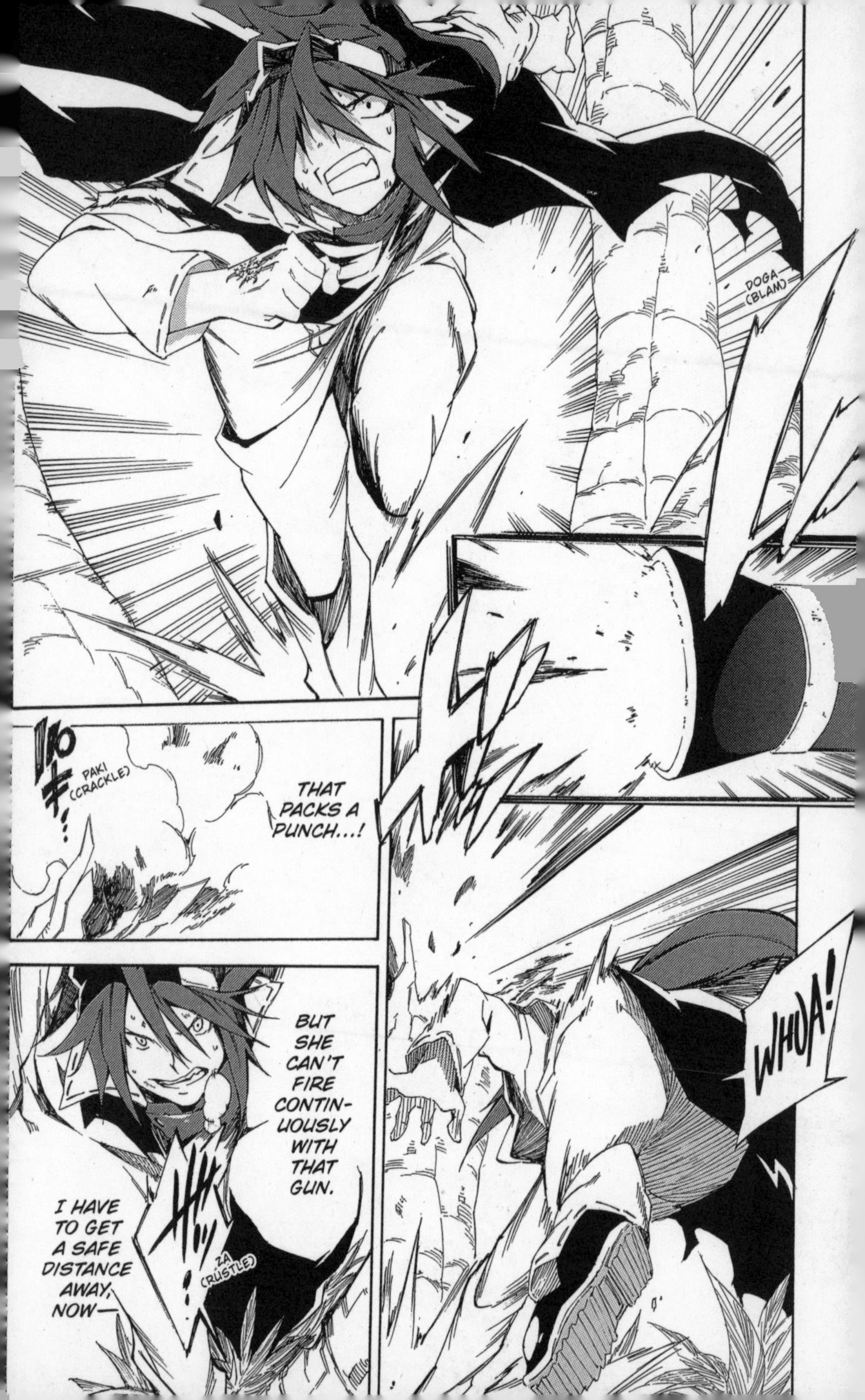
DOGA (BLAM)
PAKI (CRACKLE)
THAT PACKS A PUNCH...!
WHOA!
BUT SHE CAN'T FIRE CONTINUOUSLY WITH THAT GUN.
I HAVE TO GET A SAFE DISTANCE AWAY, NOW—
ZA (RUSTLE)

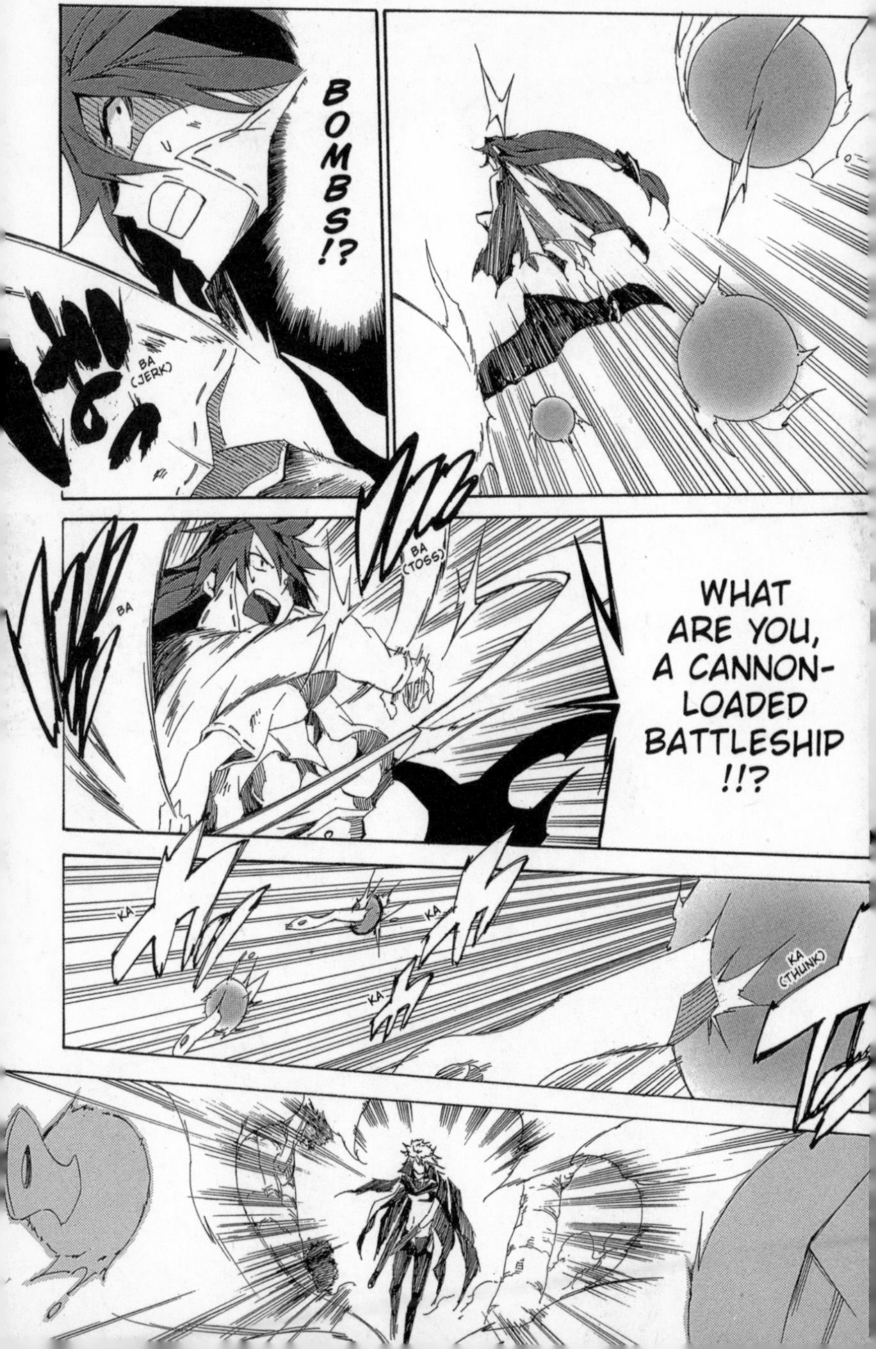
BOMBS!?
BA (JERK)
WHAT ARE YOU, A CANNON-LOADED BATTLESHIP!!?
BA (TOSS)
BA
KA (THUNK)
KA
KA
KA

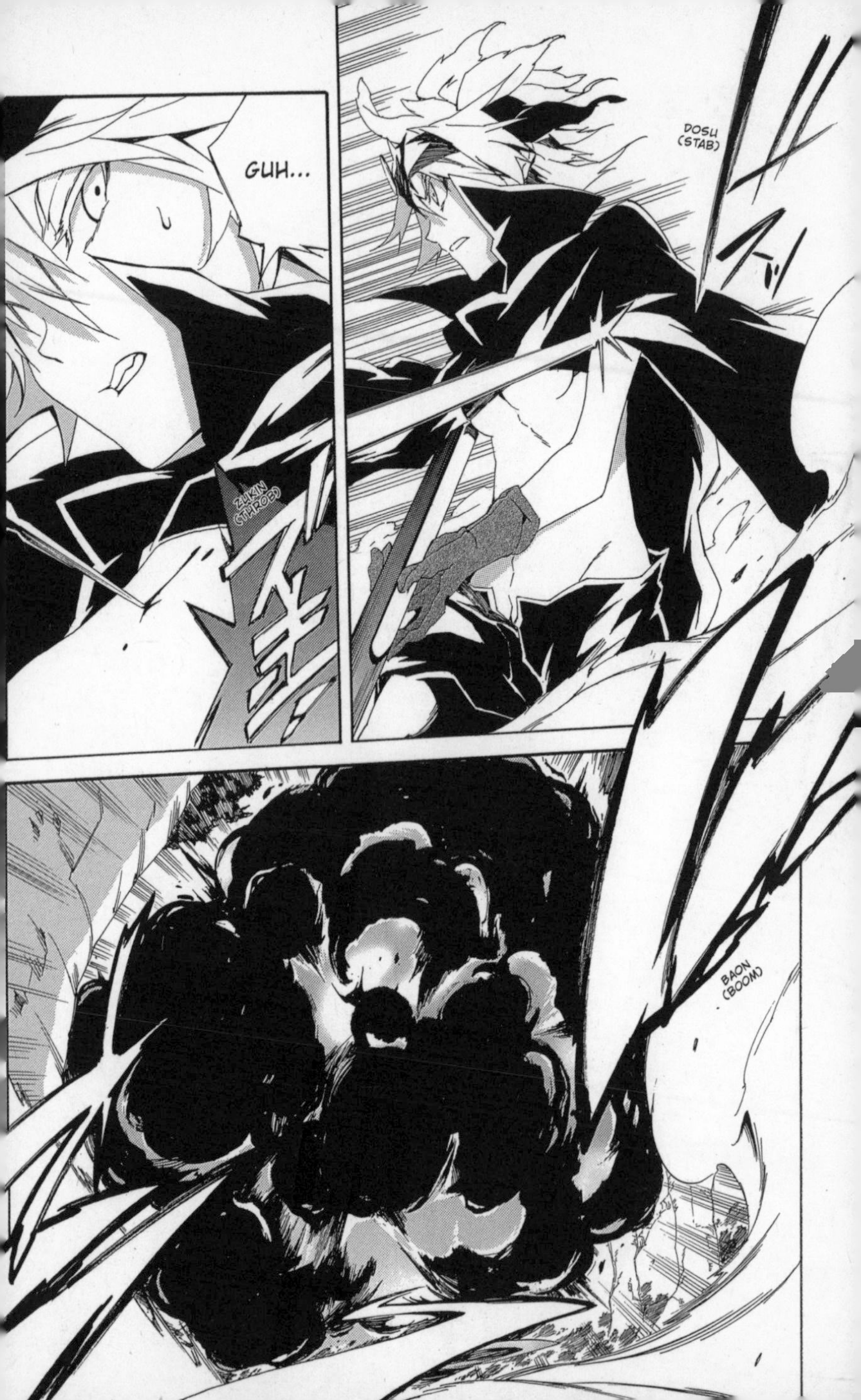
DOSU (STAB)
GUH...
ZUKIN (THROB)
BAON (BOOM)

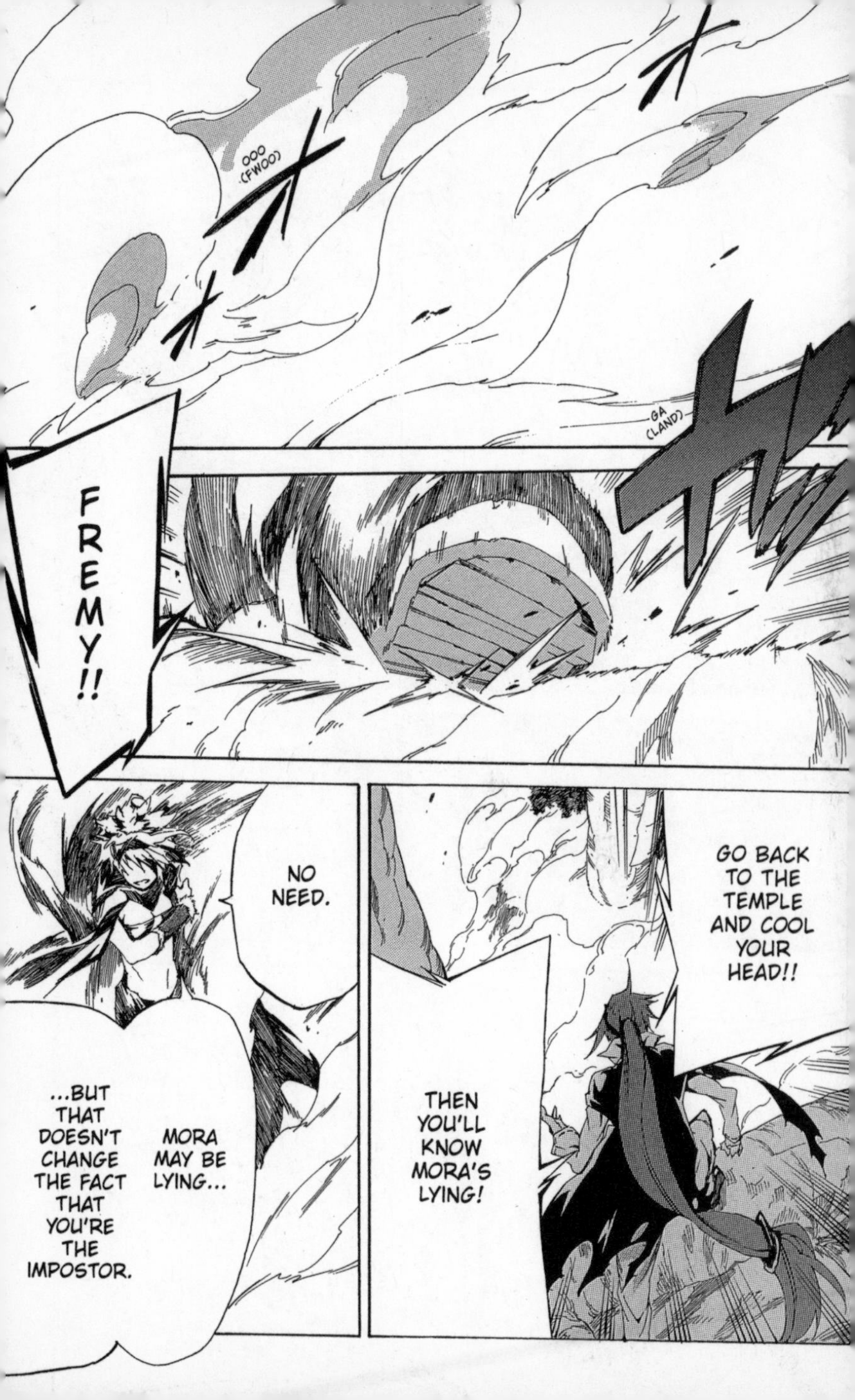
OOO (FWOO)
GA (LAND)
FREMY!!
GO BACK TO THE TEMPLE AND COOL YOUR HEAD!!
THEN YOU'LL KNOW MORA'S LYING!
NO NEED.
MORA MAY BE LYING...
...BUT THAT DOESN'T CHANGE THE FACT THAT YOU'RE THE IMPOSTOR.

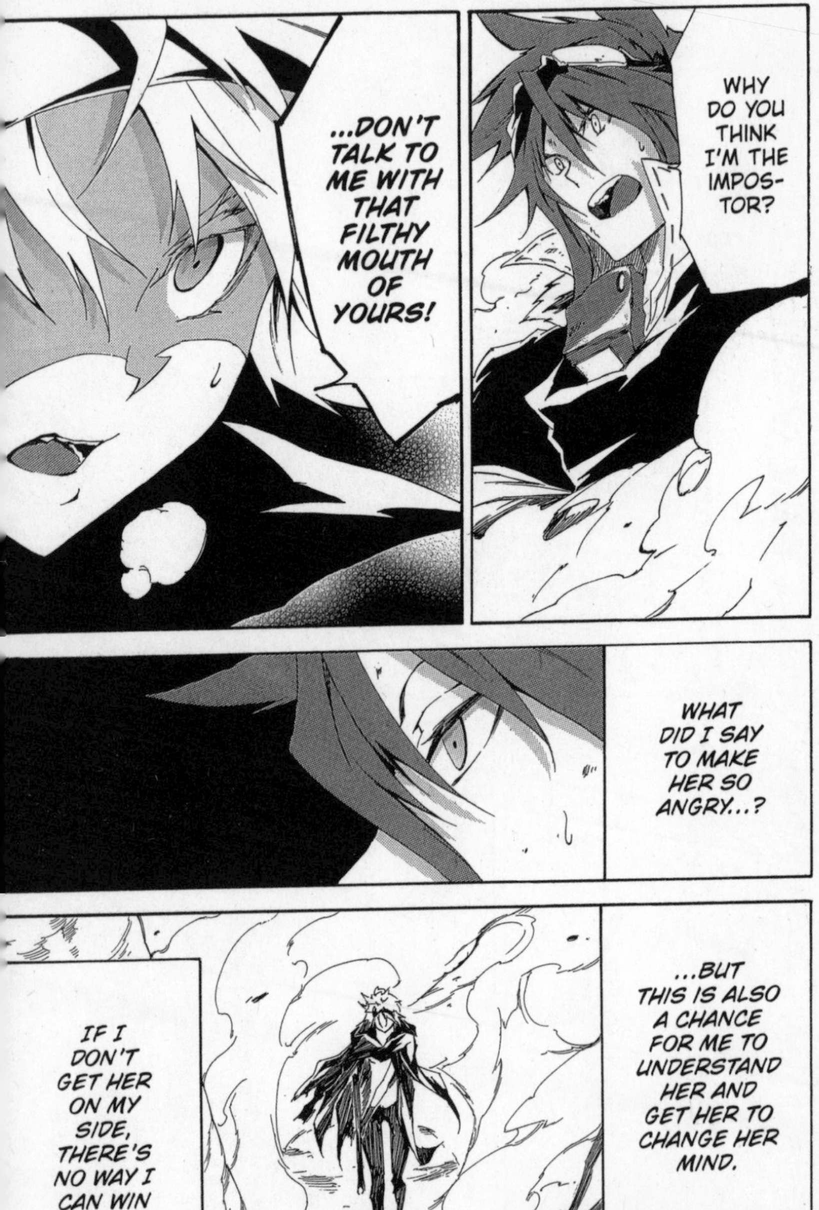

WHY DO YOU THINK I'M THE IMPOSTOR?
...DON'T TALK TO ME WITH THAT FILTHY MOUTH OF YOURS!
WHAT DID I SAY TO MAKE HER SO ANGRY...?
...BUT THIS IS ALSO A CHANCE FOR ME TO UNDERSTAND HER AND GET HER TO CHANGE HER MIND.
IF I DON'T GET HER ON MY SIDE, THERE'S NO WAY I CAN WIN THIS.

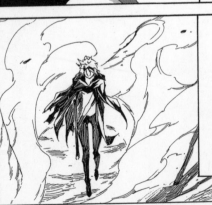

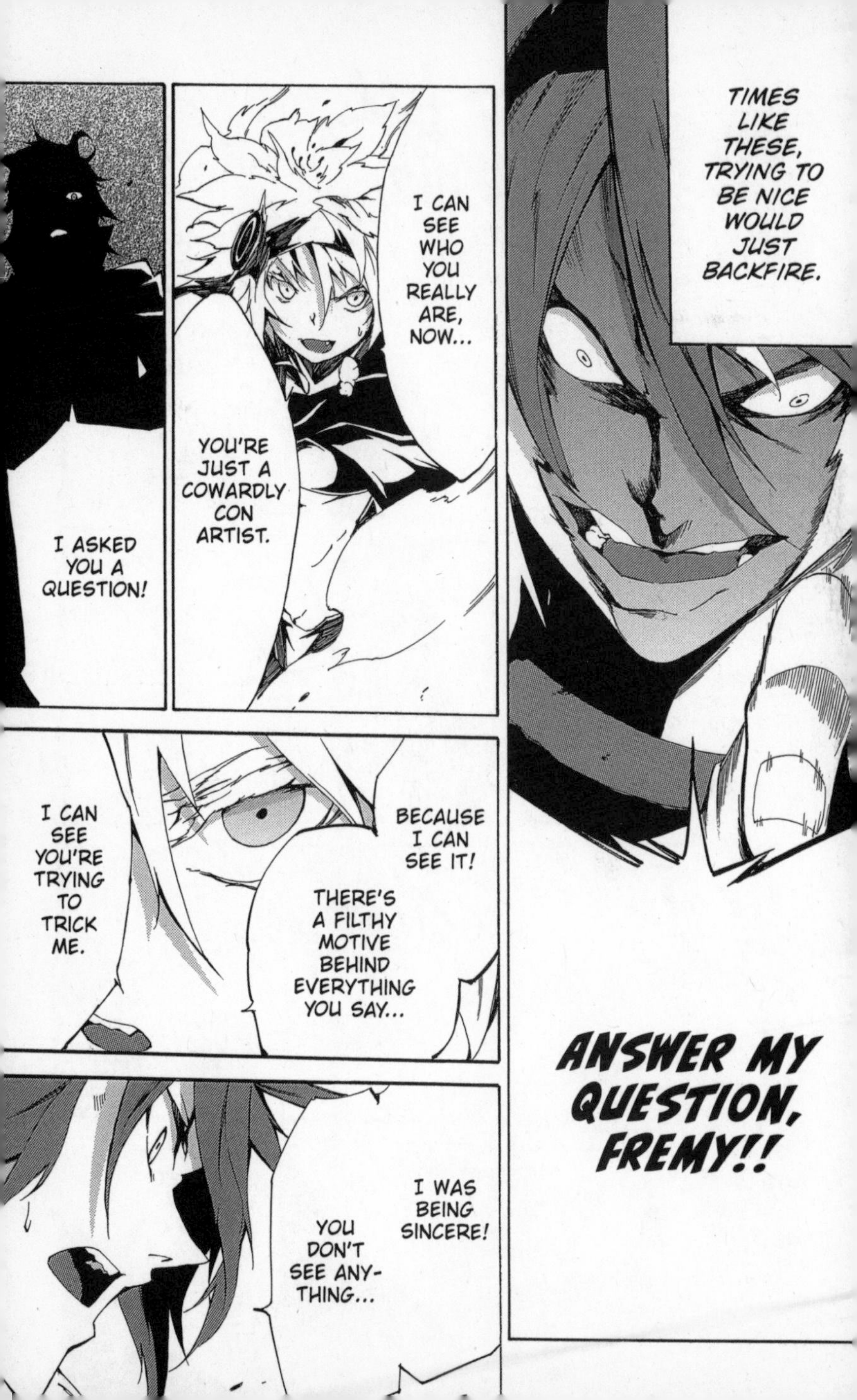
TIMES LIKE THESE, TRYING TO BE NICE WOULD JUST BACKFIRE.
ANSWER MY QUESTION, FREMY!!
I CAN SEE WHO YOU REALLY ARE, NOW...
YOU'RE JUST A COWARDLY CON ARTIST.
I ASKED YOU A QUESTION!
BECAUSE I CAN SEE IT!
THERE'S A FILTHY MOTIVE BEHIND EVERYTHING YOU SAY...
I CAN SEE YOU'RE TRYING TO TRICK ME.
I WAS BEING SINCERE!
YOU DON'T SEE ANYTHING...

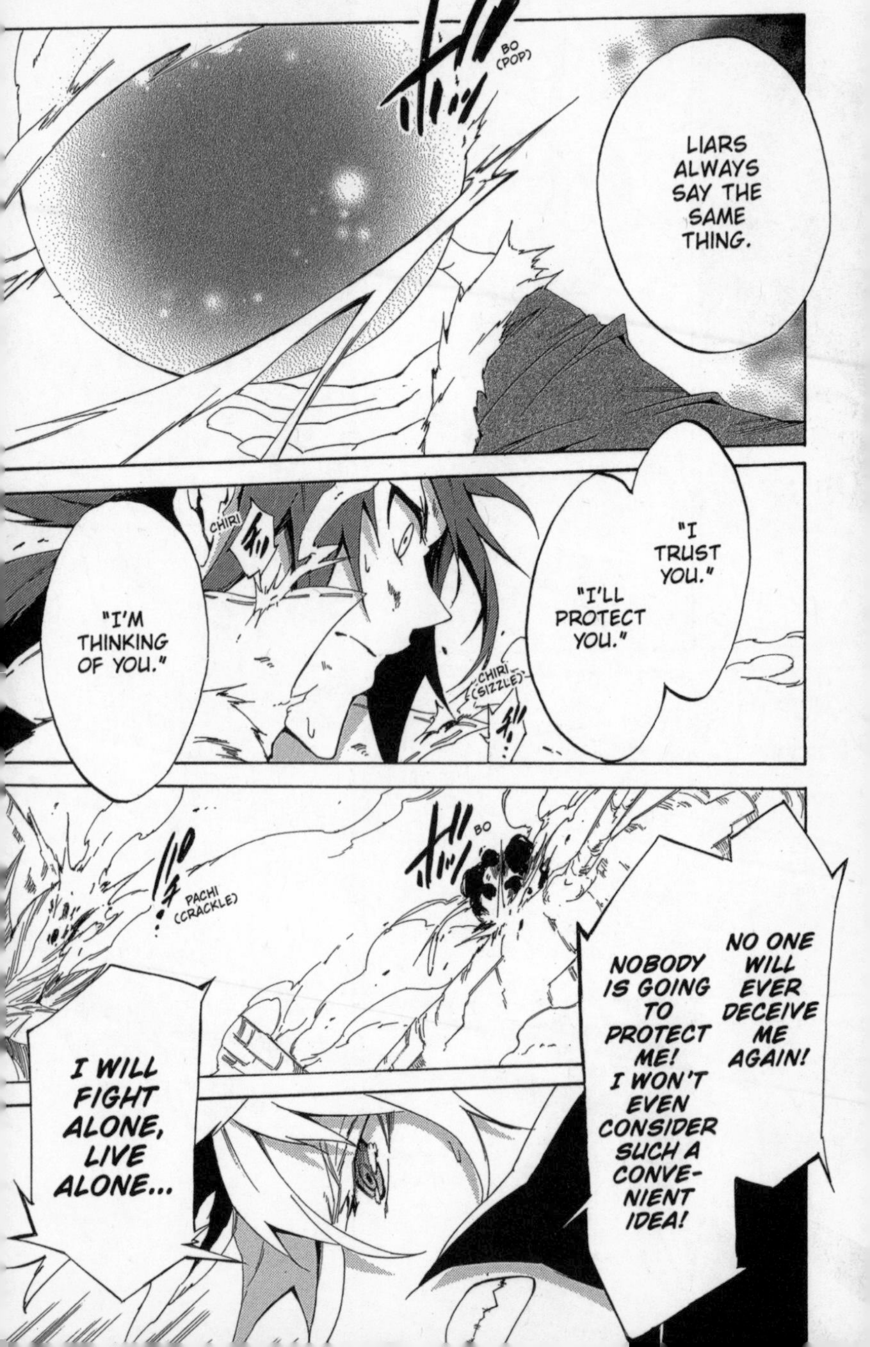
BO (POP)
LIARS ALWAYS SAY THE SAME THING.
"I TRUST YOU."
"I'LL PROTECT YOU."
CHIRI (SIZZLE)
CHIRI
"I'M THINKING OF YOU."
BO
PACHI (CRACKLE)
NO ONE WILL EVER DECEIVE ME AGAIN!
NOBODY IS GOING TO PROTECT ME! I WON'T EVEN CONSIDER SUCH A CONVENIENT IDEA!
I WILL FIGHT ALONE, LIVE ALONE...

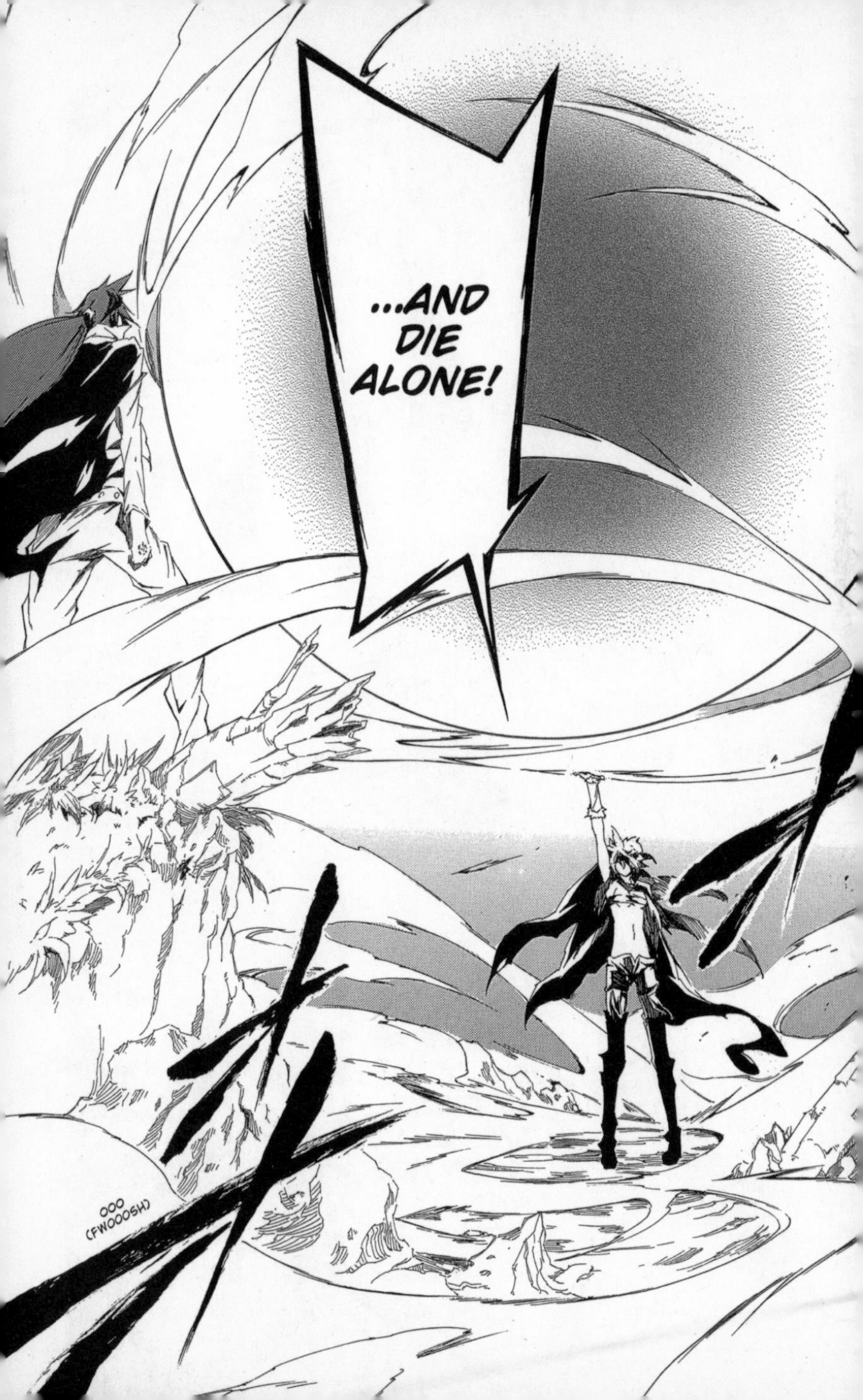
...AND DIE ALONE!
OOO (FWOOOSH)

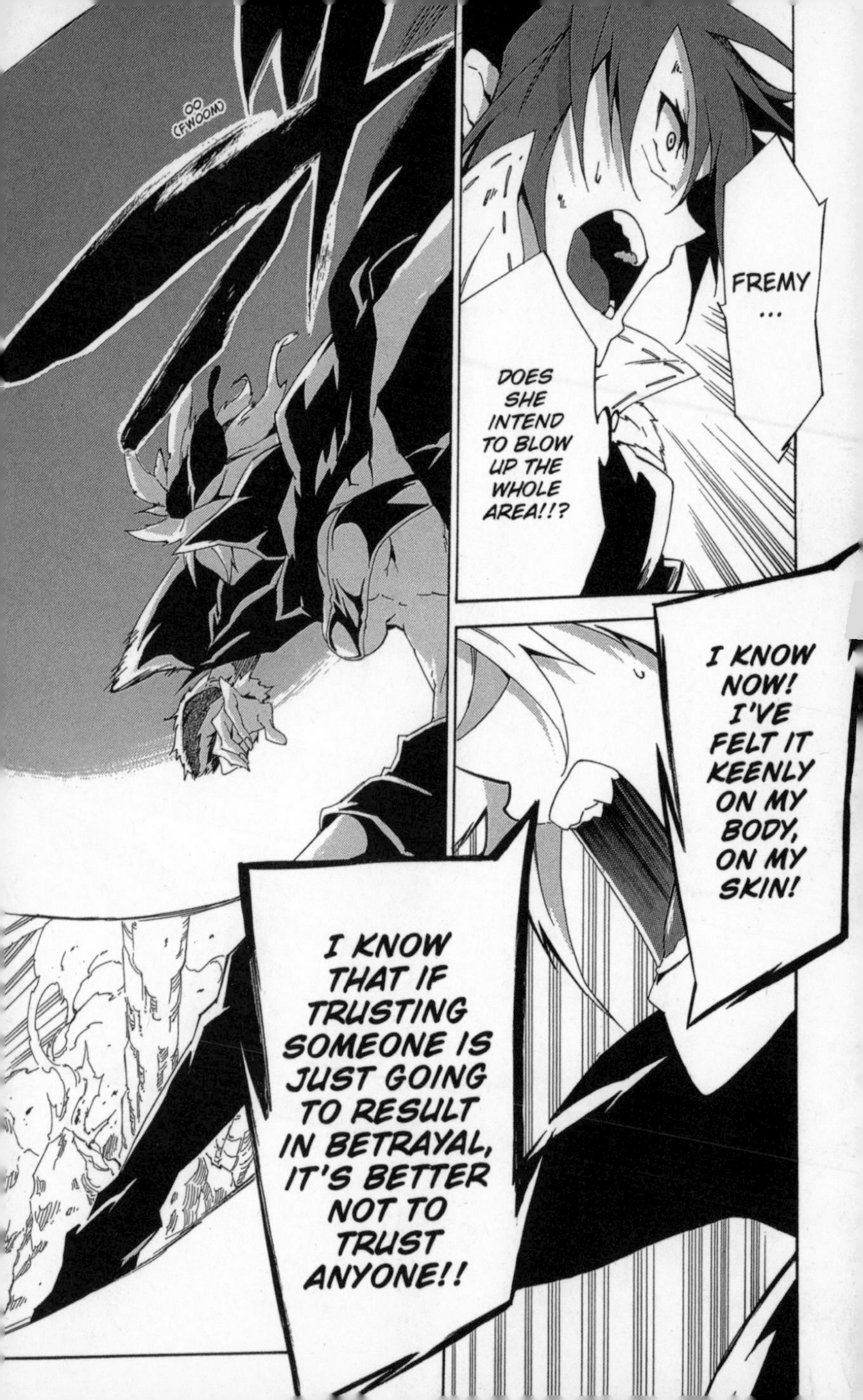
FREMY ...
DOES SHE INTEND TO BLOW UP THE WHOLE AREA!!?
I KNOW NOW! I'VE FELT IT KEENLY ON MY BODY, ON MY SKIN!
OO (FWOOM)
I KNOW THAT IF TRUSTING SOMEONE IS JUST GOING TO RESULT IN BETRAYAL, IT'S BETTER NOT TO TRUST ANYONE!!

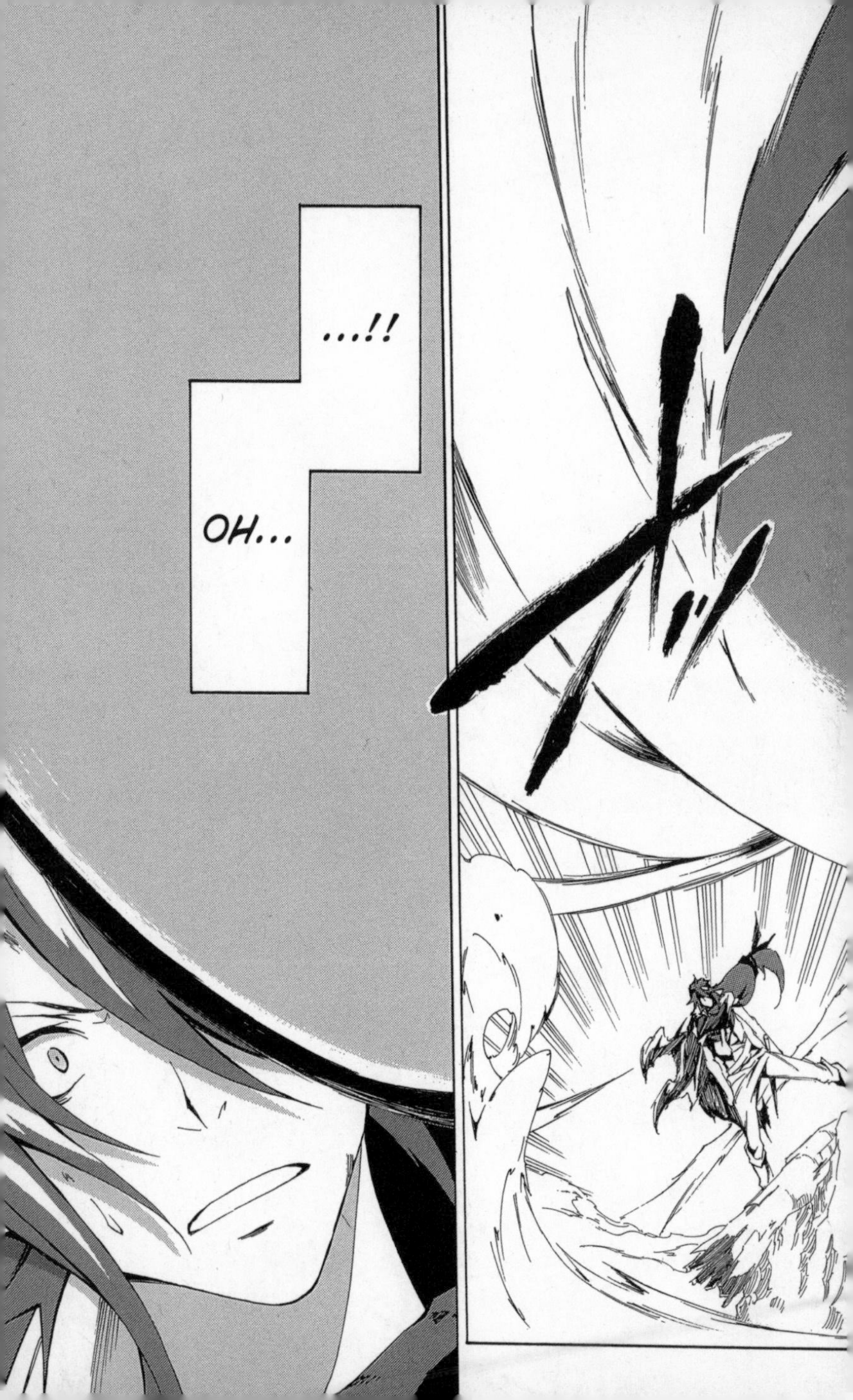
...!!
OH...

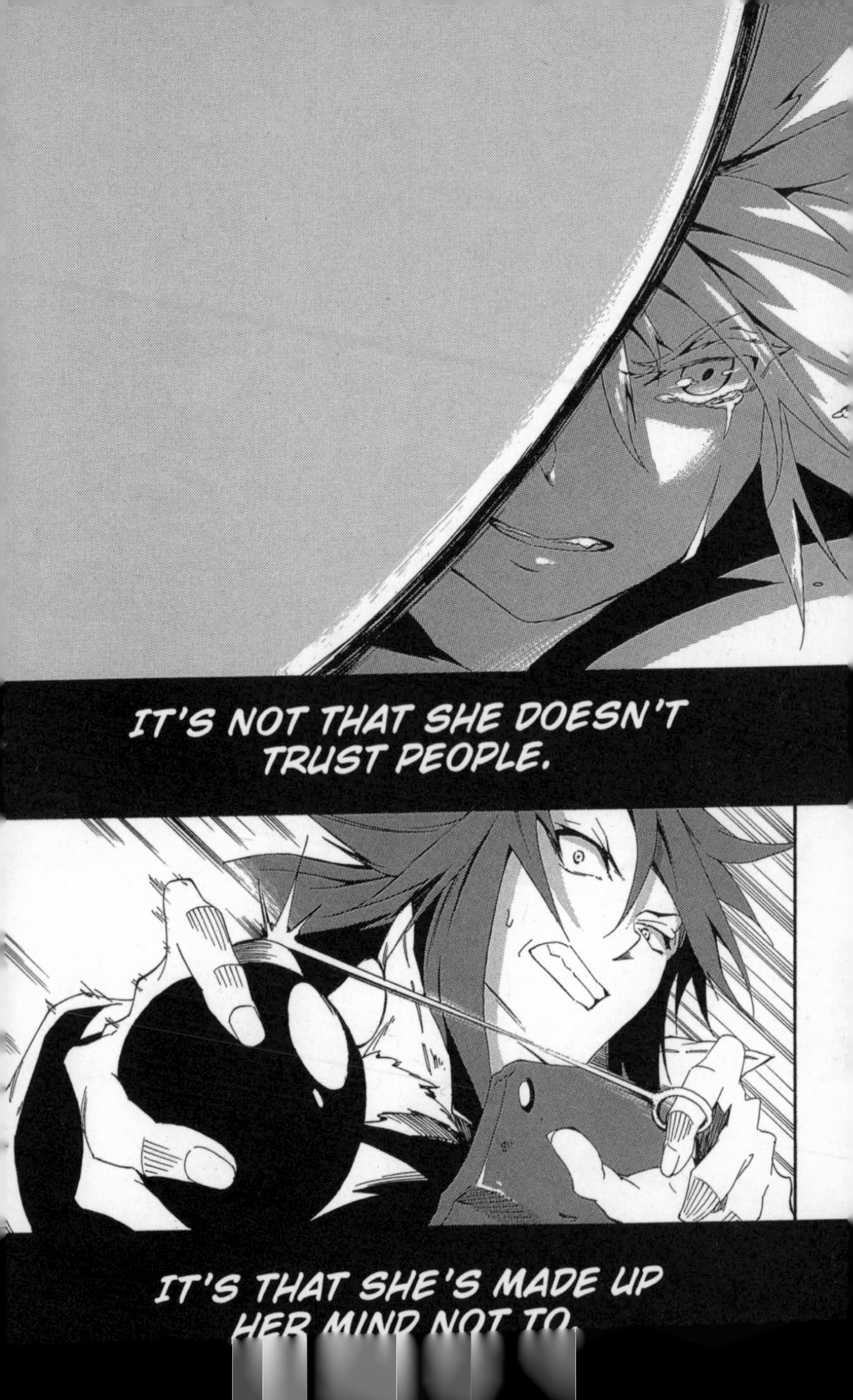
IT'S NOT THAT SHE DOESN'T TRUST PEOPLE.
IT'S THAT SHE'S MADE UP HER MIND NOT TO.

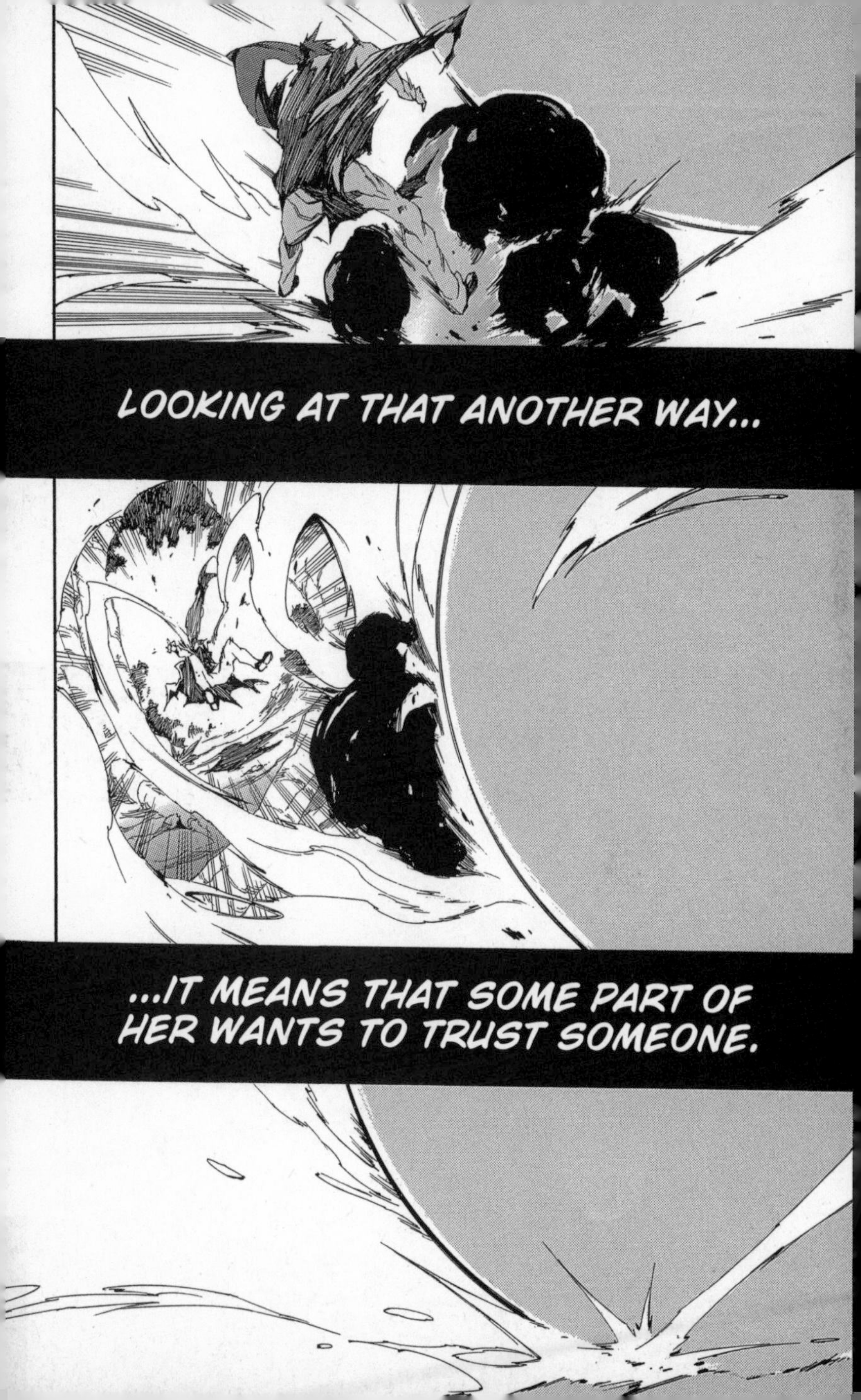
LOOKING AT THAT ANOTHER WAY...
...IT MEANS THAT SOME PART OF HER WANTS TO TRUST SOMEONE.

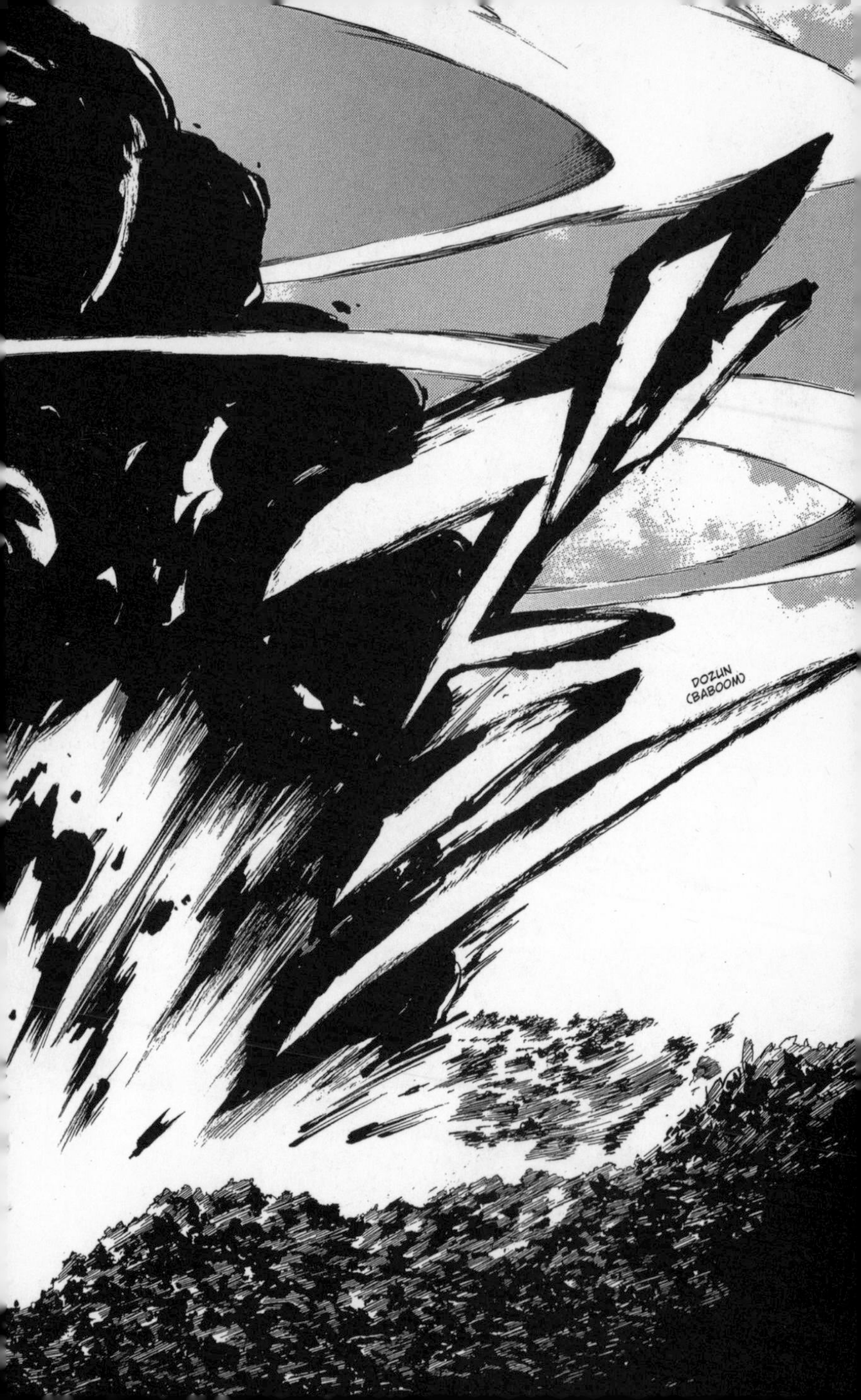
DOZUN
(BABOOM)

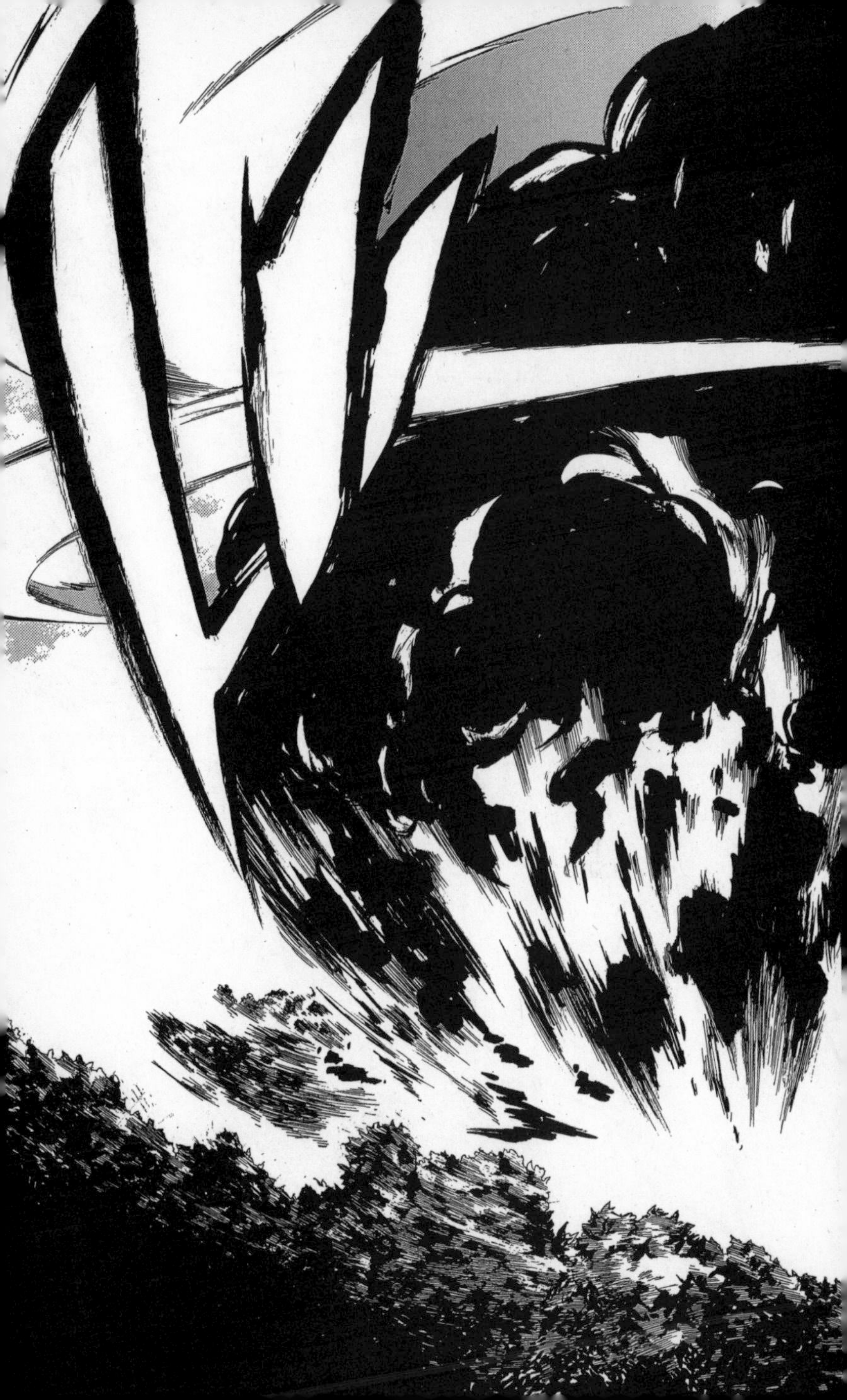

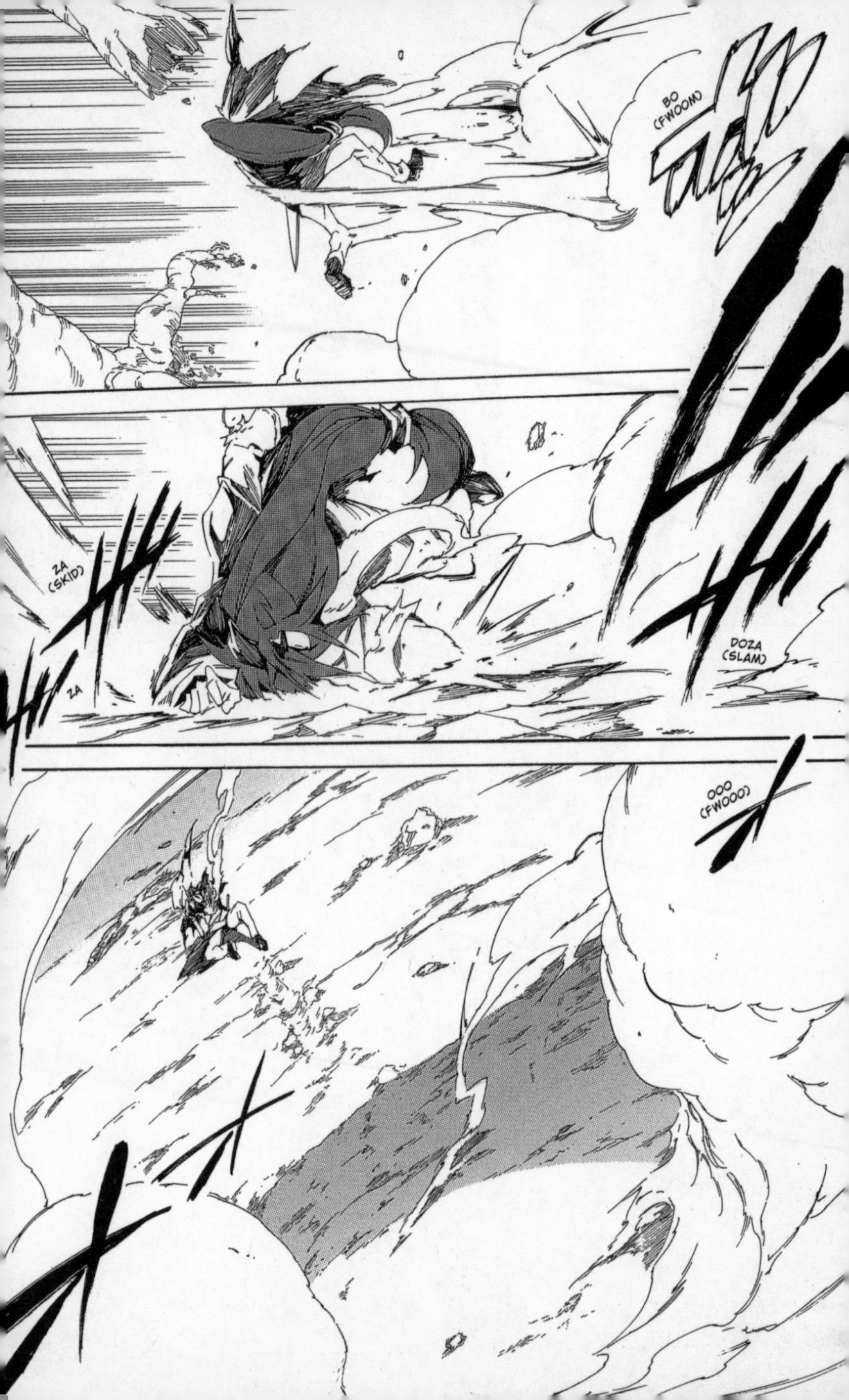
BO (FWOOM)
DOZA (SLAM)
ZA (SKID)
ZA
OOO (FWOOO)

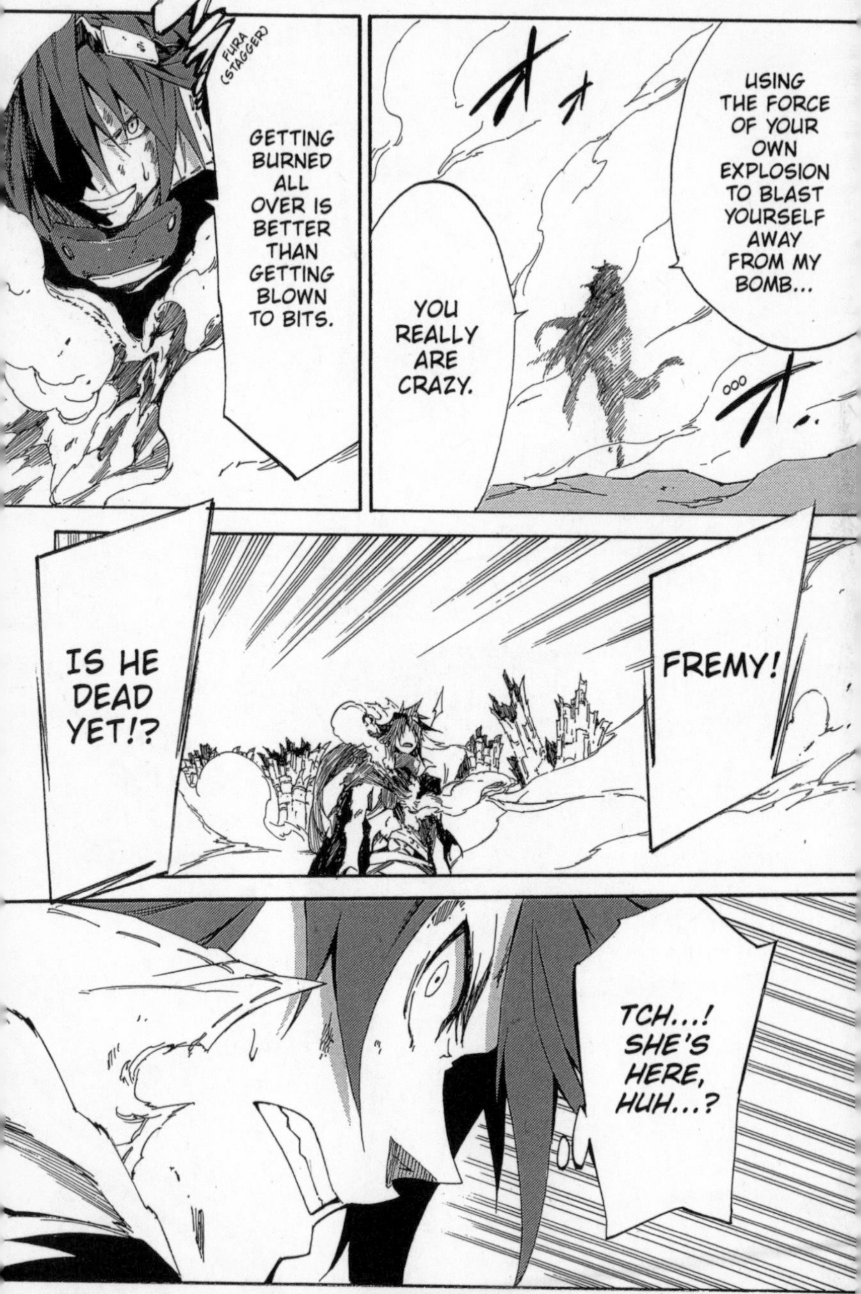
USING THE FORCE OF YOUR OWN EXPLOSION TO BLAST YOURSELF AWAY FROM MY BOMB...
YOU REALLY ARE CRAZY.
FURA (STAGGER)
GETTING BURNED ALL OVER IS BETTER THAN GETTING BLOWN TO BITS.
FREMY!
IS HE DEAD YET!?
TCH...! SHE'S HERE, HUH...?

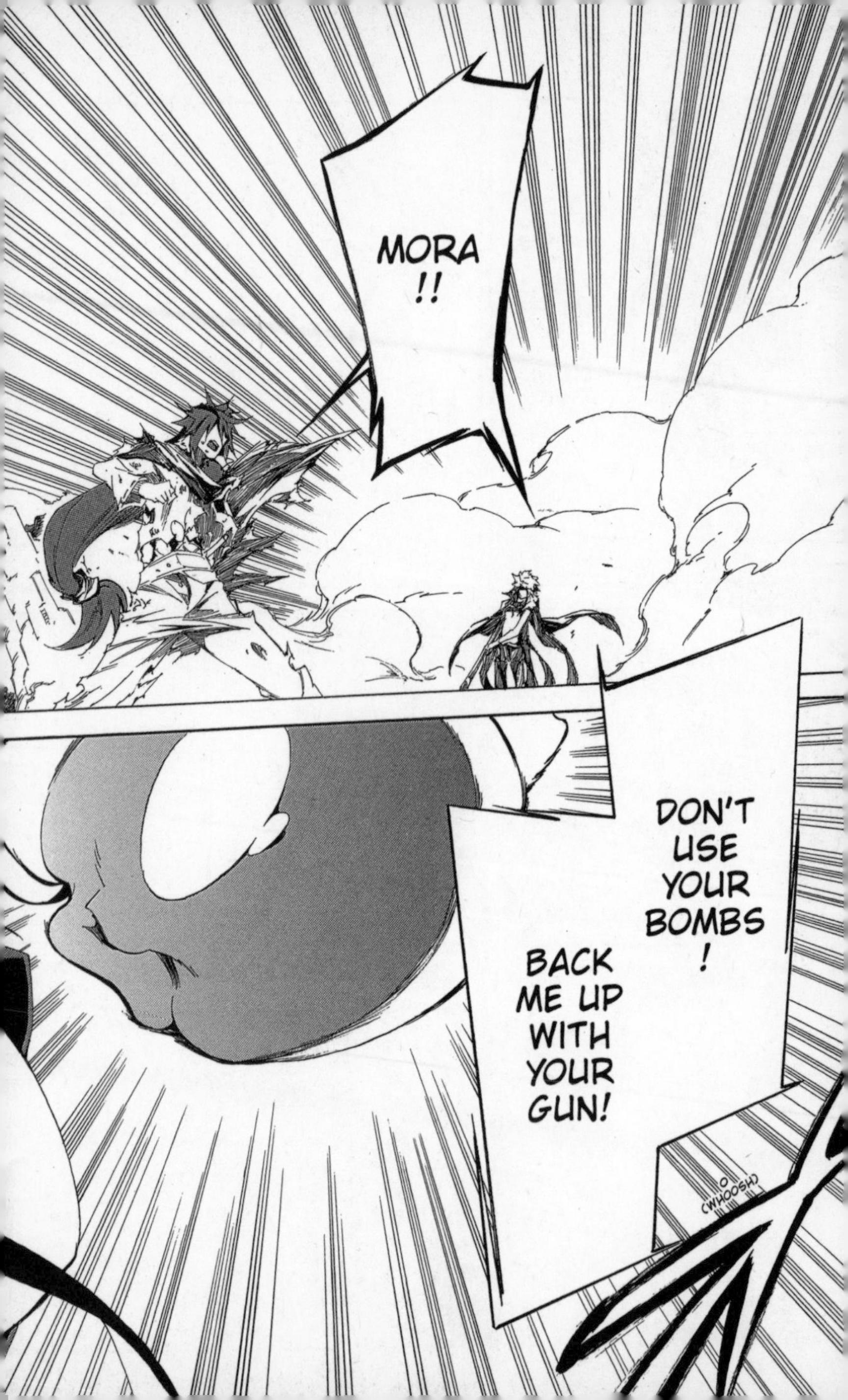
MORA!!
DON'T USE YOUR BOMBS!
BACK ME UP WITH YOUR GUN!
(WHOOSH)

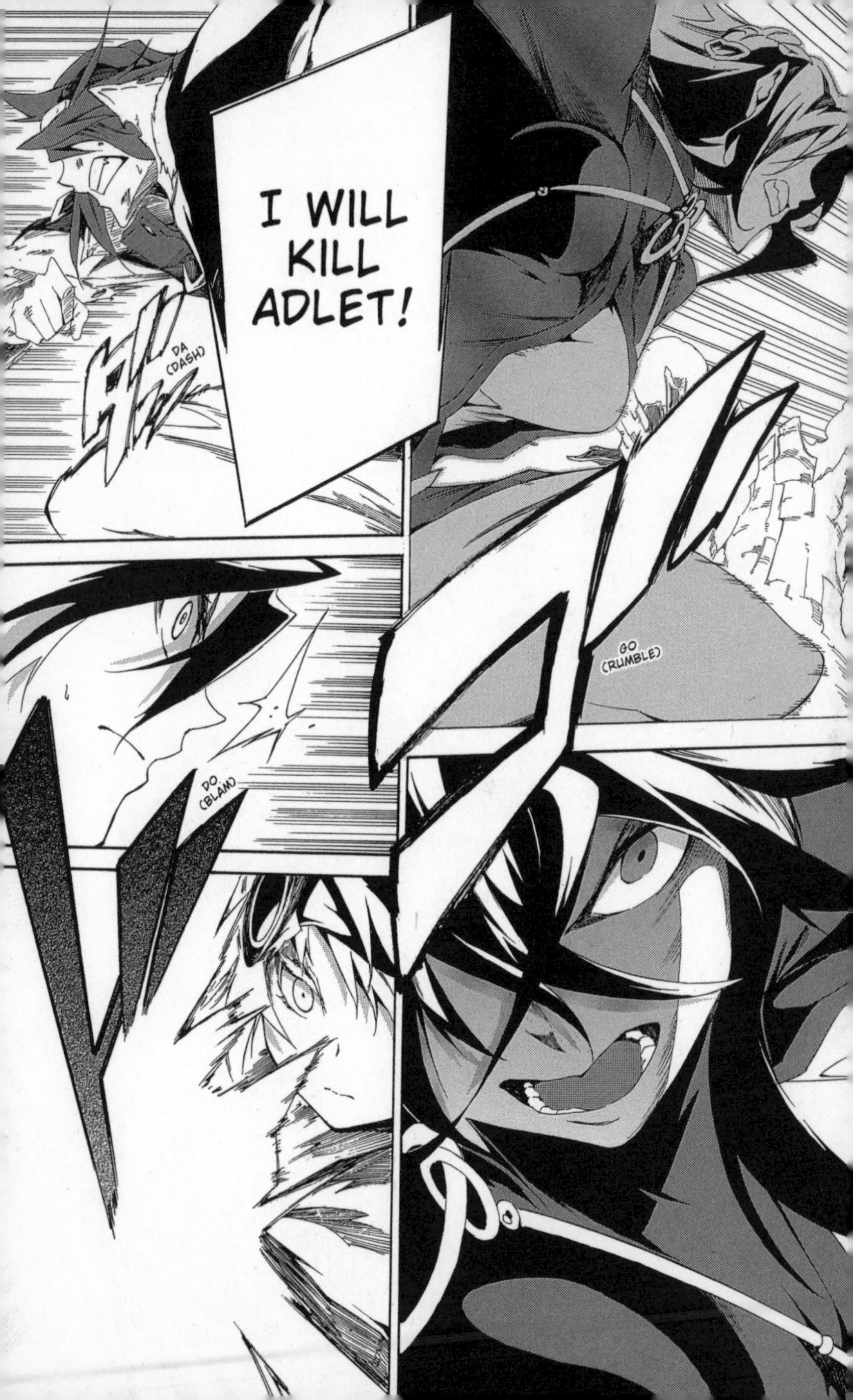
I WILL KILL ADLET!
DA (DASH)
GO (RUMBLE)
DO (BLAM)

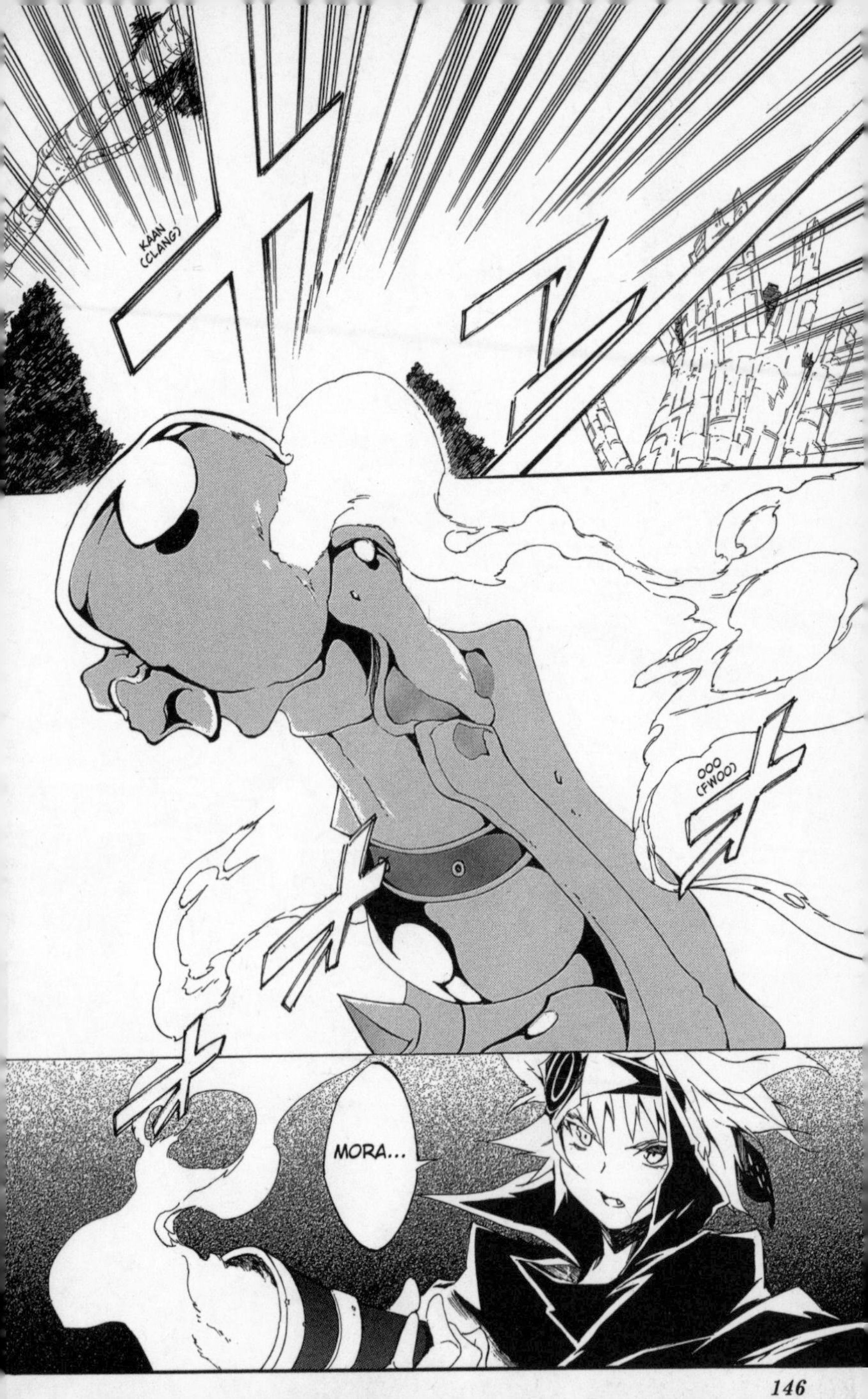
KAAN (CLANG)
OOO (FWOO)
MORA...

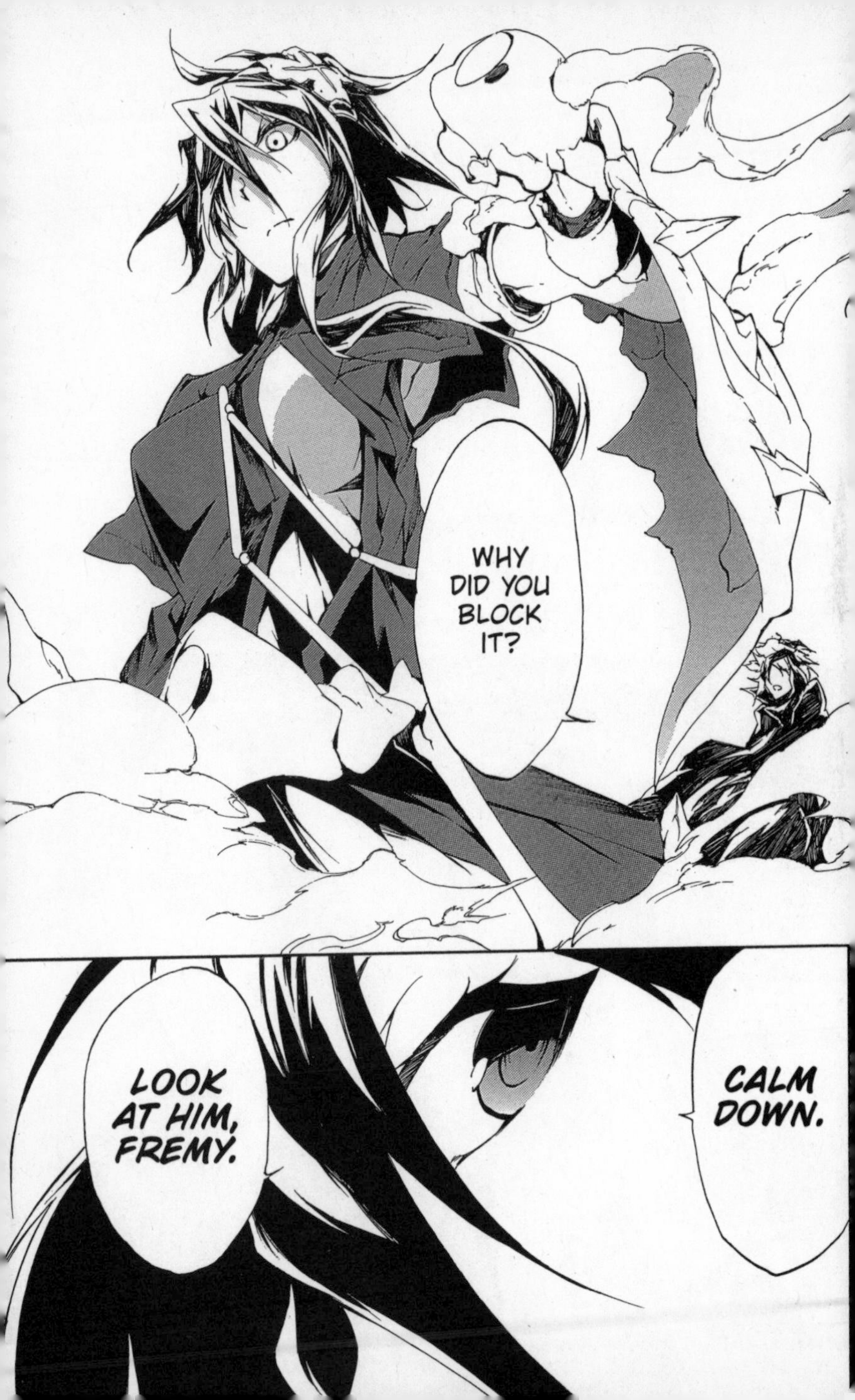
WHY DID YOU BLOCK IT?
CALM DOWN.
LOOK AT HIM, FREMY.

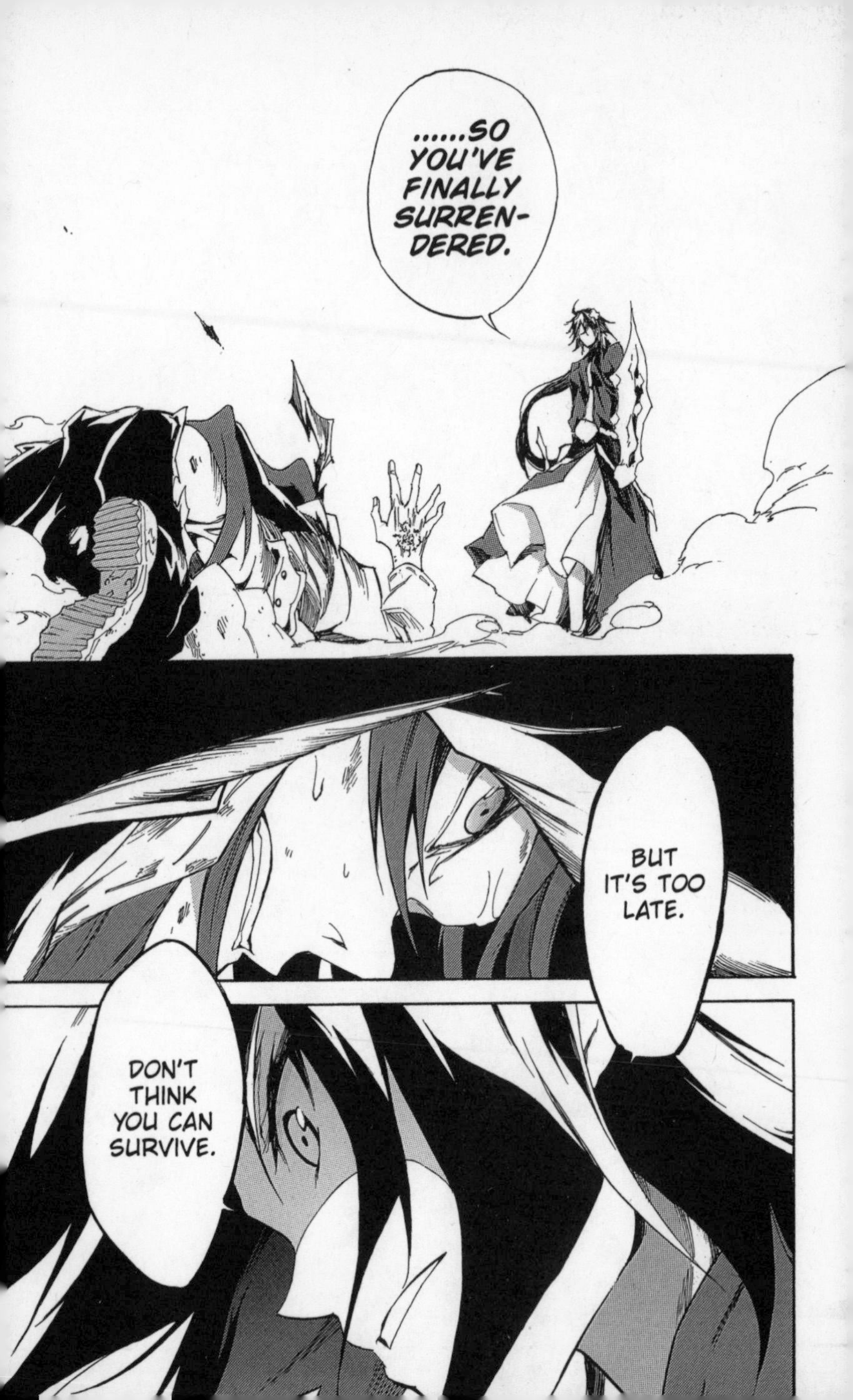
......SO YOU'VE FINALLY SURREN-DERED.
BUT IT'S TOO LATE.
DON'T THINK YOU CAN SURVIVE.

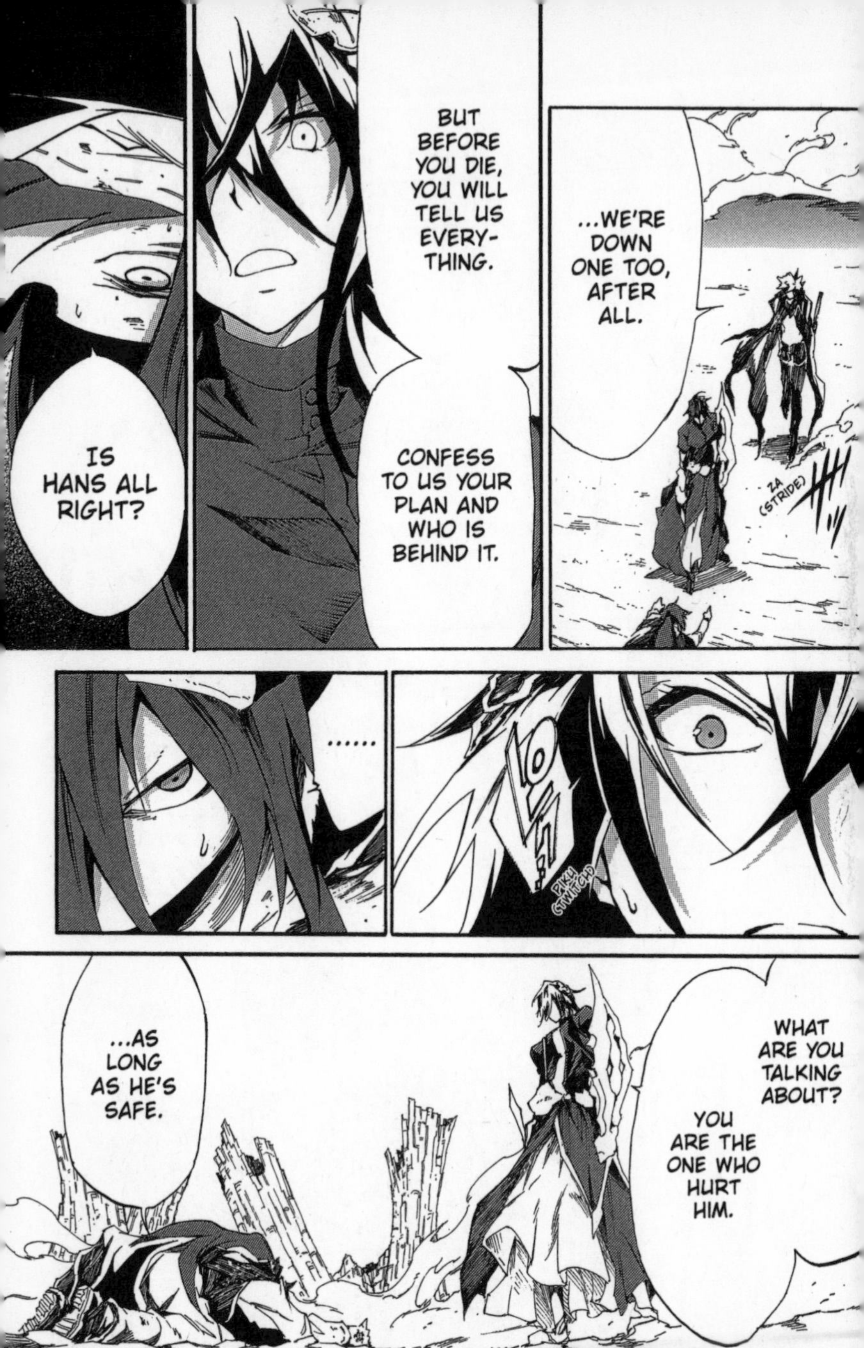
...WE'RE DOWN ONE TOO, AFTER ALL.
ZA (STRIDE)
BUT BEFORE YOU DIE, YOU WILL TELL US EVERY-THING.
CONFESS TO US YOUR PLAN AND WHO IS BEHIND IT.
IS HANS ALL RIGHT?
PIKU (TWITCH)
......
WHAT ARE YOU TALKING ABOUT?
YOU ARE THE ONE WHO HURT HIM.
...AS LONG AS HE'S SAFE.

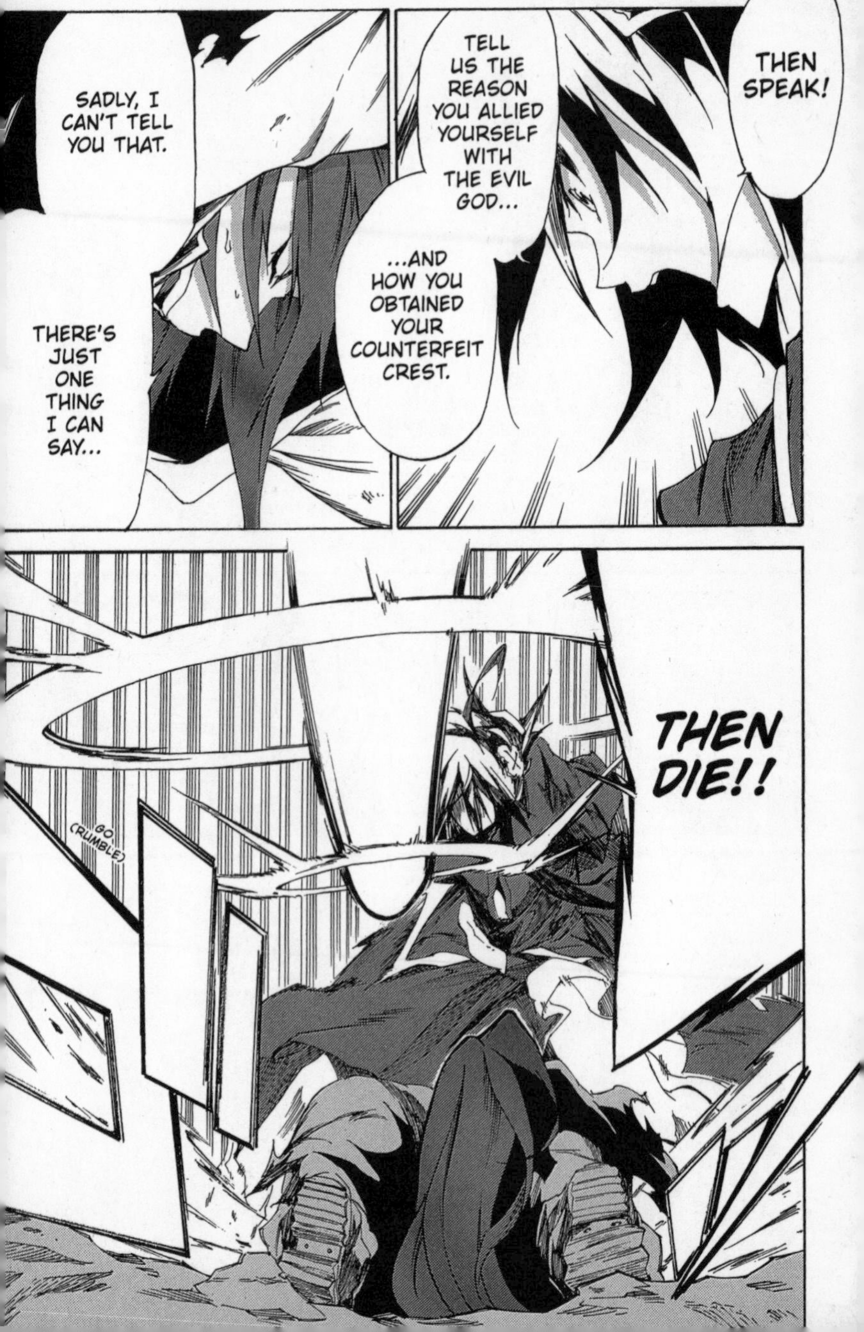
THEN SPEAK!
TELL US THE REASON YOU ALLIED YOURSELF WITH THE EVIL GOD...
...AND HOW YOU OBTAINED YOUR COUNTERFEIT CREST.
SADLY, I CAN'T TELL YOU THAT.
THERE'S JUST ONE THING I CAN SAY...
THEN DIE!!
GO (RUMBLE)

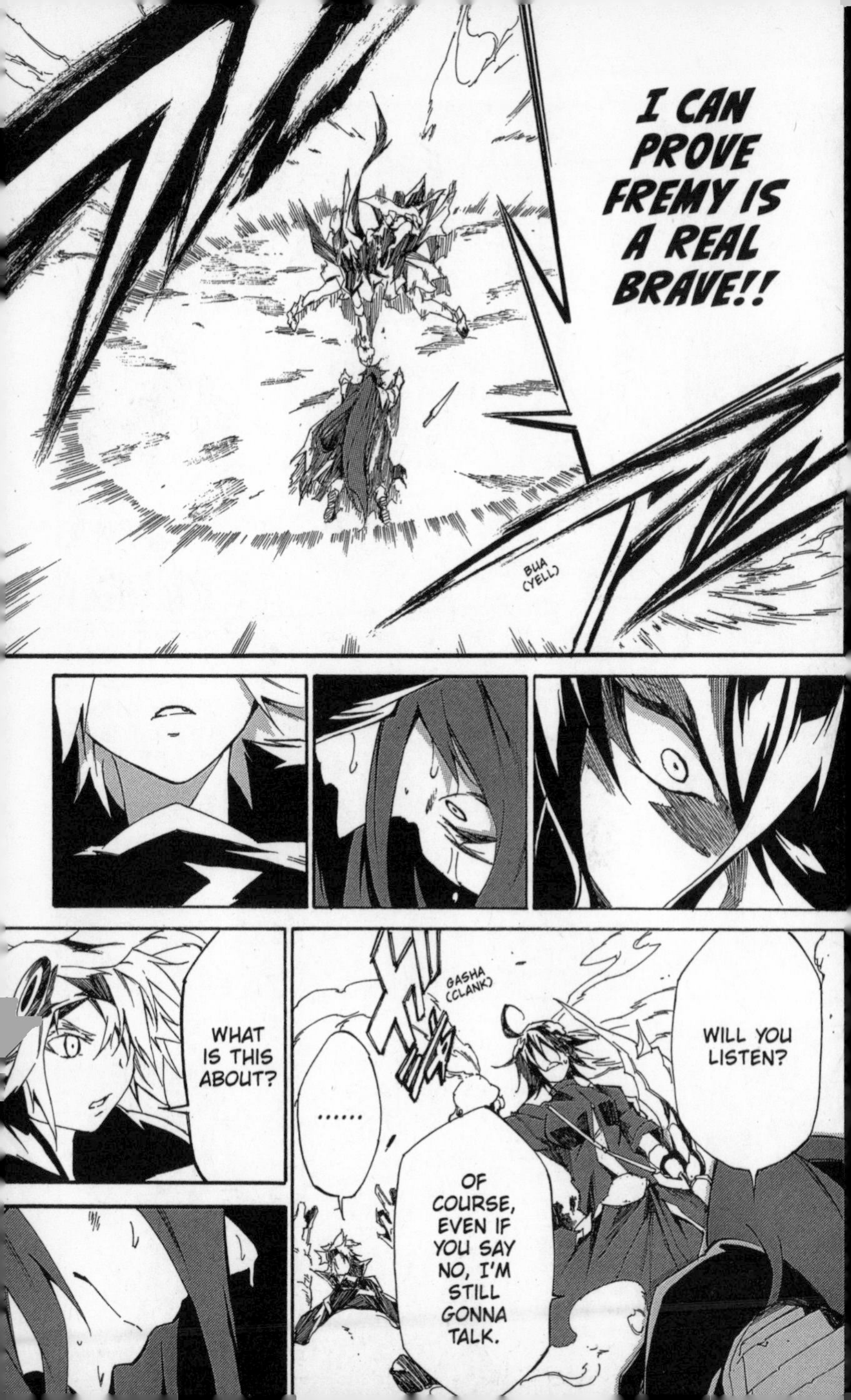
I CAN PROVE FREMY IS A REAL BRAVE!!
BUA (YELL)
WILL YOU LISTEN?
GASHA (CLANK)
......
OF COURSE, EVEN IF YOU SAY NO, I'M STILL GONNA TALK.
WHAT IS THIS ABOUT?

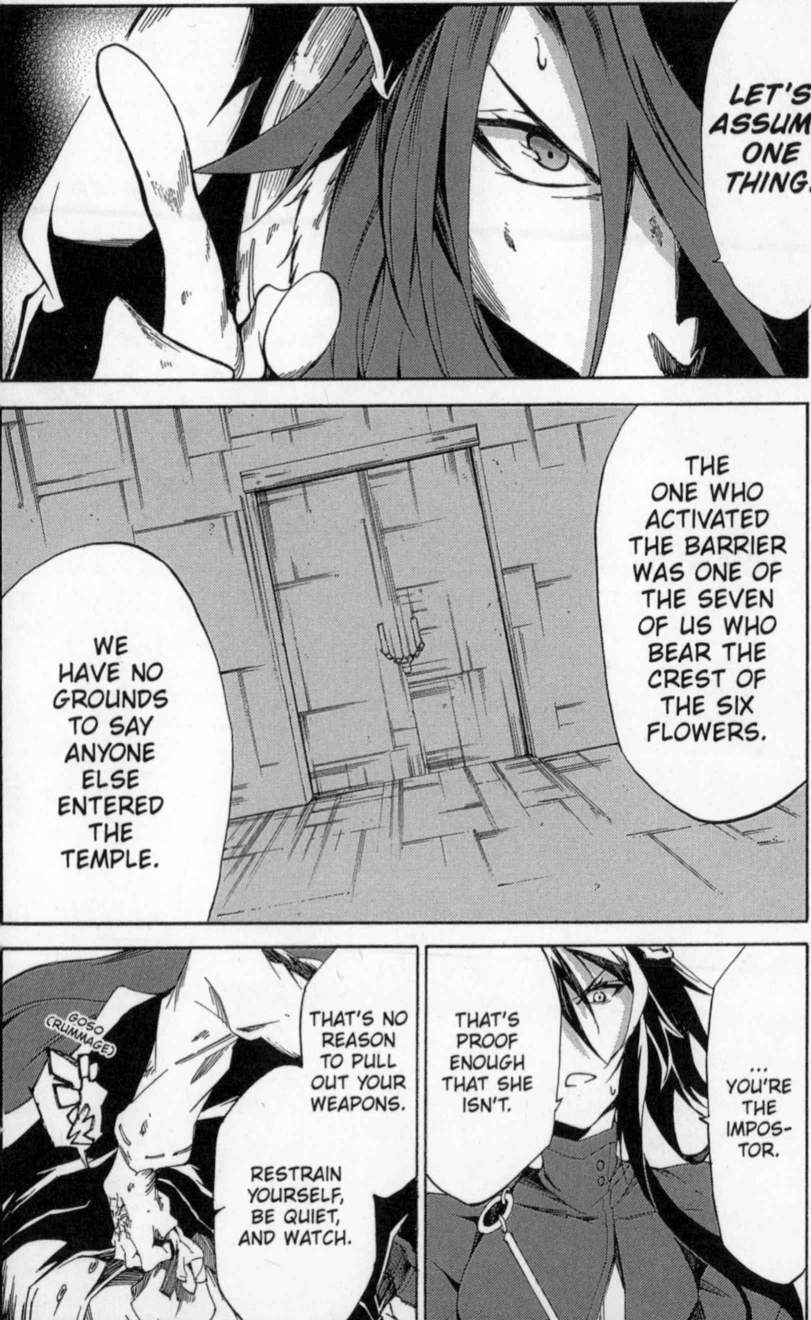
LET'S ASSUME ONE THING.
THE ONE WHO ACTIVATED THE BARRIER WAS ONE OF THE SEVEN OF US WHO BEAR THE CREST OF THE SIX FLOWERS.
WE HAVE NO GROUNDS TO SAY ANYONE ELSE ENTERED THE TEMPLE.
... YOU'RE THE IMPOSTOR.
THAT'S PROOF ENOUGH THAT SHE ISN'T.
THAT'S NO REASON TO PULL OUT YOUR WEAPONS.
RESTRAIN YOURSELF, BE QUIET, AND WATCH.
GOSO (RUMMAGE)

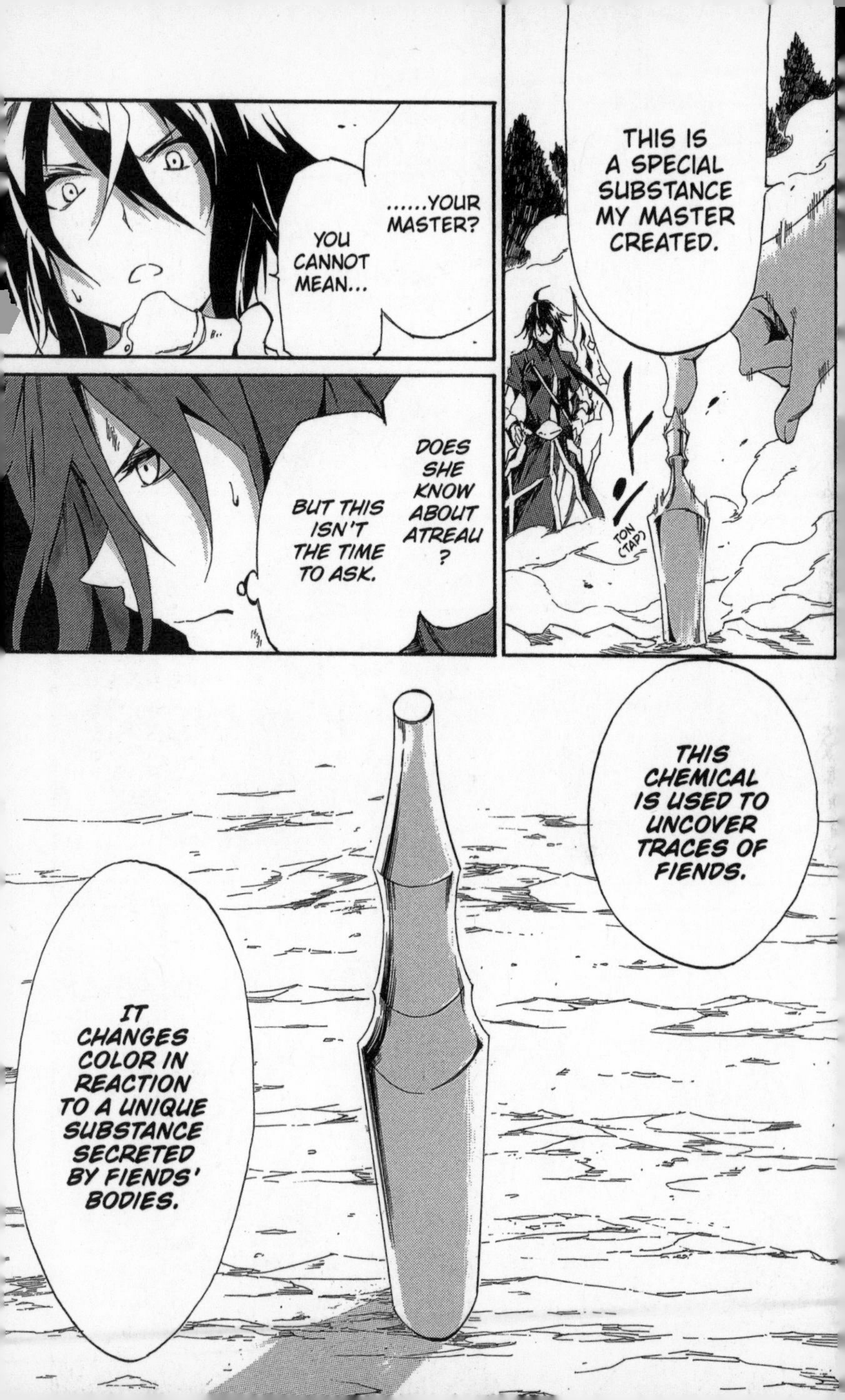
THIS IS A SPECIAL SUBSTANCE MY MASTER CREATED.
TON (TAP)
......YOUR MASTER?
YOU CANNOT MEAN...
DOES SHE KNOW ABOUT ATREAU?
BUT THIS ISN'T THE TIME TO ASK.
THIS CHEMICAL IS USED TO UNCOVER TRACES OF FIENDS.
IT CHANGES COLOR IN REACTION TO A UNIQUE SUBSTANCE SECRETED BY FIENDS' BODIES.

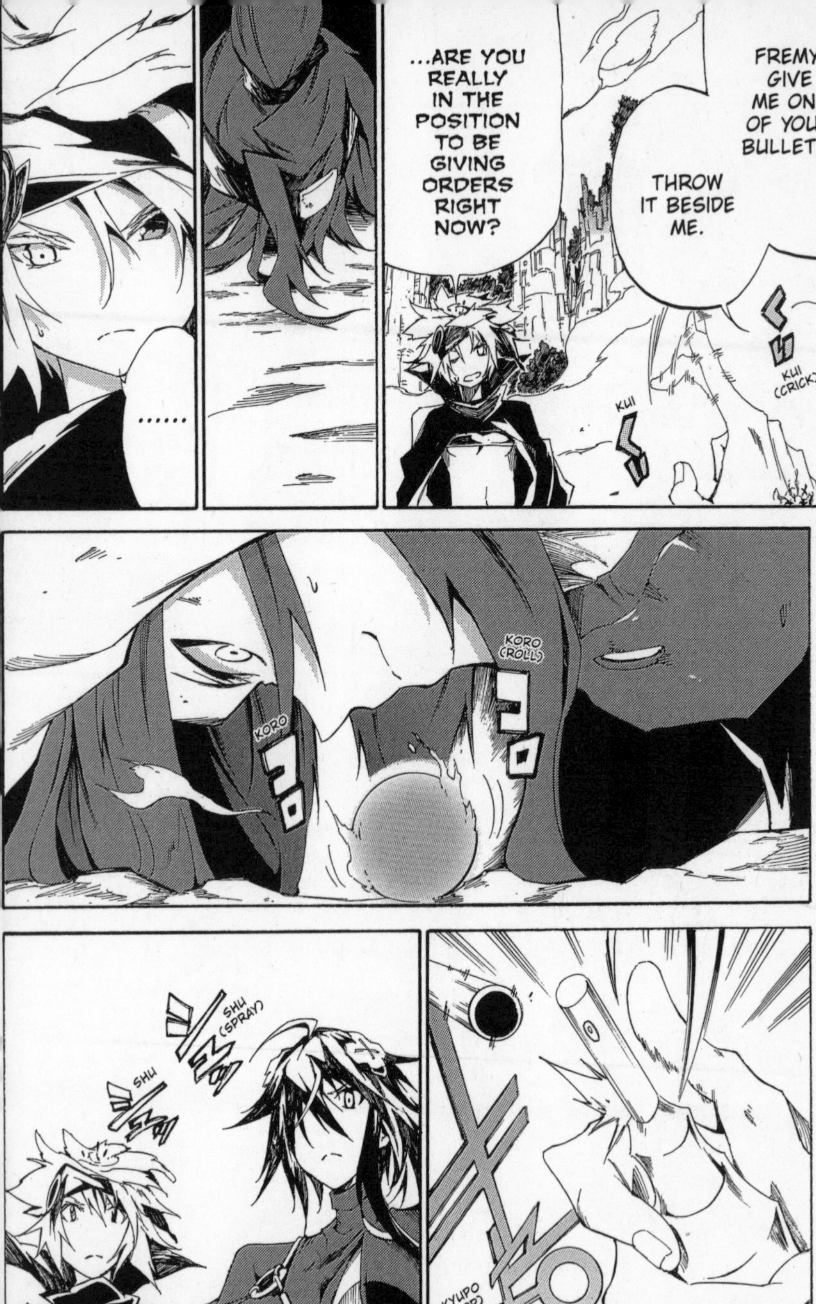
FREMY, GIVE ME ONE OF YOUR BULLETS.
THROW IT BESIDE ME.
...ARE YOU REALLY IN THE POSITION TO BE GIVING ORDERS RIGHT NOW?
KUI (CRICK)
KUI
......
KORO (ROLL)
KORO
KYUPO (POP)
SHU (SPRAY)
SHU

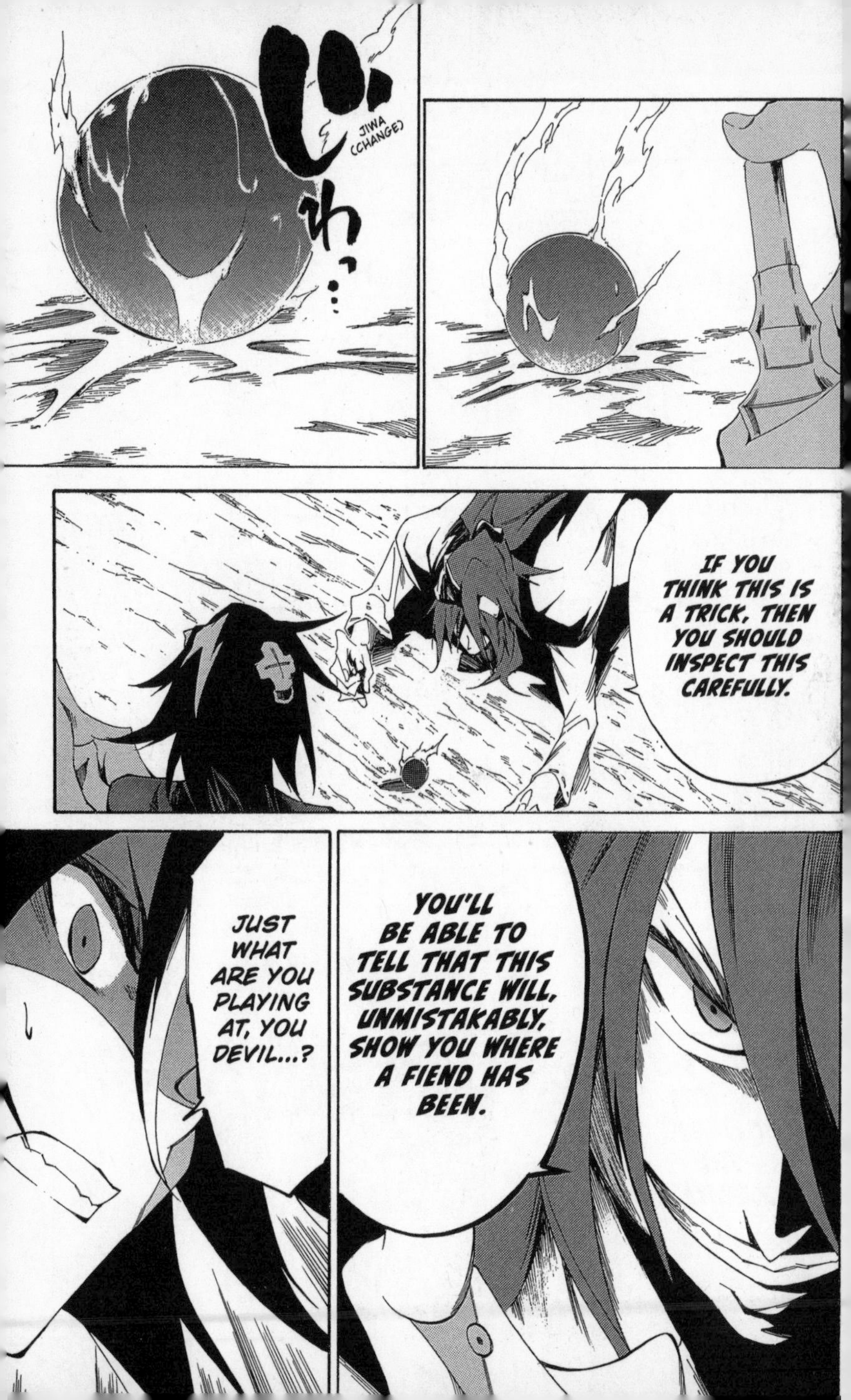
じわっ…
JIWA (CHANGE)
IF YOU THINK THIS IS A TRICK, THEN YOU SHOULD INSPECT THIS CAREFULLY.
YOU'LL BE ABLE TO TELL THAT THIS SUBSTANCE WILL, UNMISTAKABLY, SHOW YOU WHERE A FIEND HAS BEEN.
JUST WHAT ARE YOU PLAYING AT, YOU DEVIL...?

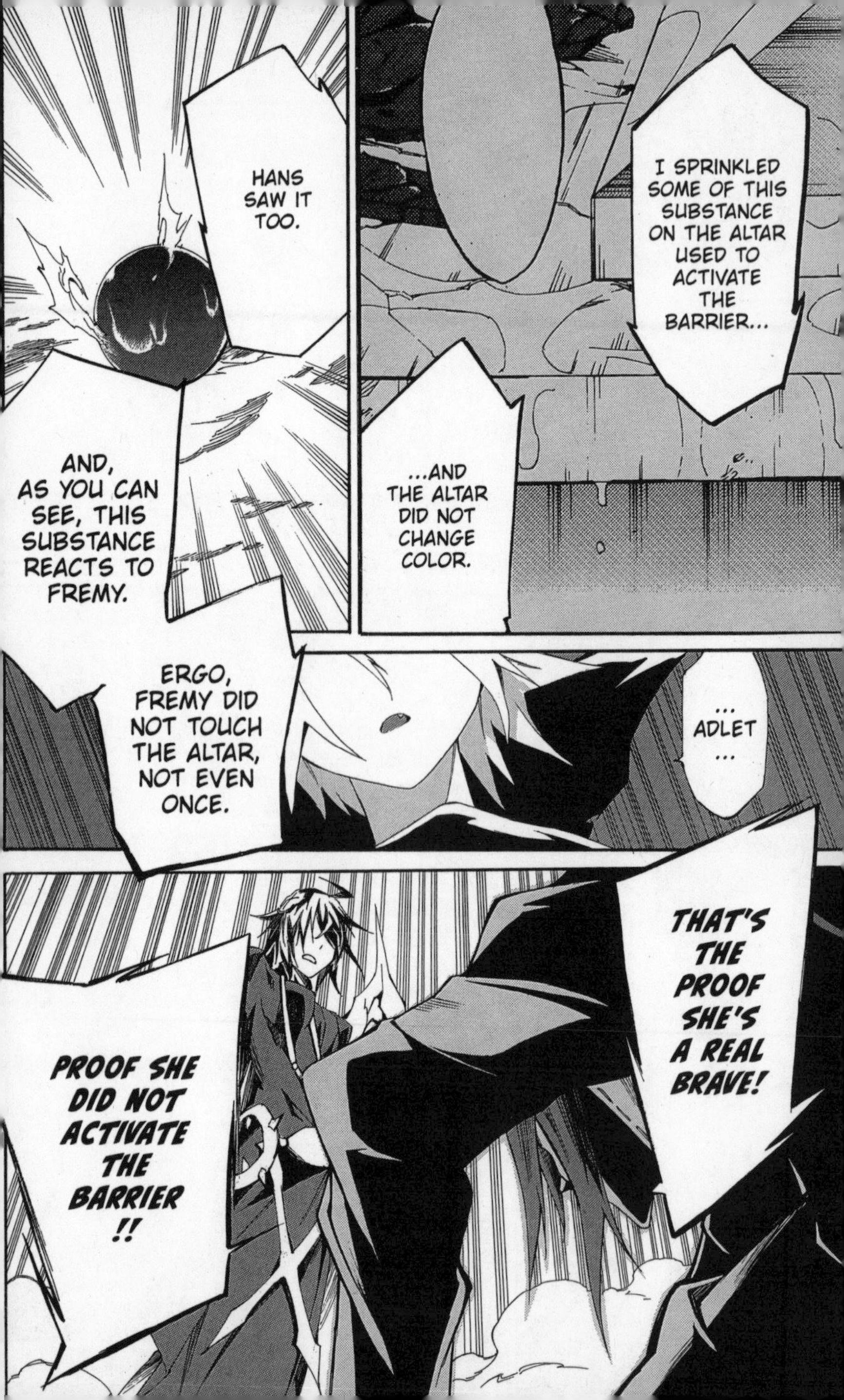
I SPRINKLED SOME OF THIS SUBSTANCE ON THE ALTAR USED TO ACTIVATE THE BARRIER...
...AND THE ALTAR DID NOT CHANGE COLOR.
HANS SAW IT TOO.
AND, AS YOU CAN SEE, THIS SUBSTANCE REACTS TO FREMY.
... ADLET ...
ERGO, FREMY DID NOT TOUCH THE ALTAR, NOT EVEN ONCE.
THAT'S THE PROOF SHE'S A REAL BRAVE!
PROOF SHE DID NOT ACTIVATE THE BARRIER!!

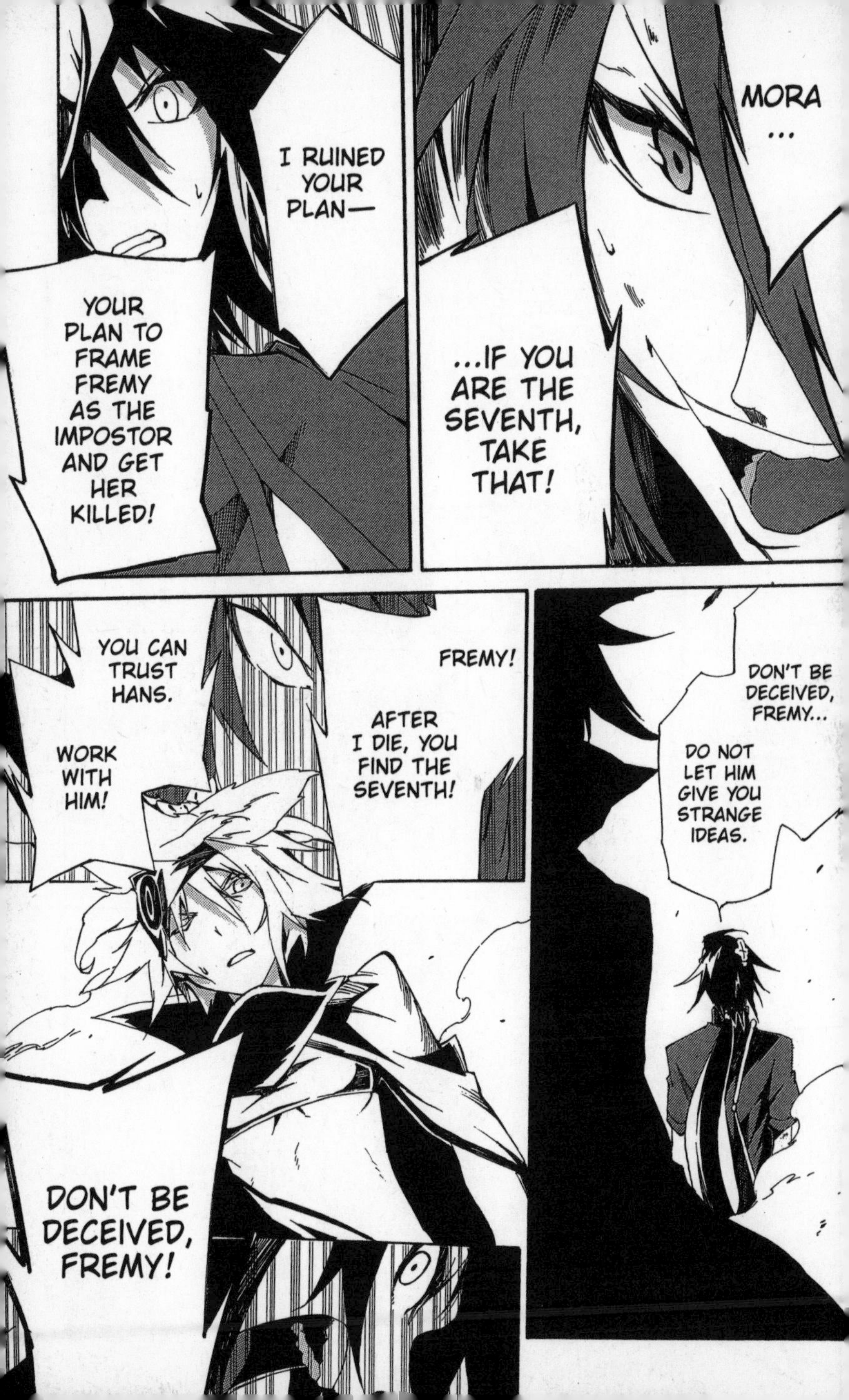
MORA ...
...IF YOU ARE THE SEVENTH, TAKE THAT!
I RUINED YOUR PLAN—
YOUR PLAN TO FRAME FREMY AS THE IMPOSTOR AND GET HER KILLED!
DON'T BE DECEIVED, FREMY...
DO NOT LET HIM GIVE YOU STRANGE IDEAS.
FREMY!
AFTER I DIE, YOU FIND THE SEVENTH!
YOU CAN TRUST HANS.
WORK WITH HIM!
DON'T BE DECEIVED, FREMY!

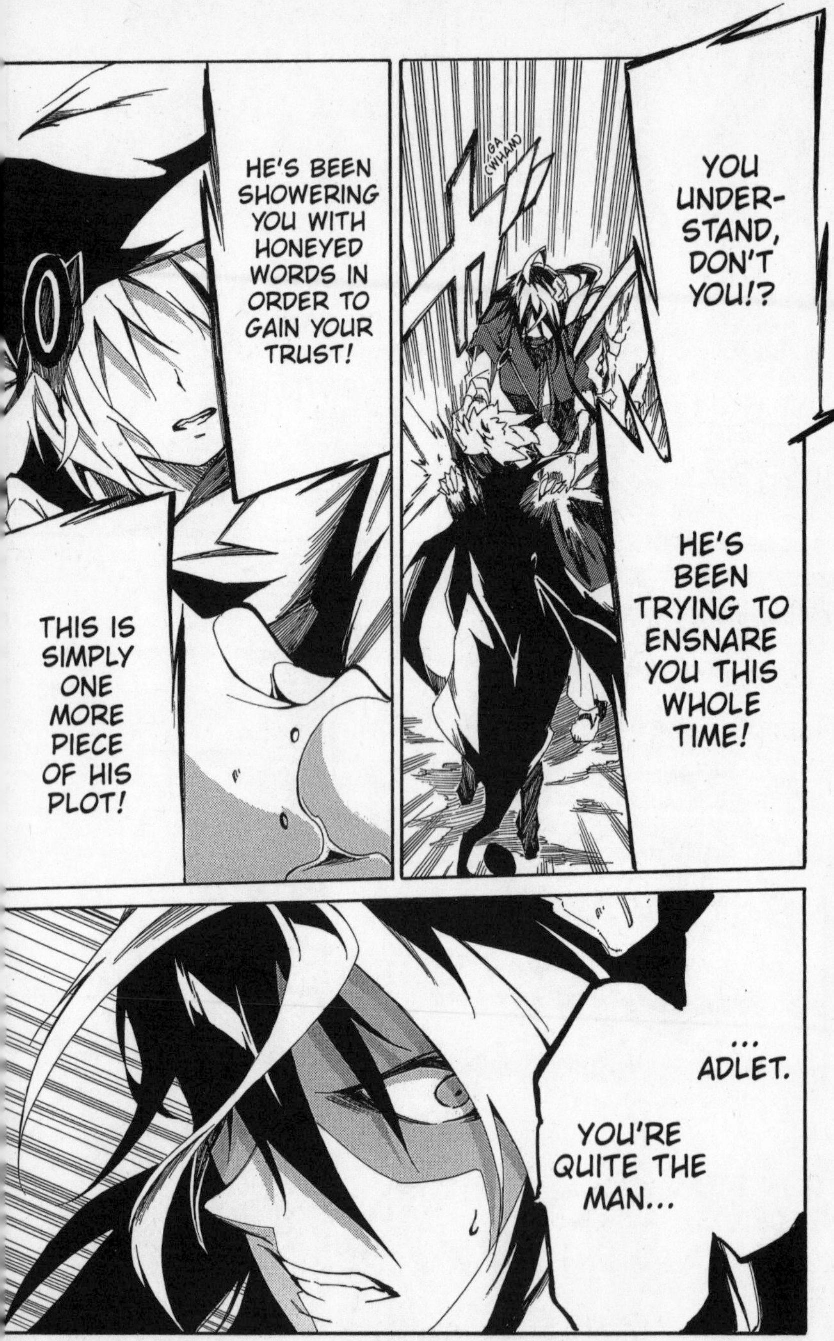
YOU UNDER-STAND, DON'T YOU!?
GA (WHAM)
HE'S BEEN TRYING TO ENSNARE YOU THIS WHOLE TIME!
HE'S BEEN SHOWERING YOU WITH HONEYED WORDS IN ORDER TO GAIN YOUR TRUST!
THIS IS SIMPLY ONE MORE PIECE OF HIS PLOT!
...ADLET.
YOU'RE QUITE THE MAN...

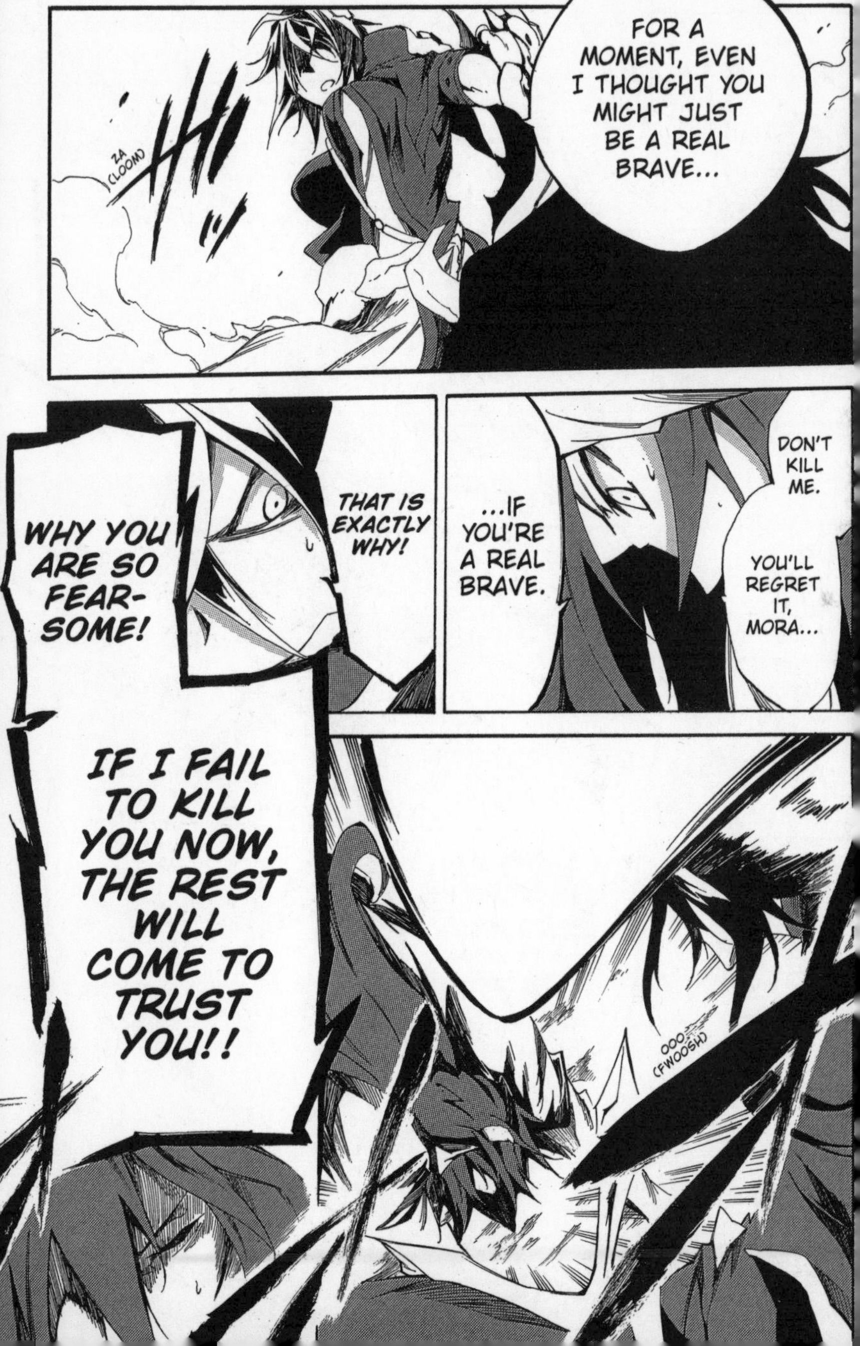
FOR A MOMENT, EVEN I THOUGHT YOU MIGHT JUST BE A REAL BRAVE...
ZA (LOOM)
DON'T KILL ME.
YOU'LL REGRET IT, MORA...
...IF YOU'RE A REAL BRAVE.
THAT IS EXACTLY WHY!
WHY YOU ARE SO FEAR-SOME!
IF I FAIL TO KILL YOU NOW, THE REST WILL COME TO TRUST YOU!!
OOO (FWOOSH)

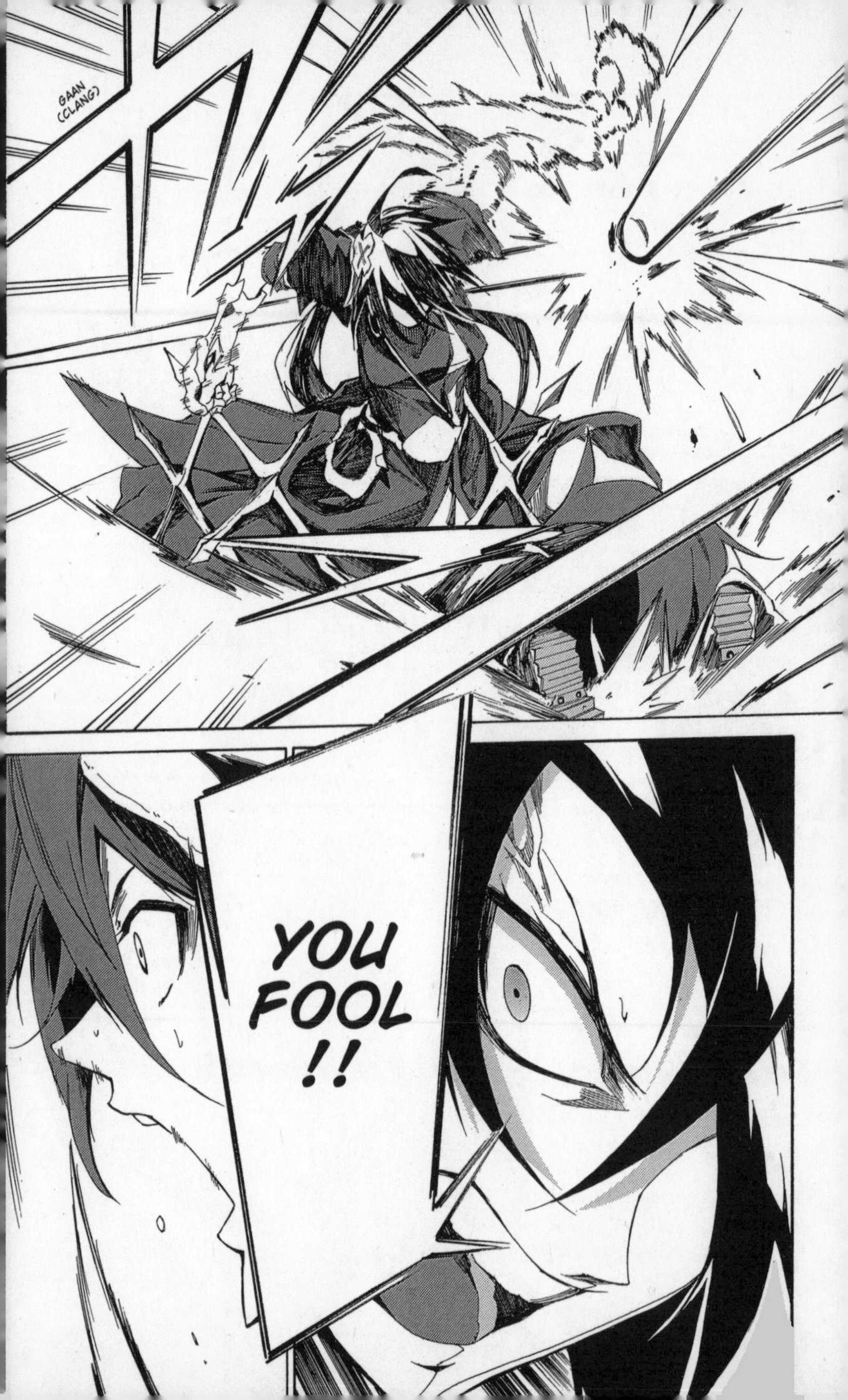
GAAN (CLANG)
YOU FOOL !!

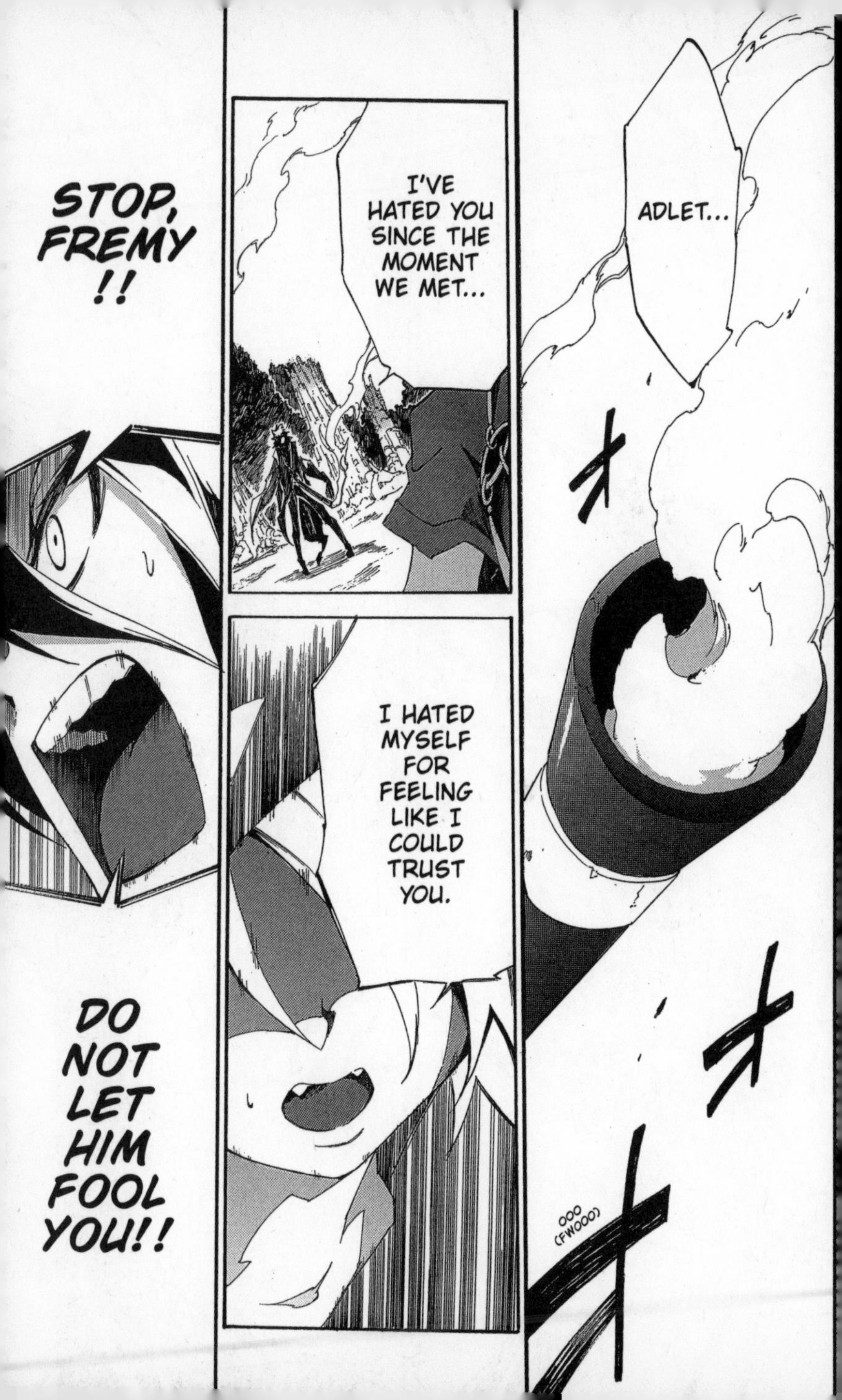
ADLET...
OOO
(FWOOO)
I'VE HATED YOU SINCE THE MOMENT WE MET...
I HATED MYSELF FOR FEELING LIKE I COULD TRUST YOU.
STOP, FREMY!!
DO NOT LET HIM FOOL YOU!!

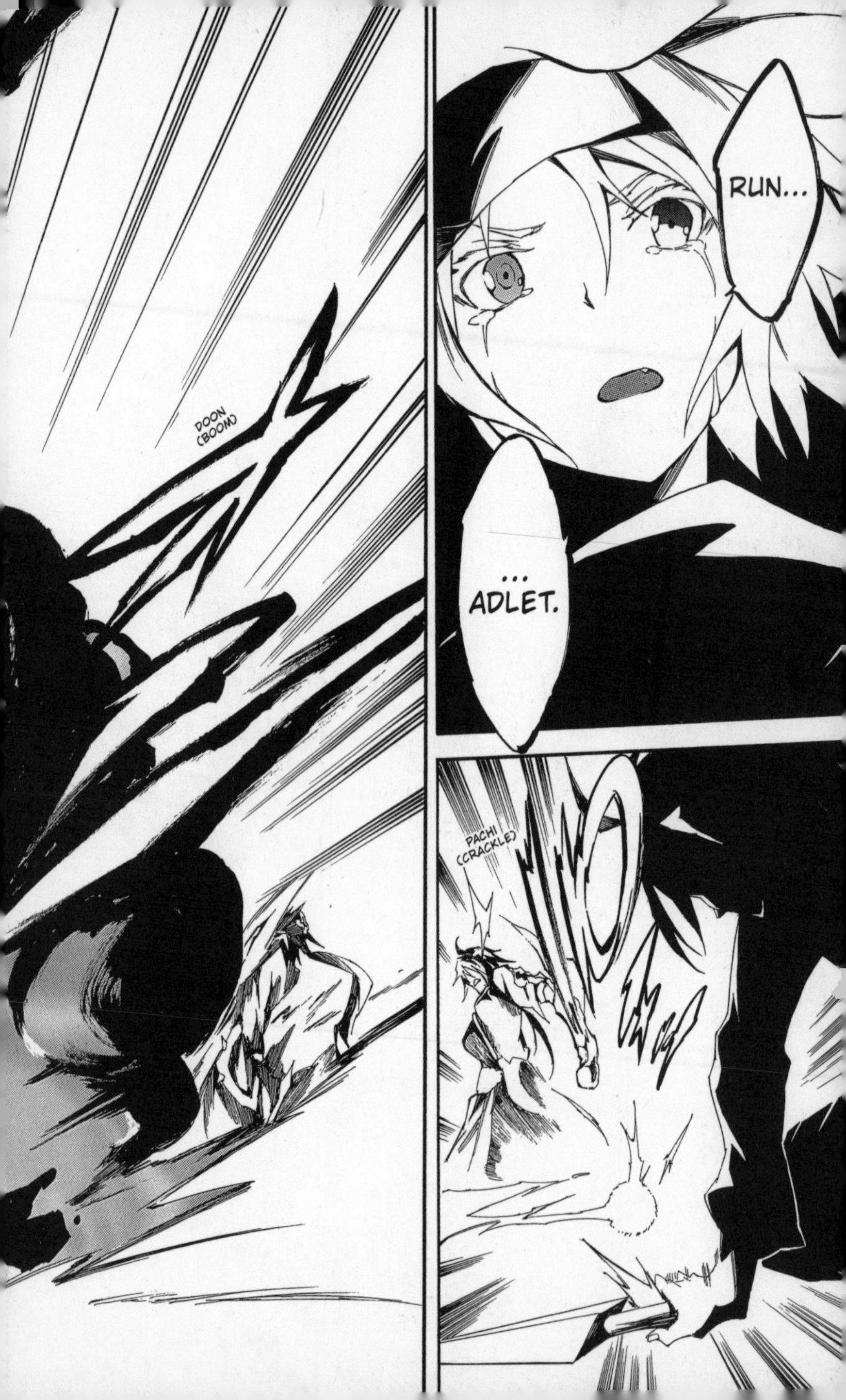
RUN...
...ADLET.
PACHI (CRACKLE)
DOON (BOOM)

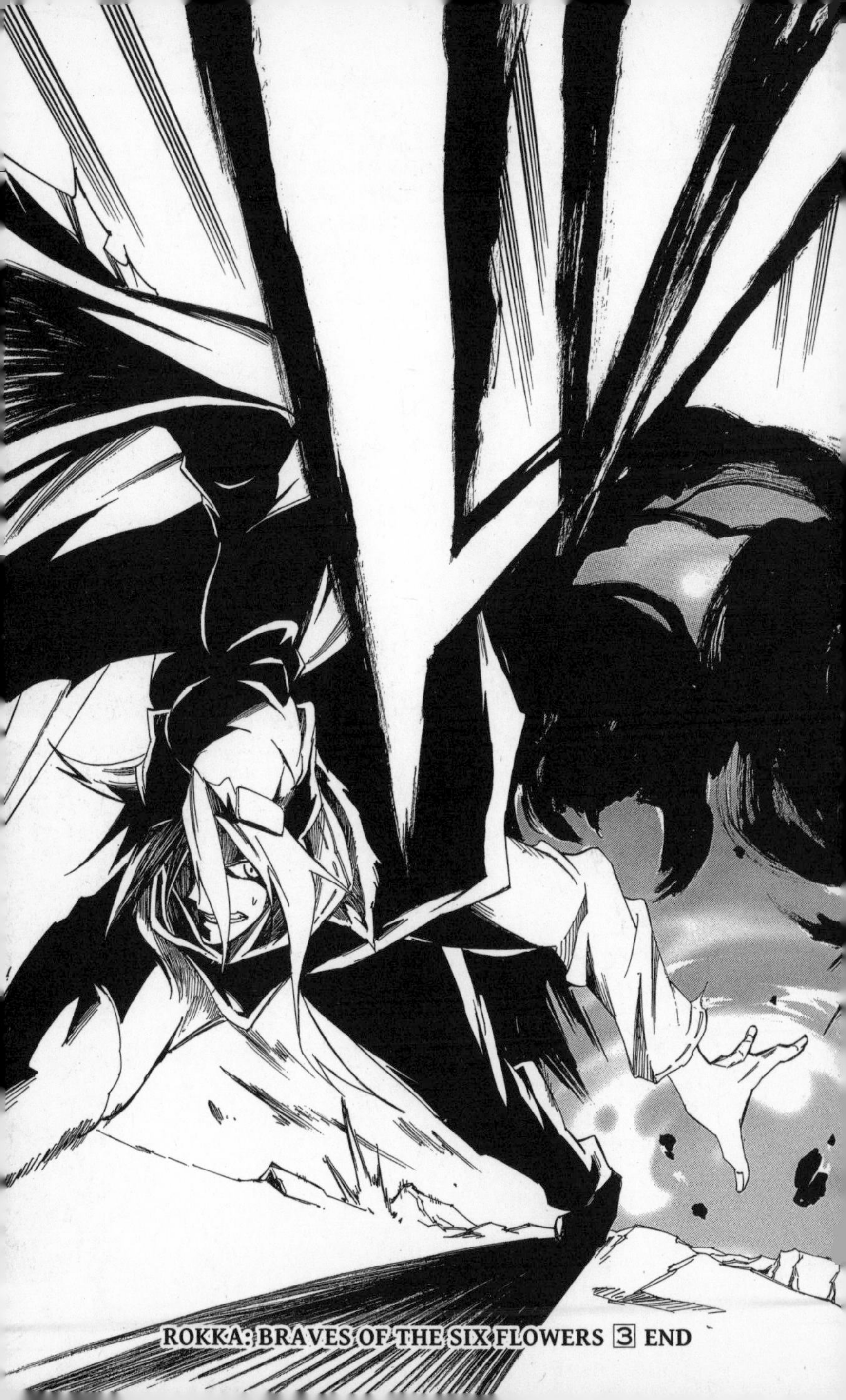
ROKKA: BRAVES OF THE SIX FLOWERS 3 END

ROKKA: Braves of the Six Flowers 3

Story ISHIO YAMAGATA
Art KEI TORU
Character design MIYAGI

Translation: Nicole Wilder
Lettering: Rochelle Gancio

ROKKA NO YUSHA - COMIC EDITION- © 2012 by Kei Toru, Ishio Yamagata, Miyagi
All rights reserved. First published in Japan in 2012 by SHUEISHA, Inc. English translation rights arranged with SHUEISHA, Inc. through Tuttle-Mori Agency, Inc., Tokyo.

English translation © 2017 by Yen Press, LLC.

Yen Press
1290 Avenue of the Americas
New York, NY 10104

Visit us at yenpress.com
facebook.com/yenpress
twitter.com/yenpress
yenpress.tumblr.com
instagram.com/yenpress

First Yen Press Edition: August 2017

Yen Press is an imprint of Yen Press, LLC.
The Yen Press name and logo are trademarks of Yen Press, LLC.

The publisher is not responsible for websites (or their content) that are not owned by the publisher.

Library of Congress Control Number: 2016958577

ISBN: 978-0-316-55626-2

10 9 8 7 6 5 4 3 2 1

BVG

Printed in the United States of America